CW01656463

Dedicated to [illegible] has been my rock for fifty-two years, the chief proofreader of not only this book but also my life

Bernie Ecclestone a true friend for fifty years

Aaron Greenwood for 15 years of solving my problems and his invaluable help in bringing this book to reality

Jeffrey Lewis, Ciro Orsini, Greg Wong, Rod Vickery,
Pasquale Lattuneddu, Zvi Konikov, Lou Jordan,
Avi Berkovitz, David Richards and Max Mosley,
Who have always been around when I needed them.

FastPrint Publishing

www.fast-print.net/store.php

FULL BLOOM

Copyright © John Bloom 2013

All rights reserved

No part of this book may be reproduced in any form by photocopying or any electronic or mechanical means, including information storage or retrieval systems, without permission in writing from both the copyright owner and the publisher of the book.

The right of John Bloom to be identified as the author of this work has been asserted by him in accordance with the Copyright, Designs and Patents Act 1988 and any subsequent amendments thereto.

A catalogue record for this book is available from the British Library

ISBN 978-178035-718-8

First published 2013 by
FASTPRINT PUBLISHING
Peterborough, England.

An environmentally friendly book printed and bound in England by
www.printondemand-worldwide.com

Mixed Sources
Product group from well-managed forests, and other controlled sources
FSC www.fsc.org Cert no. TT-COC-002641
© 1996 Forest Stewardship Council

PEFC Certified
This product is from sustainably managed forests and controlled sources
PEFC PEFC/16-33-415
www.pefc.org

This book is made entirely of chain-of-custody materials

Full Bloom

My life

John Bloom

Copyright © John Bloom 2013

Confidential Material.

All rights reserved.

Prologue

Those of you starting to read this book who are aged under 55 might be surprised to learn that from the late Fifties through until the mid Sixties retailing in Britain was not so different to Soviet Russia. In fact the only real difference was that in Russia, prices were set by the State, and in Britain they were set by the Establishment. British retailing was far from the free market we live in today. Back then, retailers were forbidden to sell goods below the manufacturers fixed retail price. The manufacturers set the price and the public simply had to pay it, no deals, no discounts, no choices and that's where this story begins.

I was 27 years old, a high school reject, looking for a future, following two years national service, six years of dead end jobs and several failed ventures, I stumbled upon the world of direct selling; the rest as they say, is history. Not only did direct selling change my life, but also it changed the lives of almost every housewife and household in the country. How I hear you ask? Simple by offering the public at large a fair deal at a fair price on things we take for granted today.

Washing Machines, Fridges and Vacuum Cleaners these were all luxury appliances well beyond the means of the average British household; that is until I came along and upset the applecart. I could not possibly have imagined the roller coaster ride that was to follow. I fought to abolish retail price maintenance and won but lost a fortune in the process.

With this book I hope to entertain and amuse you with just some of my adventures and perhaps share with you a more human glimpse into the lives of the people both famous and infamous that I have met along my way. This is my life, well at least some it I hope you enjoy reading about as much as I have enjoyed living it.

Chapter 1 - Forever Friends

'Happiness always looks small while you hold it in your hands, but let it go, and you learn at once how big and precious it is.'- Maxim Gorky

Late March 2013, London town was still in the grip of the longest, hardest winter since I first thought of selling washing machines. I had met my friend Bernie Ecclestone for a quiet evening. Quiet? How could it be quiet when I was in the company of a guy that I had first met 50 years ago? A lifetime really, in our case, several lifetimes.

David Bowie, who I helped get his first break in the music business, had the top selling album that week.

England football's team had struggled to hold off some cabbage pickers in a World Cup qualifier. Some things never change.

The sports news was dominated by the events in the Malaysian grand prix the previous weekend when Sebastian Vettell had ignored team orders and overtaken Australian team mate Mark Webber to win the race. The team leader of the Red Bull outfit was driving me home that night, a man by the name of Christian Horner. Also in the car was Bernie, giving a steady stream of instructions of how to get me home the quickest way possible.

So there I was being driven through London in the company of the most powerful figures in the world of F1.

That story sort of sums up my life, I loved London town, the people in it and for a while maybe, I owned it... My name? John Bloom. If you have not heard of it before now, you will certainly remember it by the time you finish reading this book.

Travel back with me to when I first met Bernie in that turbulent watershed year of 1963 when I invited the pop singer Adam Faith to stay on my yacht the *Arianne 3,* moored in Monaco Harbour. Close to it was a vessel owned by Aristotle Onassis, the *Christina.* John F. Kennedy was to die later that year in an event that shook the world and Onassis, the Greek shipping magnate and a zillionaire by today's standards, was later to marry Jackie Bouvier Kennedy, JFK's widow. The yacht he owned was famous the world over, more than 300 ft. long and named for his daughter, who also died in tragic circumstances. Amongst the guests to have stayed on his yacht were Marilyn Monroe, Eva Peron, Grace Kelly and Frank Sinatra, for some reason he never asked me.

Today in peak season the whole harbour is crammed with an armada of craft owned by the rich and famous. Some of the oligarchs' super yachts are too large to enter the harbour. That weekend there was only four craft there, the two mentioned above and vessels owned by another Greek shipping magnate Stavros Niarchos and Lady Docker. Joining the 'have yachts' was the culmination of a personal dream: my original five-year plan had been to get enough money so that my wife Anne and I would just cruise around islands and not work anymore. Yeah ... something like that.

Adam Faith had a companion with him, a car dealer friend. This guy was the original Arthur Daley: he could have sold binoculars to Stevie Wonder. Adam had met him when, awash with cash, he first went to buy a shiny new car as the proceeds of his early success started to roll in. Born in West London, Adam grew up on the Acton Vale Council Estate an Adel Taarabt free kick from QPR, a club I nearly acquired at one time. Their Loftus Road ground is now situated near the fabulous Westfield shopping centre in Shepherd's Bush. Of course in those days Westfield was a pipe dream; it was as inconceivable then as the car salesman becoming the Charles Foster Kane of motor racing and actually going on to stage Grand Prix in the most fabulous of locations. You must have guessed by now that the salesman's name was Bernie Ecclestone.

Adam had a string of hit records and dominated the charts in those days. He was joint contender for the crown of King of English Pop Music with another young gun called Cliff Richard. I remember one of Adam's number one hits was called 'What do you want if you don't want money?' Good question. Should have been my signature tune.

The blonde-haired singer was later to switch to an equally successful career as an actor. Perhaps his most famous role was as Chancer extraordinaire Budgie Bird in the smash hit show *Budgie*. Watching him star in the London Weekend Television series I wondered how much he had based that character on real life chancers he had met on the way up, present company excluded of course.

I met him through his manager Eve Taylor who also looked after Sandie Shaw, one of the finest female vocalists to emerge from those fabulous times. I accompanied Eve the first night that Sandie auditioned for her and Adam backstage at Hammersmith Odeon. In those days Sandie had that blind belief in her own talent. I could see even then she was going to be a massive star. In answer to your question, yes she was wearing shoes.

Eve was an attractive, petite blonde who Sandie always compared to Ruth Ellis, the last woman to be hanged in this country. She had a huge stable of talent including such diverse talents as Irish crooner Val Doonican and a fellow called Gordon Mills. Gordon was then playing in the Gordon Fraser harmonica gang. Harmonica groups never really cut it against beat groups.

Though later he became a huge force in pop, managing the talented trio of Tom Jones, Engelbert Humperdinck and Gilbert O'Sullivan.

So what do three young men with money burning a hole in their mohair suits decide to do on their first night in Monte Carlo? Got it in one – visit a casino. We ended up in a superb little one in Beaulieu on the outskirts of town. Speaking of casinos Gordon Mills squandered the millions he made in the Vegas versions. This one was tiny but sheer class, often frequented by the beautiful Italian actress Sophia Loren and another famous Italian Gino Agnelli. The Agnelli family owned Fiat, Ferrari and Juventus; he was also known as a man of exquisite taste.

Speaking of taste, who was the first person we saw when we entered this grand establishment, none other than the smoothest smoothie of all time, David Niven. The archetypal English gentleman, a man who was as home in a Casino as Cristiano Ronaldo is on a football pitch. The actor who best pulled off being a playboy in real life as well as on the silver screen. That was the golden era of playboys, a time where actors, celebrities, aristocrats and businessmen were sailing, gambling and chasing attractive women all over the world.

The thing I noticed about Niven was the tuxedo he was wearing. It might have been Brioni; he had a spiffy black bow tie too.

David had actually played the part of James Bond in *Casino Royale*. There is a scene in it where Vesper Lynd says to 007: 'There are dinner jackets and *dinner jackets*. This is the latter.'

He must have been wearing the same garment that night; he looked across at the newcomers with a puzzled look on his face. Perhaps he recognised Adam, Bernie nodded over. It did not seem to register with him. Then he was gone, gliding off to somewhere the real high rollers hung out.

So we did not make a big impression on David Niven but we left our mark on the tables, relieving them of a few coins. I won about £30,000, a nice sum in those days for a night's work. Adam pocketed about £10,000. Bernie won too, cannot remember how much exactly. It was a cash back night for him though. With his newly acquired winnings Adam turned to Bernie and said

'Okay Cock' (he called everyone 'Cock', popular Cockney phrase in those days, now not so fashionable for obvious reasons). 'I will have that Rolls Royce that you have for sale.'

Typical Bernie, the only person I know who could come out of a casino winning and still make money on the way home.

Adam was to die tragically young in 2003 from a heart attack. In the later part of his life he was also involved in the financial world. It was so sad what happened to him; Anne and I had such great memories of him.

Cars featured heavily on that holiday. One special trick was played with an amphibious car that we kept on the *Arianne 3*. The amphi-car was the first of its kind and always a favourite of mine. I am surprised they never caught on more, particularly with the record rainfalls and severe floods that have hit the country in recent years.

Our gag was simple – we waited until many of the inhabitants of the other vessels were on deck, usually at supper time and then making a lot of noise and fuss we would chuck the car into the harbour. To all intents and purposes it looked like a normal car and that the crazy Englishmen had lost the plot and were deliberately sinking their vehicle. The crew of the 'Christina' seemed particularly concerned at our antics. I never saw the great man Aristotle on deck but I am sure that he was kept informed of events. Our fun was interrupted by the harbour patrol who demanded that the car, at the time floating adrift, was returned to our ship.

Bernie wanted to take it even further by pretending to be trapped inside the car but we thought better of it; Bernie had a wicked sense of humour which I share.

He is not the hard man that he is often portrayed as being. Not that he will thank me for saying that.

As an example of his generosity and humanity, some years later, I was standing in a cable car whisking me to the top, or damn near it, of a Swiss mountain. Not my favourite environment – give me somewhere with a beach anytime. Bernie was with me and started having a go at my attire that day. Now this was one of the most fashionable ski slopes in the world. I had on a brown leather jacket, a smart pair of trousers and some Armani loafers. My usual garb, though sometimes the away strip was a raffish suit. Bernie was horrified and admonished me with: 'That is not what you wear to go up a mountain'.

I tried to tell him that I was not even skiing but he just shook his head and continued muttering. Anne and I were staying in the fabled Olden hotel in Gstaad. This prestigious hotel had an enviable location, with breath taking views of the slopes and haute cuisine of the highest standards. Bernie liked it so much he bought it. That night I was sitting in my exquisitely furnished room planning a new outfit. Now what would David Niven or fellow Bond star the impeccable Roger Moore have worn that day? Roger never looked like he felt the cold in those creamy cashmere roll-necks.

Suddenly there was a knock on the door and a porter with eyes like saucers presented me with the most beautiful ski-jacket I have ever seen. It blurred the boundaries between immaculate and sporty functional. Niven could have worn it in *Casino Royale*. The porter spoke in clipped English: 'With the compliments of Mr Ecclestone.'

I love that jacket, still do. Many years later I was wearing another garment that he had given me a beautiful quilted FI coat. This was on the freezing night Bernie and Christian Horner were running me home. I was hoping that Bernie might have commented on it and even offered mc a new one. He did give me a pair of moon boots the following morning in Gstaad though and told me to bin the Armani loafers. Why would the most powerful man in motor racing and arguably the whole of sport spend time and money on kitting me out to take me up a mountain when I was not a skier? Because that is the sort of guy he is, an incredibly generous and loyal friend.

Our friendship took on a new dimension when I returned to Europe from America in 1994. Bernie helped me with my career revival plans that rebuilt my life and he even saved it when I fell seriously ill. Family and friendship mean everything to him. I know what a devoted family man he is.

That morning on the ski slopes, clad in my new ski gear, I witnessed him performing admirably with his family. Years later the girls Tamara and Petra were the two most famous socialites in the world

One more Bernie gag, for the moment anyway. This concerns Karl Heinz Zimmermann, brother of the Olympic skiing champ Egon. (Bet he has some nice moonboots). Karl does the cooking and Gordon Ramsay bit for Bernie and his guests at all the F1 races. This is done in a wonderful hi-tech vehicle, which also doubles as a restaurant. This is always parked near Bernie's motor home and being part of the inner circle he even has access to the grid, which has more protection than President Obama.

Karl kept a cannon on top of his mobile restaurant, that is right, a cannon. Not dissimilar to the cannon that featured on the badge of my favourite football team Arsenal. Karl's hero was Michael Schumacher and every time Michael won a grand prix, which, in his prime, was a fair few, he would fire the cannon. Actually there was no ball but some sort of firework deal. It made a great deal of noise and there was always acrid smoke everywhere. Everyone hated it, nobody more than Bernie. The drivers trailing in a cavalcade behind the Wagnerian hero Schumacher were not impressed either.

At Silverstone in 2008 Bernie and I decided to have some fun at Karl's expense. We enlisted the services of an experienced ex-police officer John O'Connor to play the lead role in our 'Sting'. No one was more equipped to play the part than him, being a former head of the 'Flying Squad' better known to some of you as the 'Sweeney'. Bernie knew of John's talents as I had employed him to hunt down some bandidos who mugged Bernie and his first wife outside his Chelsea home earlier that year.

John agreed to turn up with some bogus 'policemen' in some hired official looking cars and 'raid 'the restaurant. *CSI: Miami* was not in it. They taped the whole place with that yellow sticky stuff and produced documents purporting to be a search and arrest warrant. The 'policemen' even had evidence bags.

Karl was being arrested for being a suspected terrorist and in possession of explosives. The gunpowder for the cannon was produced and by now Karl was visibly shaking with fear, he looked absolutely terrified. Guantanamo Bay was his next stop, visualising the orange jump suit and a bag over his head. The spooks had him bang to rights. Karl kept protesting that he was innocent, merely a caterer and an employee of the famous Mr Bernie Ecclestone.

A grim faced Bernie was summoned and Karl, now almost hysterical, begged my old friend to sort out the mess and spring him from the clutches of these police.

Bernie, his head held stiff with great authority, said with a hint of disdain in his voice that he knew nothing of the matter and did not want to get involved, As far as he was concerned Karl was not even an employee of his merely a contractor hired to help out with the catering for the day. Whatever his extra-curricular activities were they had no connection with him. Unbeknown to Karl the whole farrago was being secretly taped. Bernie and John then disappeared into his trailer for what seemed ages. They eventually emerged looking very serious and muttering about the gravity of the situation. I shot a side glance at the bedraggled Karl who had almost sunk to his knees in sheer terror. John added to the mix by saying that a payment of £20,000 may possibly aid the suspect's release. Bernie, his face now set in stone, acted lemon and said he did not know what to do next, informing Karl that he did not carry that sort of money. It may be possible to approach the race promoter to arrange a loan from the gate receipts. I had never seen Bernie look so serious since he was criticising my attire in the ski-lift.

The problem was we just could not sustain the joke any longer. I was worried that Karl might suffer some sort of stroke.

He was perspiring a little more than profusely and about to hyper-ventilate. I had this image of a damaged robot, about to short circuit. As one we all burst out laughing and the game was up. To add insult to injury Bernie presented Karl with the CD of the 'arrest'. I do not know if he ever played it back, maybe in his nightmares he re-lived it all. Of course he later told Bernie that in fact he had clicked onto the gag early on and just played along with it. That is why his clothes were drenched in sweat I suppose, and, guess what; we never heard that cannon go off again.

Back to the present and the jokes still flowed. Earlier Bernie had invited us to 'The Guinea' in Bruton Place for a meal. When we got there it looked just like another pub. Well the punters were better dressed than some but it was real busy and I saw no place to eat or even sit down.

Adam Faith had a great turn of phrase: 'to stand for it', meaning you had been put upon, made a fool of, tricked. That ran through my mind as I viewed the pub. Then out of nowhere a waiter appeared, he called my name and whisked me to a private room where the food was being served. it was one of those gastro pubs or whatever they call themselves now.

Seated at the table, there was an individual called Barry Silver, a Walter Mitty type character who circled around Bernie's orbit. A former car salesman, I believe he may played an important part in Bernie's lunch time life.

Bernie once commented that so overactive was Silvers imagination that he would have been an ideal person to help write my book. {not that I needed to embellish these stories, the majority had to be toned down}

Anne and I had to endure about 20 minutes of Silvers endless drivel when in the nick of time Bernie appeared in the company of the charming and charismatic Christian Horner, Team Principle of the Red Bull Racing formula one team.

Amazing as it seems, the Red Bull leader had just come from having tea with the Queen. The Queen had astounded him with her encyclopaedic knowledge of formula one.

Bernie explained to Christian that our relationship stretched back 50 years and regaled him with anecdotes of the strokes and jokes we had pulled on the legends of motor racing, Damon Hill and Jackie Stewart amongst others.

During this conversation Mr Silver of course, imagined he had participated in these stunts.

I indulged in some light-hearted banter with Bernie about our respective ages. We both agreed that age was just a number and despite our 'senility' we had both managed to survive. Christian was a little surprised at how funny our Abbot and Costello routine was. Like watching two Jackie Masons in full flow, he mentioned that he might book us as a double act to do the stand up at the Red Bull Christmas party.

After the furore of the Malaysian Grand Prix I joked with Christian that I was putting my life at risk dining with him in case an Aussie hit-squad of enraged Mark Webber fans stormed the building. I generously offered my services in some sort of advisory capacity. 400 gallons of Red Bull and a new team jacket to replace Bernie's relic would suffice.

Christian gave me a slow smile, his bright eyes dancing dangerously. He is truly one of nature's gentlemen, and in the shark-tank of modern motor racing he's a saint. In future chapters I will tell you of my dealings with some of the unpleasant characters in the milieu.

Unfortunately Bernie's stunning wife Fabiana was not present that evening as she was on a skiing holiday in Switzerland, Mr Ecclestone joining her in the morning. I told him about my latest ventures as I hit the comeback trail once more and made reference to the old phoenix rising from the ashes metaphor. Actually, if the Bloom family ever get round to making a family crest I think I will use that image. Bernie, tongue in cheek, expressed doubts about my resurrection saying that he had already received complaints about me from people that would have preferred that I had remained buried under the ashes.

My latest plans include my work with the 'Mission Motorsport' campaign, where I want to add my marketing and fundraising experience to assist and help them in every way, including my intent to bring wounded veterans, as VIP's to motorsport events.

I briefly discussed with Bernie the latest skin care products from the 'Kismet' range I was involved with. Amongst them, I jokingly remarked, was a serum that could make us both look 50 years younger. We could become those young gunslingers on the *Arianne 3* back in Monaco again. What a surprise Fabiana would get when Bernie went back to Switzerland. Problem was that the treatment took four weeks to perfect and would have to be conducted in conditions of great secrecy in a private clinic.

Many celebrities have already expressed interest in the incredible treatments, especially the active Kismet *"Kiss Diamond"* collection

Outside on a chilly March evening Christian Edward Johnson Horner was already waiting in a fantastic Hummer-type vehicle. It was like a cross between some souped-up armoured cars last seen patrolling the streets of Basra and a space ship. I told Christian that he had passed the audition and had clinched the job as my driver. Christian had started out as a racing driver before making the switch to team principal. Just have to sort out the uniform. Maybe a cap like Parker the chauffeur in the puppet shows *Thunderbirds*. Bernie was still shaking his head when they dropped us off at Marble Arch.

The Arianne III

Prince Rainier and Grace Kelly boarding the Yatch Next to the Arianne III

Adam Faith

Adam Faith aboard the Amphicar

Bernie in Mission Control

Bernie seeking divine intervention

The F1 Circus starring Sylvester Stallone

The F1 Circus starring Antony "ER" Edwards

The F1 Circus - Working for Bernie

The F1 Circus - Working for Bernie

Chapter 2 - Good Fellows

'We only kill each other'

Bugsy Siegel

There is a scene in Martin Scorsese's epic gangster film *Goodfellas* where a young Ray Liotta has recently been indoctrinated into the ways of the Mafia. When his old, grey-haired mom pops down to her local corner store she is overwhelmed with offers to carry her heavy shopping bags home.

Why is such kindness displayed to the old dear?

'It was outta respect' Liotta drawls into the voice over.

I want to tell you about my experiences with the Mafia and my meeting with Frank Costello, introduced to me and known to all as 'Mr Frank' perhaps the most powerful and feared of the mob bosses.

Summer 1964 and in mid July my company was placed in voluntary liquidation. World War III was about to break out in the little world of John Bloom. The business establishment who I had thumbed my nose at and ran rings around for years were putting a lynch mob together. It crossed my mind that I was going to be paparazzi fodder for years. They laid siege to my house and camped on my doorstep. I got the word that the politburo at the Board of Trade was going to hold a stewards' enquiry into my business methods. Infamy, infamy they've all got it in for me.

The situation was putting an unbearable strain on my wife Anne. She was holding up well in the epicentre, but I feared for the future. We were both in a very tough place. I had to get us out of town and fast, away from the shenanigans. My escape route came in the form of a guy called Lenny Stogel, as Brooklyn as the Bridge. Lenny was an amazing fellow, and he was my go-to-guy for freebies. Sgt Bilko was not in it. Poor James Gandolfini died when this was being written; Lenny always reminded me of *The Sopranos* superstar.

Freebies were a huge weapon in the Bloom arsenal. I like to think I pioneered that type of salesmanship. My philosophy was and still is: 'If you give the customer something for free they will love you.'

I think 'free 'is the greatest word in the English language.

'You have been found not guilty of any crime relating to Rolls Razor Mr Bloom. You are free to go'.

Lenny supplied me with some genuine, silver-plated, cut-price canteens of cutlery to give away 'free' with the washing machines. He had married well to a singer called Teny. She had some hits but I cannot remember what they were. She came from a seriously wealthy family, her father just happened to own the 'National Silver Company'. That is where the cutlery came in.

Speaking of silver reminds me of a guy called Bunker Hunt, who around that time had cornered the silver market. He was a great man for the races and once famously remarked, when things got tougher in the 70's that, 'A billion dollars isn't what it used to be'

Way to go Bunker.

Lenny had cornered the market on giant inflatable Santa's and one Christmas I took 50,000 of them. They were almost as big a hit as the new Beatles album, which always came out at that time of year. If ever I see one I will re-purchase it as an act of Proustian nostalgia, the album that is not the Santa, I had a running gag with Lenny over the Santa's turning up at Buck House. Like most Americans Lenny had a soft spot for the Royals and was never sure if I was winding him up or if his classy merch had ended up there.

I started my call to him with a joke about the Queen's Christmas being made by the presence of a giant inflatable Santa. He was shocked to hear had bad things were for me and invited us over. It appeared that he was making a move out of the Santa and silver business to the wonderful world of showbiz where he had signed up some pop groups. Lenny was convinced he was going to be the next Brian Epstein. (For you younger readers Epstein were the first manager of the Beatles).

I had recently received a letter from a young wannabe that informed me with his talent and my bundles he could make *me* the next Epstein. The wannabe was a young fellow called David Jones; the world was to come to know him as David Bowie. I passed on that one, but more later on.

Lenny was keen for me to come down to Memphis to meet some of his friends and discuss his burgeoning music mogul career. He informed me that he already had a hit record by a head banger who rejoiced in the name of 'Sam the Sham'. His back up group were known as the Pharaohs, Sam was not an Egyptian though; he hailed from JR's hometown of Dallas. He did wear a turban though – told you he was a head banger. I think it had a jewel in it. Fake of course.

After confirming the food was kosher I just could not turn it down. So in early August we shipped out of London and touched down in Idlewild airport New York, as it was known then. A few months earlier another English export had landed down there and caused a stir – Mr Epstein's protégés. Those loveable Scouse mop tops. My arrival was pretty noisy too because after clearing customs and immigration there was another mob of press lying in wait.

The first thing I noticed about it was the cloud of smoke that hung above them just like I used to see at the football years ago. Just like my rosy future that had gone up in smoke. If you have never experienced anything like that you cannot imagine the rudeness and violence of it.

I was used to the 'You are all washed up' ... 'hanging out to dry' stuff but this time the scumbags seemed particularly vindictive.

'Off to Rio are you Mr Bloom'

'Why is it carnival week?' I snapped back

'Is that money in the suitcase Mr Bloom? Your 'shareholders' and 'employees' perhaps?'

I should have known better than to getting involved in a slanging match, but I was edgy as the dubious characters were getting to me. It was a sweltering day in New York and the humidity had hit us as soon as we got off the plane. It was stickier than Kate Moss in Velcro; one thing I will always recall about that day was the sweat stains spreading across their cheap nylon shirts as they gave chase. Things looked bad, I was almost thinking of getting on the next plane home, or the next plane anywhere.

Then out of the crowd, three huge guys in dark suits emerged. The hacks scattered in all directions as the trio roughly barged anyone in their path out of their way. They could have been line-backers or whatever it is from the Miami Dolphins. The leader was about five foot eleven but bulked up from doing weights. Shaven headed he was wearing a heavy suit about two sizes too small, the sea-shell buttons almost bursting. A security guy looked across at us, the baldy gave him a terrifying stare and the guy turned away, 'Mr & Mrs Bloom we are here to take you to the Stanhope Hotel.'

The leader announced and beckoned us to a black limo parked across the way. The remainder of the press corps were hot footing it; they had been around long enough to recognise heavy-duty dudes when they saw them.

The car was immaculate; I think it was a caddy bit like the one Al Pacino got into when Barazi picked him up outside Jack Dempsey's Bar in the first *Godfather* movie. Course we could have been going anywhere but I was so relieved to get out of the airport. Then after a few minutes maybe it did not seem such a clever idea.

'Relax Mr Bloom' the gorilla driving said. 'You are amongst friends.'

He smiled showing cracked teeth; I think it was a smile.

The Stanhope was on 5th Avenue, on the Upper East Side. A gorgeous neo-Italian style building opposite Central Park. You expected to see Jay Gatsby posing in the bar with some other American aristos. The legendary jazz legend Charlie Parker blew his last sax there. The Beatles stayed there on their first tour, block booking whole floors of the place.

I never found out the names of the three amigos who rescued us at Idlewild but I did meet a fellow called Dave Acavetti who greeted us in the beautifully ornate reception. Dave was a short, stocky man, and a gifted dresser with a mastery of colour. All the time we were there I never saw him in the same suit twice. The Italians call it *sprezzatura* – studied casualness.

‘Your worries are over’ he told us oozing friendliness and positivity. ‘You are now going to live in a Sea of Tranquillity’

A Sea of Tranquillity, eh? At that time almost drowning in a sea of debt and problems I would have settled for a babbling brook. I told him of my concerns about press intrusion.

‘You don’t have to worry about that; we want you to have a great time here. ‘In a grand theatrical gesture he spread his arms.

The first night we were in New York Dave took us to the famous Copacabana night club immortalised by the Supremes who did a live album there, and then Barry Manilow name-checked it in one of his global smashes. Paul Anka was performing that night, famous for his contribution towards Sinatra’s classic ‘My Way’. Later on when I lived in America we became friends. For the next ten days I did it my way, mainly relaxing in our hotel suite, taking advantage of room service and watching the giant TV set that dominated the room. Today TVs are no big deal, even the most modest home boasts wall mounted, HD, flat screen whatever.

But in 1964 colour TV was virtually unheard of in the UK and we were limited to two channels. Yes just two. To get a range of channels was amazing to us and we took full advantage of it. One of the top shows then was the classic cowboy show *Bonanza* which starred Michael Landon as ‘Little Joe’.

My wife was a fan and sometime later we had the pleasure of befriending him. He went onto to do that *Highway to Heaven* show about the angel who returns to earth to do good deeds. Michael, who was as charming off screen as he was on it, died tragically young.

Speaking of Angels, I thought for a while that I was amongst them, so considerate and pleasant was everyone to us. I thought I had died and gone to heaven, bone weary from my recent problems I crashed out most days. Sometimes Anne and I would just gaze at opulence of our surroundings; it was a dream within a dream really. We stayed close to the hotel, sometimes going out for a walk in the park, but this was before it got dark and the muggers came out.

Lenny was one of nature's hospitable hosts and nothing was too much trouble for him. One day he took us to a store called Kravitz (no relation to the other Lenny). It was a discount store and it turned my head around to see such bargains and stores selling virtually everything under the same roof. So dirt cheap, there was rock bottom prices everywhere. Back home we still had the retail price mechanism that kept prices high. There had to be a way around all this. This was a precursor of the pound shops that have sprung up on virtually every street corner in the country.

The difference is now the pound shops are a product of the recession, whereas the discount shops in America came out of a time of economic growth.

Then I met Mr Frank Costello, nicknamed 'the Prime Minister of the Underworld'. Born in a mountain village in Italy he emigrated to the United States at the start of the last century. He rose to power in prohibition days and married a Jewish girl. The character of Vito Corleone in the book and film *The Godfather,* was said to be based upon an amalgam of 20th Century Mafia figures of which Mr Frank was the most famous. Brando will be forever remembered for his Oscar-winning performance in that role, and his rasping voice, which was achieved by stuffing cotton wool in his mouth. That was the first thing I noticed about Mr Frank when we met for tea in the Waldorf Astoria where he maintained a penthouse. It was said that his old friend Meyer Lansky, whose words preface this chapter, frequently visited Mr Frank seeking advice on vital Mafia business.

At that time I knew none of this, I saw Mr Frank as another charming man, beautifully dressed. In those days I always prided myself on my appearance and that day I was wearing a King's Road suit purchased in one of Mr Irvine Sellar's boutiques. Sellar later quit the fashion game to go into property. You might have seen one of his projects – it's called the Shard. I noticed upon my return to London how the rich are retreating slowly higher up the hill. Mr Frank made me feel under dressed as he rose to greet us wearing a midnight blue mohair suit, a crisp white shirt and highly spit-polished brogues.

He arranged for us to have ‘English tea’ or his idea of it, Earl Grey tea, cucumber sandwiches and some gorgeous cream cakes. Some guy was playing Rachmaninov in the corner, it was a lavish spread typical of the traditional high tea currently sold at the Ritz. I told him of the troubles that I was having back home, the defamation of my reputation by the City, the constant harassment from the press; I was staring down the barrel make no mistake. Mr Frank listened intently, expressing the view that I was respected in his country because I was seen as ‘A man of the people’. *The Los Angeles Times* once described me as: ‘A legend. A Messiah-type figure, a champion of the little people.’

How come those goons at the airport had not read it? I caught him staring at me at one point in the proceedings like a space alien staring at an earthling. Mr Frank praised my business acumen and then started extolling the virtues of family. It could have come straight out of Mario Puzo’s book. We concluded our conversation with a chat about gardening, which was his hobby. I read somewhere that he displayed some of his roses at local horticultural shows. If you look at the ‘Godfather ‘box set you will observe that both the Brando and Pacino characters died in their gardens.

On another occasion Dave took us to a family barbecue. I think it was out Long Island way. Yes they did have red and white check table clothes like in that marge advert. The traditional Sicilian food was out of this world. Jamie Oliver would have been highly envious of the wonderful dishes that were on display. A Michelin-star restaurant would have been proud of the sausages. The men sat quietly chatting amongst themselves, nursing bottles of cold Japanese beer and keeping an eye on their pretty bambini. Later they would light fat cigars and the women, most of them lithe and tanned, would sunbathe and swim. It could have been a firm of accountants having a weekend get-together. My scalded soul was slowly recovering from London. Dave told us that Lenny was part of 'The family'. I only learnt much later that he was referring to the Gambino family, one of the most notorious in the history of organised crime. Dave, it was said, was responsible for the death of six men.

Unaware of this we flew down to Memphis where I stayed at the home of one of Lenny's friends. This place was a mansion back home, even at today's prices you could buy a street of detached houses in a nice part of Surrey for what this place would fetch. The pool would be called infinity today. Immaculately clean with a marble staircase, huge leather sofas, and expensive rugs everywhere. Of course Elvis lived in Memphis but he was never mentioned. Just a hick, country boy from the poorer side of town.

Speaking of Elvis and music Lenny asked me if I would not mind arranging a small tour for Sam and his crew in England. I had the contacts sure enough and readily agreed. The record, called 'Woolly Bully', became a hit in England too. Later on *Rolling Stone* magazine voted it the 'number one record of the year' sometimes you can hear it on that Gold station. To this day I could not tell you what it was about, somebody told me it was to do with his cat. No such thing as a free lunch as everybody knows. That was my part of the deal. I met Sam a couple of times. He seemed a pleasant enough fellow; he used to drive to his gigs in a 1952 Packard hearse. That was the only hit he had, he is still going strong combining music with a career as a public speaker. Eventually we returned to London to face a different type of music.

Chapter 3 - The Men Who Sold The World

'I had been reading a lot in the papers about John Bloom' - David Bowie

'If one hears bad music, it is one's duty to drown it in conversation.'

A Picture of Dorian Gray - Oscar Wilde

'I heard you died alone. A long, long time ago

Oh no not me I never lost control'

'The Man Who Sold the World' - David Bowie 1971

My all-time favourite Bowie song. In our own way we both sold the world. The lyrics seemed even more appropriate when I returned to London in the spring of 2013. When I visited my synagogue people would come up to me and say: 'I thought that you were dead'.

I shook my head, I wanted to use the Mark Twain reply 'reports of my death were greatly exaggerated', but just smiled back.

David was everywhere at that time. You can gauge his popularity by the fact that, when the Victoria & Albert museum hosted a retrospective exhibition decades later the Brompton Road turned into a huge queue of excited Bowie-ists. We were both making comebacks from debilitating health problems. The previous autumn I had seen some paparazzi smudges of him shuffling about New York wearing a flat cap and old jeans. Reports indicated that, following his heart attack in 2004, the sexagenarian had become a recluse. We both had something to prove. I wanted to write this chapter about him to set the record straight about an incident that concerned him that was incorrectly reported in the press at the time. The coverage was categorically without merit and ridiculously facetious.

Bowie's comeback album was called 'Another Day', cunningly disguised in the old 'Heroes' cover with a white label stuck over it, typical of his guerrilla marketing and promotional nous. The vocals sounded weary but striking, it sent a chill down me as I heard him sing

'Here I am, not quite dying'

David was now 66 I could give him 16 years. So how did I feel when he renders these songs about the pleasure and pain of life?.

The V&A exhibition had the' Starman' suit he wore on *Top of the Pops* in 1972 (The disgraced Jimmy Saville introduced him.) They even had the hand written lyrics for' Ziggy Stardust'. What they did not have was a letter that Bowie had written to me in the early 60's. That was how the whole thing started.

David Robert Jones was born in Brixton on 8th January 1947, and shares a birthday with Elvis Presley. In her youth, his mother Margaret Mary was reported to have had connections with the Black Shirts, a faction of Nationalists lead by MP Oswald Moseley. Oswald's youngest son Max is one of my closest friends. So how can a Jewish boy be friends with the offspring of the guy who used to organise fascists marches through Jewish neighbourhoods? Well that's the complex nature of friendship and one of the many ironies in my life.

Not that David was entirely exempt from controversy concerning fascism. There was an unfortunate picture of him giving the straight arm salute at Victoria Station when he arrived for the UK leg of his 1976 tour, I bet you thought it all started with the former West Ham striker Paolo Di Canio and his Ultra chums at Lazio football club.

David's father John was not so political and in 1963 wanted to help his teenage son make it in the music business. In his early days David was toying with a myriad of personae and incarnations.

I was at my zenith then, or just approaching it, and getting huge coverage in the press. It was different back then, there was no celebrity culture like today. Things were changing, but the mega explosion in the youth movement and the birth of 'Swinging London 'was still a couple of years away. I was so big because I was an entrepreneur and the papers latched onto the fact that I was trying to change things for the ordinary person. I was seen as a rebel, an outlaw, taking on the system and for a short time winning.

The Beatles had just emerged, and unless you were around in those days, you had no idea just how popular they were. Instantly recognised by all generations, nothing like this had happened before or again. Everybody in the country knew John, Paul, George and Ringo. Today the biggest boy band is 'One Direction' but how many people out of 10 could name any of them? I had been associated with the Beatles, we had socialised and I had almost talked them into doing an advert for my company.

That was how John Jones knew of me; perhaps the fact that the mop-tops' manager Brian Epstein was another Jewish entrepreneur swung it for me. I was just the person to give his son that first vital assistance.

There are as nearly many Bowie books as there are cook books on the market but the most erudite is by an American called Mark Spitz, his tome simply named after the great man. In this connection I quote the following words from Bowie.

'I had been reading a lot in the papers about John Bloom. So I put pen to paper and wrote him a letter'.

I nearly did not get it. I was living in Park Lane at the time, in a building called Aldford House. David had just put something like 'John Bloom, Washing Machines. London' on the envelope. Lucky the Post Office knew my location and delivered it safely. I was getting nearly as much mail as the Beatles. Some were complaints, some were begging (I told Bernie so many times about that), some were downright offensive, but most were just nice letters of thanks from ordinary people. One of my admin staff read them all and made sure most of them were answered. I think that was one of the reasons for my success/survival. I've always talked to everybody. (Anne says too much most of the time) but that kept me tuned in with what was going on in the real world.

The late Malcolm McLaren, another shrewd guy who knew about managing some of pop's biggest names (Sex Pistols, Boy George & Adam Ant) had this great expression about 'getting his shoes dirty'.

The gist of David's letter was that, with my money and his talent we could make it big. My end was that I could be the next Brian Epstein and make another million.

In those days he was known as David Jones and had a band called the King Bees. They were named after an old blues standard by someone who rejoiced in the name of Slim Harpo. The music they were doing was some sort of Rhythm and Blues; a few miles across town the Rolling Stones were perfecting their version of the genre. David knew he needed capital to purchase equipment for his group and that was where I came in.

I have to admit that I was so immersed in business that my knowledge of what was happening in the exploding music scene was virtually non-existent. But I knew a man that did – his name was Lesley Conn. He was a larger than life, Mr Fix-it who had been operating on the fringes of the London music scene for a number of years. The emerging beat/R& B scene was not really his field but he was highly experienced and saw this new 'pop racket' as another career move. 'Fill up your pockets whilst you can' that was his mantra.

Nobody expected it to last, especially the artists themselves. Conn was associated with Doris Day's publishing company Melcher Music, named after her husband Marty. Doris was still a gigantic star at that time, churning out those early rom-coms with Rock Hudson. Conn was the first person to use that old 'I knew her before she was a virgin' gag, perhaps that is why he never made it as big as he should have. He had that quirky, anti-social streak in him.

Doris had a son, Terry Melcher who was heavily involved in the burgeoning American music business. The following year he was to produce the Byrd's' classic song 'Mr Tambourine Man' written by Bob Dylan. The Beatles were always raving about Dylan and I lost some street cred with them when I pleaded ignorance of his work.

A few years later, Melcher got involved with the notorious Charles Manson and his murderous gang of followers. Manson had pretensions to be a pop star himself but actually knew less about music than me. The pair fell out after Charlie boy flunked the audition for a recording contract. The beautiful Hollywood actress Sharon Tate, wife of the film producer and Holocaust survivor Roman Polanski, was slaughtered by the gang at their mansion. They had turned up there one night looking for Terry who used to live there.

The address was 10050 Cielo Drive Hollywood; some five years later Bowie, by a strange coincidence, was living a few blocks away in the midst of a personal and pharmaceutical maelstrom.

I rang Conn telling him about the letter I had received from Mr Jones and asked him to get in touch with the young man to see if he could help him. The cheeky letter had impressed me and I wanted to help David, though I did not have time or the specialist expertise to really help him.

David impressed Lesley when he auditioned for him at his Marble Arch flat and signed him up on the spot. Dick James, the Beatles' music publisher and another mutual friend, was approached with a view to signing David but no deal was agreed. It was through Dick James that I had a chance to buy the Beatles' publishing company, a deal that should have happened and that would have set me up for life. My mentor at that time was Sir Isaac Wolfson, considerably older than me and a very devout Jew. Isaac hated pop music and advised me not to get involved in such a venture

With a hands-on-manager like Conn calling the shots, David and the boys progressed. Soon he landed them their first prestigious gig- playing at yours truly's wedding anniversary party.

I married my beautiful wife Anne on Sunday 12th February 1961, and am delighted to say we are still together to this day.

Three years on we decided to hold an anniversary party to celebrate; my appetite for the social circuit was at its height. The guest list was a veritable Who's Who of the rich and famous of that era. If *Hello* magazine had been in existence then, they would have died for the pictures. I cannot deny it; in those days I loved mingling with well known people who like me then, were successful.

Virtually anybody who was anybody in showbiz and big business, plus footballers, and a few villains also came into my life. John Bloom had figured in his own contemporary Pilgrim's Progress or so I thought at that time. I could fill the rest of this chapter up with the names and bios of them but to précis it some of the people present at my gathering were Lord Roy Thompson (press baron), Sir Isaac Wolfson, (head of Great Universal Stores), England football captain Billy Wright and his wife (the first wag) pop singer Joy, Adam Faith and his manager Eve Taylor, Sir Joseph Lockwood (Head of EMI), Lulu's manager Marian Massey, (Lulu was later to score a big hit with her version of Bowie's song 'Man Who Sold The World') singer Dorothy Squires and her husband Roger Moore, (not wearing any ski gear) Dame Vera Lynn and various stars from *That Was the Week That Was*, David Frost's ground breaking TV satire show.

Doing the cabaret was David Jones and the King Bees. A common myth from those days was that at that time David was a mod. He was several months away from it and that night he took the stage in blue jeans and a white tee shirt. The hair was relatively short and dyed a cornflower blond with a Tony Curtis quiff, research indicates it was done with food colouring. Anne recalls it was not that long and confirmed this by recently visiting the in-store pop up @ Selfridges, where on display was the photograph of David in his earlier incarnation the Konrads. David looked like a young waiter who had blown his first pay check on a bad haircut.

The guest list was so large that we had to switch venues from our Park Lane apartment to the club called the Jack of Clubs. It was under Isow's restaurant in Brewers Street and run by a guy called Harry Green. The club sounded like the sort of place that Jack Ruby would own. The gimmick was that I had my name painted in gold on the back of my usual chair. Alma Cogan, the biggest selling vocalist in Britain in the previous decade had her chair nearby. It was in the Jack of Clubs that I first met Stephen Ward, the guy who nearly brought the Tory government down. If his name does not mean a lot to you then perhaps that of Christine Keeler does.

A few yards around the corner was Raymond's Revue bar run by Paul Raymond. I used to see him walking down Wardour Street in ostrich shoes with his retinue of hard boys. Raymond later bought my penthouse in Portman Square. He had recently been fined £5,000 at London Sessions for keeping a disorderly house. The week I wrote this chapter a new film had come out about his life with that Alan Partridge playing him.

Bowie was a habitué of Soho; he hung out in the La Gioconda coffee bar in nearby Denmark Street heart of the London music scene. Other patrons included the soon-to-be Small Faces lead singer Steve Marriott and another of Leslie Conn's protégées, the fledgling Mod Marc Bolan. Conn had superb finely-tuned antennae for raw talent. Bolan (real name Marc Feld) was another fame-hungry Jewish kid, who in few years time would briefly out sell the Beatles with his glam-rock band T-Rex. That was until Bowie eclipsed his career with his 'Ziggy Stardust' album. Always close friends, Bowie was on his TV show a few days before Marc was killed in a car crash in Barnes.

At the Jack of Clubs Bowie came on early in the proceedings, and this was a car smash of a different kind. A messy collision of two eras. The meal was still underway, always a hard time for any artist to win over his audience. Virgil, the poet, reminds us that the devil is in the detail but to be honest I could not tell you what his first song was. It was not recognisable to me, probably some cover of an old Blues classic.

It was a tough crowd; most of our friends from the business world were much older than me. I had surprised the business community by making my first million before I was 30. In a way, it happened too fast, I reached the top so quickly the only way from the stratosphere was down. You cannot imagine the resentment and jealousy I encountered from the old guard. There were a lot of people there from the music business, they knew it was changing and artists like Bowie and John Lennon were taking a flame thrower to it. On their night off, having a few drinks, eating and relaxing they did not want to be reminded of it. But it was too late – the Barbarians were at the gate.

Thinking about it 5 decades on that night was a watershed in the history of British music, and marked the point when the cracks first started appearing. The iceberg was in front but the *Titanic* was sailing on, straight into it.

Wolfson started moaning about the band first, speaking in a guttural Scottish accent, which I found hard to understand. It was a bit like Charlie Endell, 'Budgies' (Adam Faith's) boss from the eponymous TV Show, I think he said something about their hair, then it was some contemptuous pronouncements like 'bloody row' or 'Bloody kids',etc, etc, blah, blah, blah.

He had a generous champagne flute in his hand and was gripping it so hard; I thought the industrially etched crystal would snap anytime.

Let Bowie take the story up: 'it was all a bit embarrassing. The party was posh with many of the guests in evening dress. And we turned up in our t-shirts and jeans to play rhythm and blues. We really worked hard that night but many of them just ignored us and carried on talking as though we were not there.'

I did not realise how tiny Bowie was until I saw him on stage that night. I had just met him briefly before the show, his casual clothes doing little to dim his chocolate-box good looks.

The thing that I noticed was that he had really small feet and later in his career would wear girl's shoes. Bowie was very pleasant but subdued; he seemed tired, even a bit nervous. This was at odds with what Conn had told me about him. He was always supremely confident in the presence of his manager, wanting to take on the world, maybe even sell it.

Lord Roy Thompson, seated at a bottle-laden table alongside mine was a nice guy very modest, he quietened the din when he snapped: 'Give the lad a chance.'

Paradoxically, Sir Joseph Lockwood just had his head down, and he was pushing some scraps of food unenthusiastically around his Wedgewood plate. Lockwood was head of EMI, at that time riding high, flush with the cash from the millions of records that the Beatles were selling. Lockwood was keen to diversify and was talking to me about moving into domestic goods. Nothing ever came of it, Joseph had seen the future in music, represented by the Fab Four, Bowie was just confirming it tonight. Not that he seemed to be enjoying the moment.

I always thought of the HMV 'Dog and Trumpet' logo when I saw Lockwood. Legend had it that the trademark was borrowed from a picture painted at the start of the 20th Century of a fox-terrier listening to the voice of his dead master.

It was obvious that the Bowie performance could not go on any longer. I was worried about my party turning out to be a disaster. I had a lot of very important people to keep happy but above all I wanted it to be a special night for my wife. Nothing could go wrong, I was getting increasingly worried.

I had a word with Billy Wright, a man who had played for England 105 times. Wright is a name from the past that conjures up images of baggy shorts and leather studs, a time when football was still a game played and watched by the working classes. He was married to a girl called Joy, who sang in an act called the

Beverley Sisters. They were the first UK female group to crack the American charts. Billy and Joy were the 'Posh and Becks' of the 60's. England's top player marrying the star of the country's best girl band. Billy was managing Arsenal then, I would hardly expect Mr Wenger to turn up to a similar event today. I tried my best to promote Mr & Mrs Wright, and they even did an advert for me called 'The Wright Choice' or something profound – eat your heart out Don Draper.

Wright was brilliant as Bowie and the King Bees tuned up for their next song. The ex-Wolves legend spoke softly to the future global superstar and the next minute I saw the band start to pack up.

It was widely reported that I shouted at Bowie, telling him to get off the stage as he was' ruining my party'. This was completely untrue, I never shouted at Bowie; in fact I was highly embarrassed at having to let him wind up his show. I felt that I owed him something, as he had turned to me for help. I was torn between some sort of loyalty to him and trying to balance my own personal and professional Life.

Since then Alan Sugar has traded heavily on the reputation of successful and abrasive businessman. His contempt for money grabbing attention seekers with an inflated sense of their own importance could apply to himself.

It was always a source of amusement to me that a businessman with his alleged acumen patently failed to see what sort of person would be interested in appearing on his humiliation fest of a television show. The difference between us was that Sugar would have probably shouted 'Your Fired' at the crestfallen youngster. I just looked across as Bowie and his band slowly dismantled their gear. Contrary to the press reports Bowie was not in tears; obviously he was upset but appeared to be unfazed. He disappeared behind the stage.

The night then took a surreal twist as Dame Vera Lynn took the stage and sang two songs. The first was 'White Cliffs of Dover'. You could not have made it up really, ironic or what? The old wartime chestnut sung by the home guard. The young upstart had been vanquished and the old order had been restored. Of course it had not; Bowie was turning Vera, Lockwood and even Adam Faith into musical dinosaurs. Their future was bankrupt. Also sat in the crowd was a guy called Chris Andrews, who had written a couple of Sandie Shaw's smashes. He had a solo hit himself called 'Yesterday Man' – how appropriate.

Vera wound her act up with another showstopper. 'We'll meet again'. Yeah sure we will. I never met Bowie again, but felt sorry for him and his treatment at the hands of my friends that night. I gave Conn £500 as 'development money' for the group.

I never knew how much of the money eventually filtered down into Bowie's band.

In June 1964, a few months after the shambolic party, David Jones and the King Bees issued their first single 'Liza Jane' written by Conn. It sank quicker than my amphi-car, but he was on his way. The King Bees buzzed off due to the failure of the single, but David became a Mod and was managed by Conn until 1966. They parted amicably – Conn's lack of resources and David's unstoppable exuberance and soaring ambition being the reason for the split. The rest is history.

I lost touch with the music scene as my empire crashed and burnt and I moved into other ventures. I still had a line on Bowie though. I was involved in the night club business and one of my projects was the 'Crazy Horse Saloon'. One of my singers was a young lady called Dana Gillespie. To call her full figured did not do her justice. Bowie met her in the nearby Marquee club and she ended up on his record label in the 70's. She came from an aristocratic background, her father was an Austrian Baron and seriously wealthy. I do not know if they had any connection with the House of Vettel.

Dana kept me informed of Bowie's trajectory, the blueprints of his development; she was one of the first people to hear his first monster hit 'Space Oddity'.

Looking back it was a pity that our paths never crossed again; perhaps I could have advised him financially as he became enmeshed in a huge and expensive wrangle with one of his future managers Tony Defries. That night in the Jack of Clubs saw the end of a particular sensibility of Englishness. Bowie was the single most important artist in the history of English music, an icon of London in transition. I was glad to be part of it.

Chapter 4 - Early Days

'The wheel has come full circle, I am here.'

King Lear - William Shakespeare

Let's go back to the start. I was born on 8th November 1931, 8 years before Mr Hitler decided to set Europe ablaze. I was an East End boy born in Nelson Street down by the docks. That is when they had docks of course, now its Docklands better known as Canary Wharf, full of banks and skyscrapers, not far from the O2, the new Westfield shopping centre at Stratford and the Olympic Park. They have certainly rejuvenated the area since I grew up there.

My father's name was Sam; he was born in Austria and was a tailor by trade. He was an excellent tailor and I can see him now bent over his Singer sewing machine altering the neighbours' clothes. That must have been where I got my love of clothes from and how I become meticulous about my appearance. Sam Bloom was a lovely guy, in temperament the complete opposite of yours truly: calm, quiet, reserved, a real thinker. As I get older I think about him a great deal.

He never once spoke of his early life and how the Bloom family ended up in London Town. Despite his prowess as a tailor money was tight but he worked so hard to avoid his family getting dragged down by the poverty that was everywhere in the East End before the Second World War

When the war broke out my father, because he was Austrian, was interned on the Isle of Man. Crazy or what? They must have thought he was some enemy of the country. Hadn't they heard that Hitler was persecuting the Jewish race? We never saw my father for years; it must have really tough on my mother, and the family ended up in Stoke Newington. We had no money and it was impossible to visit him. With no steady income we just lived off next to nothing. When eventually he was released he was put to work in a clothing factory and kept under surveillance. It must have hurt him deeply, perhaps the trauma of all this, when I was just a small boy, was at the heart at what drove me.

My first vivid memory of my early life was when my grandmother died and I went into the bedroom in Nelson Street where she was laid out. All the Bloom family were gathered there to offer their condolences and the gravity and overwhelming sadness of it all struck me. It scared me and I wondered how long it would be before my parents died. Death was always around me throughout my life. I know a lot of dead people.

My first memory of London town was when I was five and went up on a hot and muggy summer's day to London's West End for an outing on a bus. It must have been a huge event because the pavements were packed with people. I googled 1936 but there was no Festival or special occasion in London. My abiding memory was of how clean the West End was opposed to the grime and filth of my neighbourhood.

John Bloom's first business deal involved marbles, just before war. I always loved marbles and would play endless games with my school mates. I was not brilliant at the game, I was not brilliant at any form of sport, and remembered losing some prized ones. I always loved polished glass. Now there are plenty of people out there that would tell you that John Bloom lost his marbles years ago but I am putting it on record now. Something told me that I would be better off buying and selling these lovely objects to my school chums than losing them. There you have it – my ethos. I realised very early on in life that nobody was going to help me and that I would have to start earning my own money.

Rod Steiger made a movie where he outlined the Jewish trader ethic of how some merchant would get hold of a piece of cloth and tear it in half and sell a portion. With whatever he made from the sale he would buy some more cloth and sell that, etc, etc. it sounded fool proof, wish I had seen it back in those times.

After marbles I moved into fireworks, and have been trying to let them off in one way or another every since. By this time I had managed to win a scholarship to Hackney Downs Grammar School. I always thought grammar schools were a great idea; propelling bright kids from modest starts into good jobs. Although soon after I made it big Labour government minister Anthony Crosland said he would not rest until he closed them all down.

The war had just ended and fireworks were in short supply, as were most things actually. My schoolmates loved letting them off but could not be bothered queuing up outside shops for them. I spotted a gap in the market and was prepared to put in the hours obtaining them. I never minded doing these things because I was earning. I could buy them for one old penny and knock them out for three times that. Steiger would have been proud of me.

Things were going great but my business literally went up in smoke one evening. I was coming home on the train with my entire stock stashed in a cardboard box that I had obtained from the corner store. Some wise-guy flicked a burning match into the box and Guy Fawkes Night came early that year. It was a good display though.

Things were tough but I had a happy childhood because my parents loved me and showed it. Later in life I could see the effect that a lack of love in childhood and undemonstrative parents had on people. Poor little rich girls everywhere. Sigmund Freud, another clever old chap, was always of the view that what happened in your early life set the pattern for the rest of it, but that always seemed so obvious to me.

Another explosive incident in the war years nearly did for me. I was staying with my grandfather in Dunsmure Road one night when the Luftwaffe launched a huge raid on London Town, with the docks their main target. I was lying on the couch praying for it all to end when suddenly I heard a terrific crash. A shell had fallen onto our house killing my grandfather in the next room. The shell had been fired by the anti-aircraft battery nearby at one of the bombers but had failed to detonate and had fallen to earth. My grandfather was just unlucky that it fell on him; it was awful, and I heard years later that it had severed his legs. I escaped unscathed, apart from being covered in grime and dust. As a precaution I spent the night in Homerton Hospital, and looking back it was a miraculous escape, for had the shell gone off when it impacted I would have been a goner for sure. God had other plans for John Bloom, though.

The war was an exciting period for me and London was a huge adventure playground my chums and I would spend hours in the many bombsites looking for shrapnel. At night in the recently dug Anderson air raid shelter my sister Noreen and I would look at the sky filled with German Heinkel Bombers. It was like watching a movie. Later the sky was lit up a bright red and orange from the fires that raged throughout London. The nearby docks were a strategic target and the bombers came over night after night, wave after wave.

Sometimes we would see soldiers back from the front walking the streets in their uniforms home on leave. We would ask them for badges and more often than not they would give us them as souvenirs. I could sell them also – this was years before eBay. Now I was selling whatever I could come across and I thought would do well. Comics did the biz and also chewing gum that I managed to obtain from America by getting letters published in the papers over there appealing for goodies.

There was always the danger of being beaten up because of my background. The Teddy boy gangs were a few years away but there were always bullies and racists. I was always a lover, not a fighter, I was very thin and not that good looking, I started living on my wits, avoiding the thugs who ran in gangs and taunted the Jewish kids.

I hated school, could never see the point of it. I had no real plan for my life or even a sense of the future, there was no career officers, job workshops or advisors in those days. I never expected to be a millionaire before I was 30. When the business crashed I remember that the *New Statesman* ran a big piece on me saying that, even as far back as my schooldays, I was taught the only path open to my agile mind (their phrase) was to be a millionaire. News to me! In those days it was seen as a crime, that's why I called my first book ' *It's no sin to make a profit*.'

I even encountered racism at school from the teachers. My form teacher was a good example. I do not even remember his name; he was an old spud, a bigger manic depressive than the Grand Old Duke of York. The headmaster was a Mr Balk who did not bother us much but the form teacher was a problem: when he was up he was up and when he was down... Every morning he would take the register and being an ethnic neighbourhood most of the names were Jewish: Cohen, Goldberg, Bernbaum and a few Blooms.

'No Smiths or Joneses here today?' he would enquire wearily, then with a heavy sigh would slam the register shut. Wouldn't be allowed in these PC times.

A favourite moment when I was a kid was listening to the *Goons* show on the radio. There was no television then, let alone DVDS or iPads. The programme featured the combined talents of Peter Sellers, Spike Milligan, Harry Secombe and Michael Bentine. It was perhaps the most influential comedy show of all time and in those days completely anarchic and totally surreal. A few years later I wrote to Sellers inviting him and his wife to be guests on my boat, filming commitments did not allow him to but I received a very nice, amusing letter back.

I was lucky enough to meet Harry Secombe at a charity function one night. I recall watching a documentary on the *Goons* made a few months before Secombe's death. One scene featured Harry visiting Spike Milligan, both men were in the autumn of their lives and beset by health problems. Their humour, though, was still special, razor sharp. The Irish genius Milligan asked Harry to promise him one thing.

'Of course Spike, anything.'

'If I go first please do not sing at my funeral.'

He never got the chance.

My other passion at that time was Arsenal Football Club; in the 30's they were the giants of the game, as dominant as Manchester United have been in the 21st century. It was the start of a lifelong love affair with the club. Shortly after the end of the war a chum and I decided to visit the hallowed halls of Highbury. (For younger viewers this was their home ground before they moved to the Emirates Stadium). Dressed in our best school uniform, navy-blue blazer with badge, white shirt, school tie, grey flannel trousers and shiny shoes we looked the part.

The cub reporters turned up at the ground informing the Commissionaire that we had been commissioned by the school magazine to write an article on the club.

We were welcomed in and next thing we found ourselves actually on the hallowed turf, where the team was training. Imagine such a thing happening today? One of my particular heroes was an Irish winger called Kevin O'Flanagan and we saw him juggling the ball, playing 'keepie uppie'. The Arsenal star was only too pleased to spend time talking to us and answered our questions as we furiously scribbled into our little notebooks. When he was not flying down the wing Kevin was also a qualified doctor, an interesting fellow and a true sportsman in the Corinthian manner, and he ended up playing for Brentford. I cannot see Theo Wolcott dishing out prescriptions somehow.

My next visit to Arsenal was in November 1945 to see the fabulous Moscow Dynamos, who in essence were the Russian national team. They had come to London at a time of particular friendship between the two countries. The war had ended just a few months before and the British nation was grateful to the Russians for the huge sacrifice they had made in helping win the war. All that Cold War stuff was to follow the next decade. There was even crank theories that the Russian team were in fact on a spying mission.

This was at the time of all that Philby / McLean / Espionage / Third Man/ Spooks paranoia (speaking of spies, wait till you read my chapter on Stephen Ward and Christine Keeler, another name linked with Russian spies).

If that were true about Moscow Dynamo then they were the best double agents of all time because they were dazzling footballers. Chelsea had scraped a lucky 3-3 draw against them in a match watched by an estimated 100,000 people. So desperate were the fans to see the Russians they had kicked down the locked gates and burst into the ground. A few days before they had visited Wales and beat Cardiff 10-1.

The thing I recall most about that game was the thick fog in which it was played. The papers said that Dynamo won 4-3. It could have been 14-3, so little of the match was visible to us. The legend that was Stanley Matthews guested for Arsenal that day. Such things were regular occurrences at that time. I had never seen so many people gathered in one place, we even saw some Russians, sailors on shore leave carrying a huge faded Soviet battle flag. I had never seen any Russians before I expected them to have moustaches like Stalin and snow on their boots but they were only young, with faces like choirboys.

I left Hackney Downs with no formal qualifications and 'Could do better 'stamped across my reports.

Education had come at the wrong time for me, I did not like the way I looked, and I did feel very insecure. I idled my way through an incongruous string of jobs, including stints as a salesman in Selfridges and a junior in the press office at the Board of Deputies of Jews. Don't ask me exactly what *they* did.

The Selfridges job was interesting, the money was not. I was earning £2 a week; I think they paid me in buttons. I was selling fridges and these things called washing machines. They were real luxury items I noticed only people that were well off could afford to buy them.

By now I had managed to scrape enough together to buy my first set of wheels. A 1931 Austin 7 for the princely sum of £29. I can even recite the registration number – HX 2104. Everything was going well for me, but then I received my call up papers for National Service.

The RAF sent me to West Kirby on the outskirts of Liverpool. To say I was not excited about any of this was an understatement. It started badly with a three-mile march to camp. I and most of my new colleagues was useless at marching and by the time we got there the NCO in charge was purple with anger and frustration at our dismal performance.

I smuggled my car up to Kirby and stashed it on a farm near the camp, even had a set of street clothes in the boot. I had a Singer now after writing off good old HX2104 on a European jaunt with a mate of mine. The car was invaluable on the weekends when I had leave. A group of us would then drive to Liverpool or even Blackpool where we would sample the local nightlife. Great fun until an off duty corporal, who just happened to supervise our billet, spotted the 'Likely Lads' driving down Lime Street as if they owned the place.

Then I got ill, really bad. I swerved an assault course that Rambo would have struggled with and was put on fatigues in the bread shop dolling out the rations. It gave new meaning to 'give us this day our daily bread'. This was post war England remember and people did not wear those plastic glove thingies they have on the bakery counter in your local M&S. By the next morning I was off my feet and was sent to the Camp doctor who immediately diagnosed scarlet fever, still considered a very serious illness at that time being so soon after the advent of commercial antibiotics. Soon rumours were rife that because of the bread round the whole place was going to be infected. Luckily enough nobody was but everybody was panicked into thinking an epidemic was about to strike.

I was in the sick bay for weeks and when I finally was discharged my group had passed out and I was shunted out to another squadron. Due to some admin error I was transferred into being a NAAFI orderly. In the jargon of the RAF it was a really cushy number and I had the added bonus of striking up a relationship with a voluptuous young lady who also worked in there. It was a real 'cash-back' time for me as I spent time with her whilst outside my colleagues were square bashing. Their ears ringing from the grief given to them by the foul mouthed paranoid drill sergeants.

One of the biggest comedy shows in the early 60's was called the *Army Game*, a satire of Army life still so resonant as everyone vividly remembered the war, and of course National Service was a fact of life; the show really caught on in a big way. The stars of the show were two characters called 'Bootsie and Snudge'. Bootsie was a skiving malingerer played by a brilliant character actor called Alfie Bass, who was always getting out of marching by claiming he suffered from 'bad feet'. That's where 'Bootsie' bit came into it, excused boots being an army expression for missing marching. The 'Snudge' character, played by Bill Fraser, was the sort of bullying Sgt Major jobs worth type I fell foul of many a time during my National Service. I met his type all my life actually, and have been waging war against them with various degrees of success.

At my zenith in 1962, just after the Cuban missile crisis had nearly turned the earth into a pile of ashes, the *Daily Mirror* ran an editorial headed 'Bootsie and Snudge (and the New Diplomacy)'. My name nestles there between those of President Kennedy and Mr Khrushchev, then the two most powerful men in the world. That is how far I had come. I told my friend John Lennon once that if you reach a certain point in the stratosphere then the only place is down. John disagreed but could not really tell me of anybody who was as big as they had become and who had actually stayed there,

The point of this was that, within just over a decade, my name could be linked with such august company. If you had told back then in West Kirby that would have happened to me I would have laughed the loudest. You see in life you never know what is going to happen next. Ok I am dropping more names than those marbles I sold – but it happened.

I did learn also the hard way, though, that nothing lasts forever, especially if it's good. My idyll in the NAAFI was rudely interrupted by a 'Snudge' of a warrant officer who started investigating me. I ended up in front of the top man in the squadron. I think he was the commander, and he was apoplectic when he learnt how little square bashing I had done. Passing out day was near and he was nearly passing out himself. He knew I would never make the grade and come the big day John Bloom was back in the NAAFI hiding out whilst the lads were pounding the square.

They made me take an aptitude test, convinced I was a nut of some sort. That was the problem: they could not figure me out at all and they were very surprised that I came out of it with a high score. Enough to make me a teleprinter operator. At that time it was on the cutting edge of technology. I did not have a clue what it was; only later discovering it was a similar to the thing that used to give out the Arsenal score on a Saturday tea time. Of course that was when they played on Saturday afternoons.

Compton Basset was my next port of call, down in Wiltshire. It could not have been more remote to me than the place where the Dynamos played their home games. A coach to London was 26 old shillings. Ok, you do not do foreign money that is £1.30 in today's currency. Problem was I was earning about 10p (2 shillings) more than that for the whole week. Thanks a lot. Even less than Selfridges were paying me for knocking out those washing machines.

You did not have to be John Milton Keynes to work out we were getting ripped off big time. Dick Turpin was a highwayman who robbed coaches, but in this movie the coaches did the robbing. I needed to get back to London on a regular basis, my mother's health was poor and I wanted to keep an eye on her. Back in London I started asking around about the coach fares between Wiltshire and London.

I found a guy called Bob Smith who had some coaches and cut me a deal of around 70p a seat. I sold them to the guys for about 15p more and part of the deal was that I always had a seat for me. It took off faster than Gareth Bale; within weeks I was running three coaches on a weekend and had slashed the price down. I was making just a little and the RAF boys were happy because they were getting back to London for a cheaper price, which gave them a little bit more to spend when they got there. It just mushroomed, and soon other bases wanted to get in on the act. I bought a Hudson Terraplane out of the money I was making.

It was a lovely piece of steel, silver and grey, beautiful upholstery. I always wanted an American car with the fins, and with the lights it looked like something out of a movie starring Tony Curtis, who was just starting out at that time. I was causing a stir by now, the local coach operators were losing half of their business and most of the bases were not too struck on me. Now in the ninth decade of my life I do not know where I got the chutzpah from. I had always had my radar on for racists but I soon ran up against powerful enemies in the camp, drill sergeants, the adjutant and the commanding officer. Course I did not help myself by parking the Terraplane outside the camp gates. Flash little fellow that I was.

The drill sergeant started harassing me big time; of course being this atrocious marching airman, I gave him more ammunition than the Magnificent Seven. Things became a little tricky for me and became worse when one of the local coach owners dropped a coin on me and told the police about my activities. I went to Clerkenwell Court and was found guilty on two charges, operating a coach business without a licence and making a profit on a self-help venture. I was given a conditional discharge. Summing up the kindly magistrate used the 'no sin to make a profit' expression. It was the end of my coach business though.

My mother was diagnosed with disseminated sclerosis a terrible disease. The RAF was very good to me and I was transferred to the Air Ministry situated at Bush House in Aldwych so I could be near her. I was still making money, this time on the allowances given to airmen living out of camp. I eventually left the air force and took a while to getting acclimated to civilian life again. It was time for me to get serious about finding a way of making serious money. Then I met a guy called Mick Cosgrave who told me about cheap washing machines.

My RAF days

The Beginning and the End

Chapter 5 - Mr Big

'There's some things you can help and some kind of things you can't do anything about. Knowing the difference, as long as you can tell the difference, you're in pretty good shape.'

The Friends of Eddie Coyle - George V. Higgins

Higgins was called the Balzac of Boston, the best modern, hard-boiled crime writer since Raymond Chandler. 'Eddie Coyle' was his meister-work, a relentlessly apocalyptic tale about a small-time crook that had to sell out somebody to avoid being sent up again. When I lived in America somebody tried to set me up and for a while I was 'Mr Big' to the FBI.

1978. Another year of living dangerously. I was residing on Carla Ridge Drive, Trousdale, Beverley Hills in a pleasant house that I had bought from a fellow by the name of Sly Stone. Sly fronted the famous' Sly and the Family Stone' group who in those days were massive but he fell into drugs and the last I heard of him he was homeless. It's a long way down.

One of my neighbours was Don Costa who arranged and conducted for Francis Albert Sinatra. As another famous vocalist Neil Diamond once sang: 'The sun shone all the time'. Beverly Hills – what a town.

I used to drive to work through those angst-ridden affluent suburbs in a gold Rolls Royce. England, the rain and cold, my business problems back there seemed a lifetime ago. I had plans for an oceanfront domicile. It was a dog-eat-dog world but as one of LA 's most famous residents, film maker Sam Goldwyn so succinctly put it 'And no Dog's gonna eat me' I was in television then, not an exaggeration but not one of the smash hit shows like *Dallas* or Michael Landon's *Little House on the Prairie* that ruled the airways that year. My angle was the actual business of shifting TV sets. I was schlepping around, selling those large-screen sets long before Dixons, and they were not as thin in those days.

The usual price was $2,500 but I was knocking them out for about $899. I managed to sell them that cheap because I had a magnifier in front of the screen with a German handcrafted lens. That was the video age remember then, another artefact from a bygone era, like the inside forward, LP or tape recorder. Videos were big business back then. It was a golden era for the cinema, they actually made films that people went out to see then and would want to watch again and again in the comfort of their own homes. The big film that of the day was the sci-fi epic *Star Wars*; America was shattered morally by the fallout from its unsuccessful Vietnamese crusade and craved escapism.

My television showroom was on Beverly Boulevard. I had two girls working in there, Denise and Pauline charming the punters and selling the merch. They were both lookers, not in the standard American pretty way and both were very clever. One of them, Pauline, told me she was going out with Clint Eastwood. This was standard Hollywood chitchat and when she told me sometimes that 'I was out with Clint last night' I was a little sceptical to tell you the truth. I always wanted to meet the great man; having followed his career from the 50's when he appeared in *Rawhide*. I suppose, like 90 per cent of the young females in that town, she wanted to find fame and fortune. In what order they actually came were not of great importance to them.

Clint did make my day for me, however, by coming into the shop; Pauline must have told him what a bargain my televisions were. I did not recognise him at first; I just saw this gangly figure that was dressed very badly, at least a decade behind the times. The actor was wearing a rumpled dark corduroy shirt, faded jeans with a thick leather belt and some type of cowboy boots. He was staring intently at the screen, and if I recall there was some cartoon thing on. Something told me not to approach him I just stood at the back of the store. Suddenly he whirled round and said: 'I will take two of these.'

The famous drawl gave it away; he didn't say much. It is odd meeting famous people you know so many things about them. That year he was making the film with the orangutan, my favourite of his was *Unforgiven*. To me he was the last true male movie star, raised to be a hero when the first generation of legends, Bogart, Clark Gable and Errol Flynn, were dead or dying.

Speaking of movie stars, the girls had some dubious contacts; they would tell potential customers that they could obtain the latest films in the hope of closing the sale. Video piracy was a highly sensitive matter then and I am not talking about those Johnny Depp pictures when he was Capt. Jack Sparrow. It still is a major problem today; the figures are little short of mind-boggling: in Britain alone in 2011 bootlegging cost the film industry nearly £450m in lost revenue. Back then the multinational entertainment conglomerates were getting very upset at what they were missing out on and were exerting a lot of political pressure on the authorities to take steps to tackle the problem.

None of this was any concern to me; all I was interested in was selling the televisions and then getting back to my wife Anne and our daughter Nicole in Beverley Hills. Life was sweet ... but never for long, as I was finding out.

One brilliant Californian morning I got to the shop early. I had driven down in the Roller south past McArthur Park, immortalised in the Jimmy Webb song by Richard Harris and that boulevard where the shoot-out happened in *LA Confidential.* I placed a cassette, another artefact, in the tape deck. The man in black, Johnny Cash, singing about Folsom Prison.

Sometimes I could not wait to get to work; I loved hustling the televisions and meeting the Los Angeles public, most of them crazies or fruitcakes. Shortly after the opening at 9am I glanced up from my copy of the *Wall Street Journal* just as the doors were thrown open and about half a dozen guys burst in waving guns. They were casually dressed in jeans, baseball caps and sweatshirts. (In chapter one I detailed the practical joke Bernie and I played on the hapless chef at Silverstone. This event was a good two decades before, though, and I had not seen Bernie for some years. Just for a split-second it crossed my mind that he was playing some long-range gag on me.) When I saw the Colt Pythons though I knew it was no joke. I did not see Clint there in his alter ego of 'Dirty Harry'.

'On the floor ass-hole.'

Was he talking to me? The girls had already 'assumed the position' as they say and were against the wall.

By this point I was convinced we were being robbed, my mind was racing, what were we going to this marauding band of bandits? There was no money in store we had only just opened. The leader of the intruders, high on testosterone, waved a wad of papers of some sort under my nose.

'FBI, we have a warrant to search the premises.'

I was startled by the speed of it all, my brain now flipped into overdrive and I recovered to say: *'What are you searching for?'*

'Pirate videos'

My thoughts turned to Anne and my daughter. If she got to hear my about my shop being stormed by these armed police she would be worried sick.

'Can I phone home I need to speak to my wife?'

The FBI agent was wearing a leather jacket even though it was so warm. He had thick black eyebrows and curled his lips saying: *'Too late, we are there already.'*

They had hit Carla Ridge drive simultaneously. Anne was at home with Nicole about to pick up her friend and go to their aerobics class.

She had to call her friend to say they she could not transport her that day as she was at present being raided by the FBI! The agents had already blocked the circular driveway with a couple vans and it was not long before the place was looking like a major crime scene, swarming with the FBI, uniform cops and detectives. For the next two hours they systematically dismantled the house. They even searched Anne's underwear drawer.

Then they turned their attentions to my daughter's room and began by tipping her toy chest onto the floor. Dolls, teddies, 'my little ponies' were strewn everywhere. What a mess. Later my tearful daughter asked me: 'What were those nasty men doing to my toys?'

I shrugged my shoulders, what could I tell her?

The nasty men found zilch; the only video was my daughter's copy of the classic Judy Garland film *Wizard of Oz*. If I remember they took that with them but gave Anne a receipt for it. That reminds me – I must get it back sometime.

Back at the shop they were doing the same thing, stripping the place down, tipping out drawers, emptying cupboards, they even took the backs of the television sets expecting to find stashes of drugs or master tapes of movies. Under the shelf on which some VCRs sat were two drawers all filled with tapes?

These were all coded: they thought they were the mother lode, but it fact were just tapes of shows and films recorded off the TV to demo our fabulous TV's, certainly nothing illegal.

Joe Carbone was a not quite the small time video pirate he had convinced his new found friends at the FBI of, his narrow eyes were dark like a rodent's, he was given to wearing shiny suits and flashing a wad of bills that would have choked one of my old spin dryers, in short he was a punk. The fact Carbone had been picked up by the cops with 2900 pirate videos in his possession, you would think would have been a clue. Thinking about it maybe they should have asked my new pal Clint to ask him about his luck. In any event they had leaned on him to give them a bigger name in connection with the video crimes.

That is where I came in. I was already a local celebrity, the flaky English guy, with his outlaw attitude, that had made and lost a fortune and was now getting it back. The Americans loved those stories. Surely this was the central theme of American Movies? *Rocky* in particular – no matter how many times you got knocked down, it was how many times you got back up.

Once in a while I would buy the odd video or two from Mr Carbone, I preferred to watch movies at home rather than going to the Cinema, after all finding a big screen TV to watch them on wasn't exactly a problem.

In custody, it must have taken the lathered Carbone all of ten minutes to start giving up names. Mine was first out of his mouth, 'Mr Big', a guy who lived in a mansion up in Beverley Hills and drove around in a gold limo. The local police kicked the file over to the FBI; this was the biggie, the mastermind behind the whole racket, the bête noire of the entertainment industry. So I was in the frame and soon the FBI was bugging my phones, at home and the shop, no mobiles then. Carbone went on to tell them some elaborate story about how I had set up a network of couriers that regularly delivered copies to the UK where they were duplicated and distributed on mass, the cops bought it hook, line and sinker.

Soon the monitored conversations included one of the girls telling customers that they could get them any video they wanted, in any quantity. That is when they decided to raid my home and work place. Beforehand they had tried to set me up with a 'sting', a pincer movement, trying to make a case against me. A young couple visited my home a few weeks before the raid; they arrived in a battered blue Karman Ghia coupe. The girl looked like the good-looking babe in CSI, the one set in Miami: requisite nose job, a fabulous mane of blonde hair, knockout body. She was wearing a bikini-top, skin-tight jeans and stiletto heels, the distraction and perfect at it; I recognised her partner as Lou Swartz he was Jo Carbon's 'runner' he was an unsavoury chap he looked like he had smallpox or something, a skinny beanpole with straggly, unwashed hair.

It was a Saturday, I had a few friends around the pool, chatting and having a couple of drinks. The last thing I needed was these two turning up.

'I was told us you could get us some pirate movies?'

'*What*?' I said slightly confused by the request, given that Lou would usually be the person delivering the odd video to me.

'We want a hundred Rocky's and a Hundred Star Wars.'

'*Are you insane?*' I replied, thinking he had lost his marbles.

I shook my head and told him to leave, at the time I thought no more about it, that is of course till later when my home was being ransacked. I later learnt that Lou had been wearing a 'wire', the whole act had been set up by the FBI who listening to every word in a van parked down the road.

Despite the fact that the searches unearthed nothing the FBI were even more determined to pin something on me. I later found out that they were convinced that I was shadowy head of the piracy business.

So convinced were they that I was indeed 'Mr Big' that they started investigating internally believing that somebody had tipped me off and given me time to remove any incriminating evidence, crazy eh?

I needed a lawyer and found a guy called Nick Sheridan, low profile and well connected, with a well cultivated tan as well as affability. He told me that I had nothing to worry about, oh yeah where had I heard that one before? Things calmed down, and for a little while I got on with my life. To me Hollywood was a boomtown, laissez-faire and all that. I used to go to a grill in Rodeo Drive, which was full of the biggest power brokers in Hollywood; it was a favourite spot of mine because of the crisp blue linen and the attentive staff. I was sat in the booth when the maître d' told me there was an urgent message. It was Nick with a shuddering call...

'What do you want the goods news first or the bad news?'

It was a rule of mine that I always asked for the good news first.

'The good news is that I am quitting the crime business and going to work in the music business.'

I was not exactly sure what relevance this had to me, or the price of bagels. Nick did very well in the music industry and ended up looking after some of the biggest names in the business. We kept in vague touch and he used to send Anne and me tickets for some of the shows at the Hollywood Bowl his clients were starring in. Do not remember Sam the Sham and the Pharaohs being amongst them.

'Can't wait for the bad'

Nick, cleared his throat before saying, 'The FBI has contacted me, and they are indicting you.'

How it works was that the US Attorney would give what evidence he had collated to the Grand Jury. This consisted of thirty-plus upright citizens who would examine the evidence and in almost all of the cases ask for an indictment. I felt a sensation like a small rodent running up my spine.

I recovered my composure and summoned up some gravitas. '*What do you think?'*

'Get a good lawyer who knows about piracy' Nick advised

His voice trailed off. I drove home thinking about what I would do next.

Nick's replacement was guy called Dominic Rubicava, he had previously worked in the DA's office prosecuting video pirates so he knew the drill. Dominic advised me to '*Plead no contest*' he explained *'the wheel of fortune would pick the judge. It all depends on the luck of the draw, the spin of a wheel, it's a crap shoot. If it's a good judge then you got a chance but if ... You can't win in those situations'*

The next day I took a call from FBI Agent Wulfing, one of the guys who had crashed in on Anne and Nicole when they turned my place over. This fellow was a giant well over 6ft, he looked like a line backer from the Green Bay Packers, and perhaps he had been. Wulfing wanted to question me some more about our erstwhile friend Joe Carbone, and announced that was coming over that evening.

Wulfing stayed three hours, during that time he refused to accept any of Anne's numerous offers of coffee. He had a gunmetal crew cut, the military type. Like most of those FBI boys he had seen action in Vietnam. The Viet Cong would have had their work cut out containing him. Incorrigibly overpowering and combative he quizzed me non-stop about Joe. What dealings had I had with him? This was the crucial, pivotal link in their case; his eyes lit up like the glittering Las Vegas strip when I said I had a transaction with him. We have got him now! Bloom admitting his association with Carbone and that he was collateralising the purchase of illegal videos.

'I remember now I bought some videos from him '

'How many, a thousand?'

I shook my head.

'500?'

'Nah, nothing like that.'

'200, 100?'

I denied buying that many.

'Well how many?'

'I honestly do not remember, but not many?'

Beefy Wulfing was no fool, a qualified attorney at law. He looked confused but switched his line of attack.

'How did you buy them? Cash, commodities exchange – drugs perhaps?'

I nearly burst out laughing in his face.

'Sure I gave him some dope. 3 for 2 that week'

Wulfing shot me a furious glance, bbbbbeep, the buzzer went – wrong answer John. I quickly countered.

'It was a cheque actually'

'A cheque. How much for?'

'Not much. My accountant can get if for you in the morning'

The FBI man was closing in: a cheque, irrefutable proof of a deal.

'I want it now, where is this accountant?'

It was a statement, not a question.

'Out in Woodland Hills, name of Connie Envron'.

Wulfing started talking into some walkie-talkie thing he produced from inside his suit, which I need hardly tell you was a conservative shade of black, made of a heavy wool cloth. Even my old dad would have had a task doing anything with it. It was a warm night, in the high sixties thanks to a warm wind blowing in from the desert towards the Pacific; the suit must have been intolerable. Soon a car was speeding under the starlit sky to Connie's house, which was about 30 miles out of town.

Eventually a call came back to Wulfing. He grunted into it, a smile or something approaching that, creased his rugged features.

'The cheque was for $95 for the purchase of three videos – *Star Wars*, *Rocky* and *The Wizard of Oz'*.

Thank god for Connie's accurate bookkeeping I thought. Suddenly Mr Big was Mr Small time. Wulfing wrapped it up pretty quickly after that and eventually left. I noticed the change in his attitude towards me, not that it was ever friendly. He said he was going to speak to his boss and the District Attorney.

I still had to go to court; they trumped up some minor charge about abetting Pauline when she had offered an illicit *Star Wars* video to a private investigator. Well they had to justify all that time, effort, not to say taxpayers' dollars; but it was a pretty small return.

The judge looked at the FBI report prior to sentencing me. Joe Carbone had been let off with the gentlest of slaps on his wrist, and as he was the one that had given them this lubricious information the judge said that there would be no financial penalty.

The girls were charged also and pleaded guilty I think they were charged with trying to sell the things.

Plea-bargaining was the order of the day and they made up some names. I am not sure if they were made up or just punters that gave them hassle in the shop. They were given a discharge and continued to work for me for some time. Pauline never made it as an actress, not that talent was a prerequisite for success. She went into the production side and last I heard of her she was an executive producer on one of Clint's films. Denise married well and lives in Laurel Canyon.

Joey Carbone walked but I do not think he survived much longer on the crime-drenched streets. Nobody liked a grass.

And me? Well the night before the biggest news show in America *60 minutes* (I think it lasted about an hour) did an exposé on the video piracy business and the menace facing America. I do not know if there was anything about 'Mr Big', and to be honest I couldn't bear to watch it. I was just hoping the judge had an early night. I was expecting a fine and to draw a cheque for a sum larger than I had paid to Joey Carbone.

It went better than I thought and I was offered community service. You have all seen the pictures of Boy George sweeping the streets he used to own or the footballer Carlos Tevez driving down in his Porsche to do his stint emptying bins. Well John Bloom had a different punishment; it was lecturing ex-prisoners about business and re-building their lives, both subjects close to my heart.

When I reported to the chief officer for the service he showed great interest in me. The office had been inundated with calls from the British Press who had picked up on the story. The wanted to know precise details of my community service – was I cleaning toilets, what streets would I be sweeping? I must be some real important guy as they never seen such interest generated.

It was a real buzz for me working with these guys, what a mixed bunch they were, covered in all the jailhouse tats and markings. A melange of Hells Angels, pickpockets, bank robbers and intransigent con men, they were all due to be released onto the street soon and were living in some halfway house. I do not think they were a violent crew, mainly white-collar crimes like fraud and embezzlement.

If this extraordinary video business had happened a bit later I would have probably been lecturing some of those guys in the genius junk bond and pyramid scams that were rife that decade. I always loved meeting people; just some of these stories would fill up most this book, a bottomless well of entertaining moments and heart-breaking sadness's.

The community service was no real hardship to me; at the end of it I actually received a letter of thanks from the United States district court. The letter confirmed that the offense I had pleaded 'no contest' to was a misdemeanor offense (minor offense) and my sentence had been served. It went on to state, that my conduct had been exemplary and commended me for the outstanding contribution I had made in terms of my community service which was a significantly appreciated by the county, it closed by saying 'we have found that you conduct yourself with integrity and decency and wish you luck In your new business ventures.'

After all this I thought it would be an idea to get out of America for a while so I went to Majorca and crashed out there. My nerve endings shrivelled, eventually I moved there on a permanent basis. The relentless British press wrote it up like I was the new Alfie Biggs. 'Mr Big became Mr Biggs'. They splashed the headlines everywhere 'Fugitive Bloom flees to the sun' was one that made the front page. Like I was still a wanted man, some *Midnight Express* deal, another popular film from that year.

They were still fascinated by me. There was always a cynical sniper in the bushes trying to shoot you down, seekers of scandal, trying to make a fast buck off my back. I sued the *Daily Express* for libel and won. They settled for a small sum, about enough for half a dozen copies of The Wizard of OZ and published a retraction in the back of the paper.

Now under the new law being proposed to the Levenson Committee by one of the finest legal minds in the country Max Mosley, they would have to put a retraction on the same page as the original libel and pay a huge settlement.

This was not my only adventure with video, in my next book Full Bloom Volume 2, I will tell of my adventures with the Mafia and the star of the most famous porno movie ever made *'Deep Throat'* Linda Lovelace and how I threw away a golden multi-million opportunity for the sake of my family.

The Entrance to "Mr Big's" House

The Driveway

"Mr Big's" Mansion

Chapter 6 - Radio Ga Ga

'Radio Caroline has always been regarded as one of the foundation stones of the Swinging '60s, and rightly so. It pioneered independent, commercial radio and changed the face of British broadcasting in the process. It shoved two fingers up to authority.

Above all, it had everything central to the dynamics of the era in abundance; youth, music and rebellion.'

Poptastic: My Life in Radio - Tony Blackburn.

'It is all out of control now but we do not know how to stop it. Greed has driven us all insane. We promote violence, assaulted by the media; the emerging intelligence in children is confused beyond reason.

Tradition has fallen into the 'Forgotten' section of modern history. We desecrate the planet's body, knowing nothing of her body'

Simon Dee, first jockey on Radio Caroline in March 1964

Good old Tony, still king of the DJs after 50 years in the business. I paid him £15 a week when he worked for me on Radio Caroline. How did I get involved with the pirates? Well, it's a long story and it all centres around a guy called Ronan O'Rahilly, the founder of commercial radio in this country. I met him in autumn 1964 when the universe of John Bloom was exploding as the washing machine business was going wrong, horribly wrong.

I was walking down Park Street (you know it, the one on the Monopoly Board) when O'Rahilly approached me and asked me If I wanted to help him out on the business side of his operation. To tell you the truth I was on a downer, and he must have recognised me from the constant press I was getting. By the time we had reached the end of Curzon Street I agreed to join him. Ronan was cool, clever and canny. His parents owned the private port of Greenore in County Louth and his grandfather was Michael O'Rahilly, a national hero in the history of Ireland. Involved in the Easter Uprising of 1916 he was killed by a British machine gunner in the fighting. There is a statue of him somewhere, in my view they should put one up for Ronan one day.

Ronan invited me out for a drink in the Trader Vic's bar at the Hilton Hotel to discuss the business further. Since the crash I had hardly ventured out, and being seen out in public again was a big thing for me.

The more of the business Ronan explained to me the more complex it seemed. In a nutshell there were two companies involved in the Radio Caroline operation: Planet Productions (Ronan was a director) and the mysterious Ferlin Trust Inc. of Panama City. They chartered the ship to Planet who paid the bills. Exactly who put the money up was a huge mystery.

Ronan owned the Scene Club in Ham Yard, just off Great Windmill Street, epicentre of the mod culture; it was run by a feller called Lionel Blake. That was a real hard-core fashion situation, home of the mod cult of 1963. Nick Cohn who wrote the story that became *Saturday Night Fever* attributed the origins of story to his memories of the mod society circa 1963. Ronan was greatly responsible and I can't emphasise enough the importance of Ronan to modern day culture. Not only was he at the forefront of the Mod culture, which to this day is the major influence of modern fashion, but he revolutionised radio. I was so proud to be his friend and be a part of the legacy he created for London and the world. I briefly quote from an interview Pete Meaden gave about the 'Scene Club' - *'The greatest records you can imagine were being played. Tony Clarke, Major Lance and Smokey Robinson. The records were played very loud over those big speakers and in a small room, which the 'Scene Club' was, with concrete walls so it comes bouncing back, hitting off the floor, so you are getting saturated with sound'.*

Ronan also managed several bands the most famous being Georgie Fame and the Blue Flames. They had met in the fabulous Flamingo Club in a Wardour Street basement where Georgie played his legendary all-nighters. The audience was a motley crew of musicians, pimps, pushers, US servicemen, villains and a galaxy of celebs, including Muhammad Ali and a young lady called Christine Keeler.

Georgie was a brilliant musician; he helped put the swing into swinging London. Ronan was keen to get his stuff out and created his own record label expressly for that purpose, almost unthinkable in those days. The problem was he ran into a brick wall trying to get airplay, the big players were the two labels EMI (we have already encountered their chairman Sir Joseph Lockwood in my chapter on David Bowie) and Decca. The BBC would not play it and it was the same story with Radio Luxembourg. Our old friend 'payola' again, but not as stringently employed as the Mafia did in America (as we have seen with my chum 'Sam the Sham'). Nevertheless nothing got played unless it was on one of those labels or other heavyweights like Phillips and Pye. Not one to be outdone, Ronan decided to start his own radio station.

An Aussie called Alan Crawford had the original idea to broadcast offshore and was already fitting out an old hulk called the Mi Amigo. Ronan was desperate to beat him to it and after raising the capital, immediately started converting a beaten-up passenger ferry called the 'Frederica' at his father's port. The Irishman won the race and started broadcasting first, Crawford followed with his station called Atlanta.

O'Rahilly's business acumen came to the fore and he formed a shaky alliance with Crawford, convincing the Aussie that serious money was to be made by covering the whole country and thus increasing the advertising yield. Consequently the *Mi Amigo* was anchored off Frinton-on-Sea and called Radio Caroline South, and the *Frederica* headed into the Irish Sea to be re-named Radio Caroline North. Eventually Ronan bought Crawford out of the radio business; they were always at loggerheads about what direction it should have gone.

I hit it off with Ronan straight away, what we shared was attitude – that mod thing, hyper-impatience, get mega-rich quick and smash the system whilst were doing it. Ronan was a direct link to his grandfather, but instead of a rifle he carried a briefcase. The agenda was the same, however: celebrate the ephemeral and enjoy the craic. His office was Caroline House, a seven-storey building based in the heart of Mayfair; he shared it with one of his investors Jocelyn Stevens who was behind *Queen* Magazine. I always thought that Mayfair was a great place to house the nerve centre of pirate radio.

Another backer was George Drummond, the Queen's godson. I met him in Barbados once, an interesting fellow with a somewhat chequered past.

I was not a great music person, still not. My favourite singer of all time was Frank Sinatra and Johnny Mathis singing the Yiddish song 'Kol Nidre' was my all-time favourite record. Ronan did not employ me for my musical knowledge though, he needed to raise the revenue of the company. One of my first ventures was to go out to the *Mi Amigo* with Ronan for him to brief me on the overall set-up. I never got there though, and during my four-year association with Radio Caroline I never set foot on the vessel.

To get on board, we had of course to get through customs at Frinton (ostensibly Holland was our destination) and then go on a tender ship to sail into the international protected waters three and a half miles off the coast. The *Mi Amigo* was under the protection of the Panamanian flag and, as Ronan always proudly pointed out, was not under British jurisdiction. The tender was little more than a glorified rowing boat and I knew that it would have taken forever to get out to the vessel. Imagine that scene from the *Titanic* when Leonardo is in the water. I could see the *Mi Amigo* in the distance; it was totally dominated by the massive 130-foot mast.

Moored near the tender was a much larger, sleek craft with some burly uniformed guys on deck. I motioned to Ronan to take that as a means of transport. A grimace appeared upon his lean features.

'No chance, it's the Royal Navy. It is their brief to shadow our movements and try to deter us from boarding the ship.'

That day was relatively calm and the sea was placid but it looked freezing. The threat of the Royal Navy was the last straw and I told Ronan in no uncertain terms that I would not be venturing out.

'I think I should go back to London '

'You can't, we have come all this way, what are you going to do when the weather is really bad?'

He was not best pleased, when I swore back he glared at me with ice-block eyes as I left to take the train from Harwich back to Liverpool Street. Not a great start and I was looking at a One-Way-ticket to Nowhere Ville if things did not improve.

The station took its name after the American President John F. Kennedy's daughter Caroline. The story went that Ronan was in America trying to raise funds for his radio station when he came across *Life* Magazine which had a photo-spread on the Kennedys.

That was the Camelot period when JFK was first in office and everything was possible. One of the pictures was of the brood in the Oval Office and Caroline was playing and disrupting the business of her father running the world. The picture struck a chord with Ronan as it encapsulated the image he carried in his mind of what the station should be. Ronan's fixation with all things connected with the Kennedys was to continue throughout his life. I recently found out that Neil Diamond penned his world-wide hit 'Sweet Caroline' after seeing those pictures of her.

I could never figure where he got that Kennedy thing from, their Irish roots perhaps. He would refer to them as the 'family of the world', whatever that meant. He even had plans to build a 'Kennedy Town' in honour of them.

There was a huge need for cash to keep the station – literally – afloat. I came up with idea of radio 'ognib'. We could not call it bingo because of some copyright problem. My plan was to send out cards by post and had plans for 100,000 playing. Another idea that was about 50 years ahead of its time, and I employed my mate Charlie Drake to be the on-air caller. At that time Charlie was the biggest comedian in the land, though he was only a little guy with curly red hair. Funnier than a dozen Ant and Dec's he was one of the highest paid entertainers of the day. His act was a strange mixture of Vaudeville and knock-about, he was a clown really.

Everybody had a catchphrase then, the most important item in an entertainer's act, Jimmy Saville then at his zenith and his most predatory had that 'Now then, Now then, Now then' mantra. With Charlie it was 'Hullo my darlings' uttered in a camp, lisping voice.

At that time Charlie was living in Weybridge, the in-place to reside, a real super-rich man's ghetto, and not bad for a boy born in the Elephant and Castle. The Beatles had just purchased properties there when their first tsunami of wealth washed over them. One of the records that Radio Caroline was wearing out in their first few months of broadcasting was Tom Jones 'It's Not Unusual'. It was a wonderful, exhilarating sound that was to set Tom on his knicker-strewn path to the top. The Jones boy was to shortly buy a home in the area from the proceeds of that song. Sandie Shaw was offered it first but passed.

Charlie's home was beautiful, located down by the river, with a garden you could have landed a Comanche attack helicopter in. He was with his first wife then, a classy blonde called Heather, an ex dancer, the second Mrs Drake was a dancer too if I recall.

I recall one hot sticky afternoon spending a pleasant time shooting clay pigeons down from some device Charlie had purchased. I imagined the targets to be Board of Trade examiners as I pulled the trigger.

My wife Anne proved to be a real crack shot also, it was great fun. Nearly as good as the times we had in Monte Carlo when we did variations of the Amphi-car stunts described in Chapter one...

Charlie, to use a showbiz cliché, squandered the vast fortune he earned on 'slow horses and fast woman'. In the closing years of his life, after his career had spluttered to standstill, penury consigned him into oblivion. Just the thought of him brings a smile to my face, he was that funny.

Another gimmick we tried was selling nylons over the airwaves. We did not need Charlie's specialist talents for this one but the line did not go very well. We only made pennies on the deal and soon scrapped them. T-shirts was another wheeze I dreamt up.

Ronan's office was a mad house, Caroline was always on blaring out the hits. There was no payola involved but some records like Booker T and the MG'S 'Green Onions' were just played to death. There was always a crowd of people in the office and I did not know who half of them were, I wondered if Ronan did sometimes. There were some guys called the Duggan brothers who were Ronan's minders. They kept themselves to themselves, always wore black polo jumpers.

In really bad weather conditions the ship swung like a pendulum, sometimes really huge waves crashed over the ship. Masts would break and float away. One day the transmission was lost because the high winds tangled some rope at the top of the mast. Ronan offered two weeks' wages to anyone who had the neck to climb up the mast and untangle it. Tony Blackburn shinned up and despite nearly losing his nerve half way up untangled it. He was really upset I heard when Ronan said he would pay him in a few weeks' time.

The studio was housed above the waterline and when the weather got rough it was like listening to *The Poseidon Adventure*. On occasion the *Mi Amigo* would slip anchor and run aground, once it was badly damaged and tugs from a firm called Mortensen towed it to Greenore. I was amazed at the reception we received, the locals treating us like folk heroes, like the inhabitants of Wigan when their favourite sons returned with the Cup after beating Manchester City. Ronan was Michael's grandson and given the utmost respect and I was in danger of developing skin cancer from basking in the reflected glory.

Wherever we went we were offered glasses of Guinness and free meals, everybody talked about the death of Michael as if it had happened a few months ago rather than nearly a century. The rebels had stormed the Post Office that was seen as a strategic target in those days. The service at the Post Office was definitely bad that day, it still is in some, even today.

I had brushed up on my folk songs and treated them all to a stirring rendition of 'Kevin Barry'. John O'Bloom at your service, It was pure *Father Ted*, and all it needed was the lady with the tea and sandwiches saying 'go on, go on, go on, go on'.

To digress for a moment, dear reader, this reminded me of my earlier visits to Ireland when I was still in the RAF serving my time at the Aldwych. They used to doll out weekend passes like sweets and John Bloom was in like Van Persie to snap them up. I had mine made out to go to Holyhead, about the furthest point on the compass that they would stretch to. My mission was to buy cheap vans that were free of purchase tax in Ireland back then. I had a tip that they were available and when I got them back to London I could make a oner on them. A lot of money in those days, my main man and sponsor Uncle Julius bankrolled the venture and for an all-too-short a while it worked perfectly.

The only down side was that it was a punishing trip, the ferries often in conditions as bad as anything that ever battered *Mi Amigo*. The long drive home, over 300 miles, was as bad, even Sebastian Vettel would have been tested behind the wheel of the unstable vans on a freezing winter's night. I always had an eye on the main chance and soon learnt that the 'freebies' certainly smoothed the wheels of commerce or in this case the wheels of the Irish Vans. Thinking about it I was the first 'Van the Man'.

In Ireland I would load up with all the goodies you could not get in post war London, delicacies like cans of pineapple chunks and chocolate bars. When I returned to London the first thing my commanding officer would ask is

'Good trip Bloom?'

At that point I would hand over the bag of goodies. Nice and easy does it, but it all went sour when the Irish authorities spotted the loophole on the vans and started charging purchase tax. It was no longer viable for me to make the trips and that was that.

Back to Radio Caroline I had very little to do with the disc jockeys. They were looked after by a guy called Chris Moore who was the programme director. Apart from Tony Blackburn the star act in the 'Radio Caroline Good Guys' line up was Simon Dee. An interesting fellow who actually designed his own downfall. When Ronan was recruiting disc jockeys the first name he thought of was that of Cyril Nicholas Henty-Dodd. The next thing Ronan did was change his name to Simon Dee. With his pop star looks and King's Road clothes as razor sharp as his mind, Simon became a household name even quicker than I did. If you want a reference point think of someone better looking than Jonathan Ross, camper than Graham Norton and as clever as Bernard Levin. (We will come to him later on in the book, a sort of intellectual Alan Sugar if you could imagine such a hybrid.)

Those fine words written at the start of this chapter by Dee serve as a good epitaph for the guy who had decades before shed the hedonistic playboy persona that had destroyed his career. The only dealings I had with him was over money. Being the star player of the team he was soon asking Ronan to increase his wages to a massive £20 a week. I told Ronan that I did not think any disc jockey was worth that sort of money and soon Simon was to jump ship to join the BBC. This was in the spring of 1965 and within two years he was hosting his own twice weekly chat show, *Dee Time*. Told you he was not worth much. Readers of a certain age may recall the start of the show with Mrs Henty-Dodd's little boy Cyril bombing around in a white E-type with a blonde companion.

His ego got the better of him though and after making many enemies, some in very high places, he was kicked out of television. I heard he was making outrageous salary demands; this came as no surprise to me as he had the temerity to ask me for an extra fiver a week. The Hollies had a record called 'King Midas in Reverse' and that was him – everything he touched after that turned to dust. Don DeLillo, one of America's great writers, was always of the view that talent was more erotic when it was wasted; Simon was a prime example of that. Liz Hurley said that the character of Austin Powers in those zany movies was based on him. He died in 2009 of bone cancer.

I often think about survival. I had parallel lives to many of these guys, instant fame, glory then a bad crash but while I always bounced back some didn't. Swinging London had more monomaniacs, egomaniacs, and megalomaniacs than any other place at any other point in time. For a while I was one of them.

I found the Radio Caroline days a welcome break from my dealings with the Board of Trade. I had 8,500 questions to answer from them; it took sixteen months each one longer than the last. At the start the meetings were cordial but soon both parties loathed the very sight of each other. I used to come back from the meetings enraged at my treatment at their hands, I would say to Ronan: 'What can we do to affront these people?'

Ronan was getting increasingly paranoid about things around that time. He was always convinced that he was a target for MI5 because of his family but then became convinced the phones were bugged. He started making calls from public call boxes, if he could find any that were not vandalised.

If anyone was getting targeted though it was yours truly. My inquisitors at the Board of Trade would accuse me of deliberately prevaricating and I would ask them what it meant. They could not believe someone in my position had such scant knowledge of accounting procedures. I replied by saying that I employed the finest accounting firms in the city like Price Waterhouse and Stoy

Hayward, lawyers like Norton Rose and advisers like Kleinwort Benson to do that for me. I was a salesman, not an accountant so it went on.

The waters around the *Mi Amigo* were getting decidedly choppy in more ways than one. The government were working on legislation to outlaw the pirates. Perceived by them as a threat to our very existence. Then something happened which was to play right into their hands. The business was starting to attract criminal types who were lured by the lucrative advertising revenues. They were operating in the old sea forts in the Thames Estuary. These concrete monoliths had been built in the war in an attempt to stop the imminent Nazi invasion.

In June 1966 the boss of station Radio City Reg Calvert was fatally wounded following a altercation with one of Caroline's directors, a Major Smedley. The dispute was over a transmitter and Smedley was later acquitted. Within days the government set in motion the Marine Offences Act, this outlawed advertising and supplying goods or services to an unlicensed radio station. It was the death knell for off-shore radio.

Things had got tough too commercially with the emergence of Radio London or the 'Big L' as it was known. This was a souped-up version of Caroline – everything was bigger and better and it sailed into Frinton all guns blazing. It was a bit like Roman

Abramovich taking over Chelsea, a lot of money was poured into it and immediately they were snapping up the best DJs. Tony Blackburn defected to them and soon they were not only poaching our disc jockeys but thousands of our listeners. Kenny Everett was their star disc jockey, bringing a zany humour the airwaves had not heard the like of since my favourites the 'Goons' a decade before.

Ronan and me still had laughs a plenty though and I recall a madcap trip to Liechtenstein to try and find out who actually owned the Mi Amigo and who were the Ferlin Trust Inc. That is where it was registered. We travelled to Zurich and then got what was little more than a toy train to Liechtenstein. I had never heard of the place, thought it was one of those mythical lands from a Hammer Horror film with castles, vampires, peasants and the like. When we eventually got there we went to the address we had and just found a strange little building which could have been a hangover from one of those Christopher Lee movies. We ventured inside and saw all these brass plates on the wall. There were literally thousands of them and one of them had the 'Ferlin Trust' on it the name we had for the ship's owners. Of course it was all window dressing and we never did get to the bottom of it as there was such a labyrinth of names and holding companies. I did not see any vampires though.

Over the years, *time's injurious hand*, as Shakespeare put it, took its toll on Ronan's memory. He would recall one of the highlights of our trip to Liechtenstein was the Ferlin Trust's huge office with a desk as big as a football pitch. This was at odds with my recollection of the place.

Around that time I was offered a duet with Tony Bennett, yeah honest, me John Bloom singing with the great man, A guy called Lou Levy had set it up for me as a thank-you for arranging for him to obtain a piece of the Beatles song 'I want to Hold your Hand', more of the Fab Four in my next chapter. Imagine owning just a portion of a Beatles classic, they are still being played 50 years on and are inflation-proof pensions.

The incomparable Tony Bennett was Sinatra's favourite singer. Perhaps the finest compliment a vocalist could be paid, like Fred Astaire praising your dancing. Tony was not only one of the greatest singers to have walked the earth but a wonderful human being and like me a guy that led a life that defied description. Tony sang with Billie Holliday, liberated concentration camps and all his life fought racism and injustice. I should have taken the gig, but I suppose deep down I was overawed by the prospect. Lou told me everything was set up for it to be a massive hit. They had squared the disc jockeys and airplay was guaranteed. It was past the post already.

A couple of years ago I was looking at CDs and I stumbled on a Tony Bennett Duets 11 record. It included collaborations with Michael Buble, Mariah Carey, Lady Gaga and Amy Winehouse. Poor little Amy, she was so proud of her Jewish–London roots and the Bennett duet 'Body and Soul' was one of her last recordings before she died of alcohol poisoning at her Camden home in 2011. It just flickered across my mind that I could have been amongst those superstars. I had the perfect song too – 'Kevin Barry'. The Father Ted remix version.

I decided to leave Radio Caroline just before the Bill came into force in August 1967. All the U-based offshore stations were closed down overnight and only Caroline fought on. Johnny Walker was one of the DJ's that stayed on. On the afternoon I wrote these words Johnny Walker was on Radio 2 broadcasting his popular 'Sound of the 70's show. I should do my own 'Sound of the 70's' show – it would feature the sound of doors slamming shut on me, or phones being hung up.

Within a few weeks of Radio Caroline being scuttled Radio One opened and Tony Blackburn played their first record, the Move song 'Flowers in the Rain'. To add insult to injury the BBC had signed the cream of the pirate disc jockeys most of them ex Caroline employees. It gets worse: they actually based the formats of their shows on the programmes Ronan had the patent on. Meet the new boss, same as the old boss.

Nothing has changed to this day. Switch on any commercial station, be it Magic, Heart or Absolute, and you will hear the same three- or four-hour show crammed with records. Some of them even the ones Ronan's boys played in the 60's,

Caroline struggled on against overwhelming odds but with no income and people afraid to deal with them there could only be one outcome. I had tried myself the year before but companies were afraid to deal with the pirates. At one time we had advertisers like Weetabix and Gillette. In March 1968 the *Mi Amigo* was boarded and towed to Amsterdam by a salvage company to secure unpaid bills. Ronan told me he had this scheme to put the station up in the air using a Constellation plane circling over the North Sea. He would refuel on the wing like military aircraft. When I asked him, What he would do about replacing the fatigued crew, he looked at me blankly.

Where would they land eventually? He just looked at me again; clearly he had not thought any of it out. His legacy lives on though. Richard Curtis did a film called *The Boat that Rocked* allegedly based on Radio Caroline but it could not have been further than the truth. Curtis was married to Esther Freud, the great granddaughter of Sigmund. Richard was doing for Blair's Britain what Riefenstahl did for Hitler's Third Reich. In my opinion the film was dreadful, and not funny at all.

Virtually every tower block in London has some pirate radio station operating from it. There is a station called Radio Caroline still on the air and run by a guy called Peter Moore. My investigations indicated that it was just a tribute act with no connection to Ronan or the real deal. I suggested to Ronan that we lead a boarding party to this landlubber's radio station and make him walk the plank or at the very least close him down. Back in the day Ronnie and Reggie would have paid him a visit.

Ronan and I kept in vague touch for a while after the demise of his beloved Caroline. When I had the 'In Place' nightclub he would come in some nights. It was usually on a Friday when my religious beliefs did not allow me to work. I remember him being there the night Stevie Wonder played.

Ronan then dabbled in the film business and was an executive producer on the Marianne Faithful movie *Girl on a Motor Cycle.* Ever seen it, soft porn with Marianne cruising around on a Harley in this leather suit. Ronan was convinced it was going to be the biggest movie since *Gone with the Wind*. He wanted me to be a co-producer; when I declined he offered my wife the chance to co-produce. The male lead was Alain Delon, the French guy who got involved in a huge vice scandal around that time. It contained one of the worse lines in the history of the cinema, spoken by Delon as he unzipped the leathers: *'Your body is like a beautiful violin in a velvet case'.*

Marianne said it took dozens of takes before she could do it with a straight face. There was some talk of Mars bars sponsoring the movie.

Ronan was a big mate of George Lazenby who played James Bond in *On her Majesty's Secret Service*. They offered Lazenby a seven-movie deal to make more Bonds but Ronan thought that that the genre was played out and talked him out of signing. A bit like me and Northern Songs.

Then he gradually became a hippie of sorts, advocating peace and love. Only 'love can conquer hate', as Marvin Gaye once sang. 'Loving Awareness' was his mantra and he tried to get the message across to the world. He stopped going out, apart from the odd visit to the Chelsea Arts Club.

In recent years I heard he had become very reclusive and was not so well and when I returned to London in the spring of 2013 I made him the guest of honour at a homecoming party I had arranged at the Pizza Pomodoro in Beauchamp Place. I was surprised when he turned up; he did not stay long and appeared distracted when I chatted to him. He looked well and with long hair he could have passed for a member of some 70's prog-rock band. There is a picture of him in the book somewhere, very rare as he shuns all publicity.

I'm pleased to say at the time of publishing this book Ronan had returned to Ireland and is doing well, back in the arms of his motherland where he is respected and cherished as the grandson of one of Ireland greatest hero's.

Charlie Drake Ist mate in the Amphicar

Sir Joseph Lockwood Head of EMI

A rare picture of the media shy Ronan O'Rahilly at Pomodoro's

At Pomodoro's with Mickey Rourke and owner Ciro Orsini

Chapter 7 - The Swiss Family Ecclestone

'The funniest picture of the week award had very strong competition from the debut Playboy *shoot of the daughter of F1 billionaire Bernie Ecclestone – Tamara.*

Never-before-seen erotica that so clearly appears to replicate scenes from early motherhood that I would label 'Putting Botty Cream on a Rash.'

Celebrity Watch 29th March 2013 - The Times

'Each family is unhappy in its own way.'

Anna Karenina - Leo Tolstoy

Well readers, do you want some stories on Bernard Charles Ecclestone? The first time I told you about him was when we went to Monte Carlo with Adam Faith. In 1966 we went on holiday to the Victoria Hotel in Palma Majorca with Bernie and his first wife Ivy. I would like to regale you with some colourful stories of the holiday but in fact it was deadly dull.

We spent the days wandering around the town doing the usual tourist things. The evenings were unexciting. After a few sunless days which seemed like months we all returned to London, I had deals to make Bernie had cars to sell.

A few weeks later Anne, Sandie Shaw who was at the peak of her career and her manager Evie Taylor, flew on to Malta to sell my yacht to Charles Revson the head of Revlon Cosmetics.

Anne recalls that the boat was in dry dock. The weather was bad but Sandie relieved the tedium by handing out painting-by-numbers kits. Sandie was very artistic

The next time we met was in America late 70's around the time I was having my problems with the FBI in the 'Mr Big' period. Bernie was now heavily involved in motor racing and asked me along to Longbeach to a race he had organised. I knew next to nothing about the sport, only that it was extremely dangerous as I was always reading of the fatalities in the races. I did not particularly enjoy the racing the first time around. I do not know if you have ever been behind the scenes of motor racing but the first thing that hits you is the noise, bone-jarring, deafening to the point of madness. It took me several years to become accustomed to the noise and now I regard it as music to my ears. Bernie and I then drifted apart and I did not see him for several years.

I lived in Cocoa Beach in Florida for a while after I left Beverly Hills; it was very near the Space Centre at Cape Canaveral. Like thousands of other residents of the place I became hooked on the space launches. Many of my friends worked there and I was invited to watch many launches from Launch Pad 39a. I often used to drive down and watch the huge rockets blast off into outer space. The Americans were still in the space race against Russia and were spending billions of dollars on the Space program. It reminded me of the time that Hitler was firing rockets into London in the last days of the war.

I did not see Bernie again until 1994 when I had returned to Europe and the world had marched on. I had a new idea on the go. Wait for it – puncture proof tyres. This was going to revolutionise motoring. The tyres had a liquid inside them that was a safeguard against perforations. I had tested the tyres by driving over nails, glass, tacks, razor blades, rocks, stones anything sharp you name it. The tyres still held up, the liquid absorbing any punishment.

I got in touch with Bernie: imagine the effect that this would have on motor racing. Grand Prix were decided on the durability of a car's tyres. After more intensive tests, though, a fatal flaw in the 'puncture proof tyres' was discovered.

When the car exceeded a speed of over 70 miles per hour it would vibrate like one of my old washing machines and lose stability. Imagine Lewis Hamilton driving in the Monaco Grand Prix with a set of them and the car zigzagging across the track. Back to the drawing board John.

Bernie got us some passes for the Barcelona Grand Prix; we ended up in the Paddock Club occupying the worst seats in the place sat by the kitchen. I was on the point of walking out when who should walk in the joint but Bernie Ecclestone. What did Michael Douglas say in the *Wall Street* sequel about 'One of the toughest guys that ever wore shoes'. Every eye in the place was on him. I have been around many famous people, as you may have gathered, but I have never witnessed anything like this before.

'Do you like this place', he asked. I shrugged nonchalantly.

'Want to go halves?'

I knew then that he was trying to lure me into the world of Formula 1, sizing me up. I had just rocketed into the centre of Bernard Ecclestone's Universe.

The crowd that day was around the 30,000 mark, with a lot of spaces. Football was still the biggest game in town and Barca took all the attention. With the ascendency of Alonso though interest in Formula 1 soared and now the crowds are in excess of 100,000.

Bernie chucked me some passes, in those days it was the plastic things. Now its high-tech computer chip passes that look like something out of *Star Trek*. (Another of my gadgets invented by my own genius mad professor Bob Mabott was this magic substance that you could mould anything into. It was ideal for passes.)

I saw the visit to the paddock as a chance to do what John Bloom does best – network. I made some good contacts that day or thought I did. I was still toying with the idea of using the puncture-proof tyres on heavy trucks that went much slower and would not have been subjected to the instability sustained at higher speeds. Nothing came of it in the end because it was still such a risk.

Bernie left before the end of the race, he always did, he has never seen a chequered flag to my knowledge. That was our lift gone, I muttered. Everybody round us was struck with the same thought: let's get a cab quick and get the hell out of Dodge.

We waited till it emptied out but of course by then the traffic was jammed and the queues were immense. It was then that I saw a tall, brilliant-looking chap with a cell phone jammed against his ear. He was obviously of Venetian colouring with close set eyes; he could have been a member of that mock-classic group Il Divo or a player for Juventus or Inter. He was like a character from a Visconti movie. That was the first time I met Pasquale Lattuneddu Bernie's right hand man, his di Capo, he was discovered by the new Mrs Ecclestone Slavica, a six-foot tall Croatian model. It is very hard to describe Slavica's impact at first meeting; she was just an amazing person. Perhaps the greatest thing about her was that she could not care less what people thought of her.

I enquired about where I might get a cab, he pointed angrily down to the payphones. His reaction irritated me, it had been a long hot day, my nerves were frayed and it was the last thing I needed. That was my first meeting with Pasquale and we have grown to be good friends despite a poor start. Pasquale was the guardian of the pits, he had more passes than Eden Hazard but Bernie always had the final say in who gained entry to his private kingdom.

My next insight into Bernie's world was when he invited us to Hockenheim, forever remembered as the track where the legendary Jim Clark was killed. A top of the range Mercedes picked us up. It had one of the first ever Sat Navs in it, and a robotic German voice barked out directions. I had never seen anything like it, for a while I thought I was in a German Tiger Tank with the Panzer commander giving orders to attack the Englanders. I asked the driver if it spoke English but the irony of it was wasted on him.

It was a few days before that that trip that I encountered the fiery temperament of Slavica. As a joke I had sent Bernie a lewd photograph that I had mocked up using some models from *Playboy* magazine, the same publication that his daughter Tamara was to grace the pages of decades later. The photo showed him in a somewhat compromising position with these young ladies. I was in Majorca and just before dinner the phone rang. An East European female voice unleashed a torrent of abuse at me about sending her husband pornographic pictures.

'How dare you send my husband this filth, who are these ugly whores? What kind of man are you? Trying to come between me and my Bernie. This is unpardonable behaviour etc, etc.

The tirade continued unabated with more insults and accusations. Then Bernie came on the line.

'Meet the new wife'. I then realised that I was the victim of another Bernie prank but this time he had a willing accomplice. He did warn me that she did possess a terrible temper though and the first time we met I was to encounter it at full blast. That is the thing nobody gets about Bernie: his underlying humour; he was savaged by the *Evening Standard* and accused of being miserable but that is easily confused with being stoic.

The first time I met Slavica was in Milan during the race at Monza

The evening started peaceably enough, with all of us sitting around the dinner table; present were the whole of the Ecclestone family and a guy called Bill Donaldson who ran the Indy 500. Donaldson was a very modest fellow and the meal was low key until suddenly Slavica exploded.

She rounded on Bernie accusing him of having a girl in his room the night before. 'It was that Brazilian whore wasn't it? Admit it?'

A torrent of vitriolic abuse followed it as she exploded into an expletive-laced tantrum. If Fergie had a hairdryer then Slavica used a flamethrower. She ranted on and on; Bernie just stood his ground, Donaldson watched aghast. Much of has been made of the difference in height between them, (12 inches) but on this occasion she seemed to literally tower over him. Bill and I just concentrated on eating our dinner through the whole excruciating episode; this is madness I was thinking. Bernie's two daughters

Petra and Tamara seemed unconcerned about the whole thing and carried on chatting amongst themselves. Being brought up in a household where dinner table scream-ups were par for the course must have had a huge effect on them at that impressionable age.

Almost as quickly as she erupted Slavica calmed down and returned to her seat next to me. Her eyes were like the glass I drove the tyres over; she had fantastic bone structure. Something at the back of my mind told me that this woman was someone to be reckoned with.

'Tell me about yourself, darling.'

We spent the evening comparing notes about our upbringings, she was born in Rijekamay in 1958 in poverty, and her father was a docker but abandoned her at a very young age. I used to wonder if the discrepancy in their ages (28 years) was some unresolved issues with her absent father. One reaches for one's Penguin Freud. Things were difficult for her; she had no shoes and as a kid stole them from the local swimming baths. She joked, 'Hard to get my size.'

A friendship quickly developed which lasts to this day, she gave me her mobile number and some afternoons I would visit her beautiful home in Chelsea Square for tea. It was no understatement to say that she was a domestic goddess. She loved doing the basic household chores, washing, cooking cleaning. She would not have a dishwasher in the house. Ironing was her forte, though she loved ironing Bernie's shirts and up to the day their marriage ended she would provide him with those pristine, snow-white shirts with the knife edge creases and stiff collars.

It was in the kitchen though that she really excelled. Slavica was in the Nigella Lawson class, providing me with kosher food and whisking up all sorts of delights and treats. (Poor old Nigella was having marital troubles of her own when the book was being written.) A special favourite of the family was an Italian dumpling concoction. There was a cook on the payroll but she was relegated to the subs bench for most of the time as Slavica slaved away in the kitchen.

The puckishly cute girls were brought up to be frugal with money and eschewing labels like Armani and Louis Vuitton. They went to the Francis Holland School, which they travelled to by good old London Transport on the tube and bus. Sarah Ferguson arranged the school for the Ecclestones' I'm told. I know Tamara was disappointed when she failed to make it to her wedding. Considering the vast wealth that was sloshing around the Ecclestone household it was a normal, stable environment transformed into a cosy home by the warmth and energy of Slavica.

Bernie loved to be at home, after he left the office having waged war against the world, he was never happier than when he could crash out and put his feet up watching the WWF wrestling. This was a problem for Slavica because she was torn between the desire for domesticity and a hunger for the bright lights and social interaction. The first cracks in the marriage appeared around then, perhaps Slavica was realising that Chelsea Square was becoming a gilded prison.

Money was another problem, not the supply of it but the fact that throughout the duration of their marriage Bernie denied her the use of a credit card. I challenged Bernie on this once and he replied that she had all the money she needed. Yes but what about some financial freedom for her? A State of Independence as Donna Summer once sang. Bernie is a very frugal person he hates waste or ostentation. Tamara's wedding described, as a £7m feast of vulgarity by the *Daily Mail* was complete anathema to him. Referring back that scurrilous piece in the *Evening Standard* Bernie was slated from walking out of his party when he married Slavica (using Bernie's words about 'I don't celebrate, I don't see the point'). Yet had he stuck around at his daughter's wedding to listen to Lionel Rich Tea earn his huge fee then he would have been slated also for being complicit.

In seemed extraordinary that a billionaire's wife would need to deal in second-hand clothes but from time to time Slavica would host a clothes sale in her house. She had a top model friend in Milan who would often send her freebies or unwanted dresses, tops, shoes, bags whatever. The models were always showered with beautiful garments by the top fashion houses that were eager to see their latest designs worn by these beautiful creatures. My wife Anne would often purchase items from Slavica, most of the money going to the various charities that she had set up in Croatia.

Another contributory factor to the failure of their marriage in my view was Bernie's obsessive cleanliness and fastidiousness. In Leonardo Di Caprio's superb portrayal of Howard Hughes in *The Aviator* we see the frantic hand scrubbing of the billionaire in the closing stages of the film. Perhaps you could compare Hughes to Bernie, the rise from nowhere, the ruthless relentless pursuit of mind-boggling wealth, the frazzle of being blinded by sheer power and crazy amounts of cash.

It is a matter of record in the various tomes on Bernie how he positioned things in impeccably straight lines and how he would meticulously cleans his desk. Slavica would tell of how he would spend ages straightening a picture frame on the wall or re-arranging vases and ornaments on shelves. What's the basis of this? I recall listening to a *Desert Island Discs* radio programme with ex Arsenal and England Captain Tony Adams talking about obsessive, compulsive disorders. On tour with England he once spent an evening discussing with wayward star Paul Gascoigne about how many OCDs they shared.

Not saying Bernie had any but the desire to control was paramount in all his dealings. If you worked for him it was his way or the highway; look up micro-management in the dictionary and you will see a picture of Bernie Ecclestone. Of course you cannot control everything but you can make sure your favourite picture is straight, that the vases are in the right place and that your nails are super clean.

Slavica unquestionably saved my life in 1999. In that year I had a serious back operation, Sid Watkins the F1 doctor took out three discs from my spine. Unfortunately the operation was only a partial success; at first I thought it was total. After just a couple of days I was up and about, terrorising the wards. I discharged myself much against the wishes of the staff. First thing I did was bowl round and see my old mate Bernie. I banged on his front door and Slavica answered. When I asked if little Bernie could come out to play she told me that he was out.

I asked where and the Croat beauty told me that he was out with 'Carlos'. Carlos who? Santana? Tevez? It was sometime later that I learnt that this Carlos was King of Spain. Where did they go? Local tapas bar probably I thought. Actually Bernie had not been well, having a triple by-pass. He kept it very quiet and as I was out of commission with my back it went undetected. That was when he started to worry about the future and how to best safeguard his family.

I rashly decided to go to Montreal to see the Grand Prix, it was in my blood now and I was cured wasn't I? Bad move, John, because out there I totally collapsed. I had some rare back condition and was flown back to London for more urgent treatment. The problem was Doctor Sid had flown off to some F1 emergency and I saw some other doctor. He prescribed me two medications but they turned out to be very harmful to my condition and poisoned me.

I went back to Palma where I was residing then, my daughter was getting married and I did not want to miss it. I felt really ill over there, lucky for me Anne was monitoring my condition and I had to take regular tests. Soon Anne was concerned at the results and contacted the doctors back in London. They told her that there was nothing to worry about. My daughter had ordered a special expensive dress for her wedding and Anne and she flew to America to pick it up. The first night they were away I woke up in the small hours screaming, 'Get me to the race track.'

I was hallucinating and was convinced I was a Formula 1 driver. If it was Schumacher then I was in a bad way, I do not remember. They rushed me to hospital and gave me a brain scan. (They did find it). The doctors soon realised something was seriously wrong. My vital organs started to pack up. Things looked bad for me, the staff phoned Anne in America and told her to get back within 48 hours or else I might not be around after that. They rigged me up on some machines and started pumping the poison out of my body that was slowly killing it. Anne came back and for the next few days it was touch and go. I was in and out of a coma. My body, particularly my back, was a shambles and it has taken me years to recover.

Eventually I was well enough to go back to London for further treatment. I rented an apartment in Portman Square so I could attend regular physiotherapy sessions at Prince Edward Hospital, but my problems still continued. I was immobile and could not walk, I tried some water treatment, the session lasted an hour a day but I was in such pain and it took so long to manoeuvre me into position it was ineffective.

Things got worse; some days I would just lie there looking up at the ceiling convinced I would never walk again. I was wondering how much those supercharged electric wheelchairs cost, It would need puncture proof tyres of course, and a phone, must have a phone.

Slavica heard of my predicament and came to visit me at the flat. She took one look at me, curled up in bed, down and almost out.

'Darling what are you doing here? Get up.'

I told her of my problems she looked at me for a while then announced

'I will get you cured.'

Anne had heard of a private sports clinic in Austria that performed miracles on seemingly lost causes. Slavica arranged for me go there in one of Bernie's private jets. The problem was that the plane was too small to accommodate my stretcher. She had recruited some of Bernie's top executives to carry me on board but after a fruitless not to say painful while (they cracked my head against the door) it was obvious I would not be flying in it.

'No worry 'she snapped 'We will use Bernie's big plane'

Bernie's big plane was a BAE 146, Slavica had this great expression 'Bernie –you bastard' and started her call to him with it. Soon she was ordering him to get the plane ready for my disposal. True to her word she got me there, it was just me and the crew that flew to Austria. I arrived at the clinic exhausted and in some considerable pain, to be greeted by a gentleman who was straight out of the *Colditz Story*. With his silver hair and Wagnerian nose he surveyed me and then barked

‘Vot do you want here?’

I expected him to ask me for my papers.

‘Treatment?’

I was well into my 60’s then and could not pass for a Dortmund defender or downhill skier.

‘You do not belong here, what sports do you play?’

This guy was annoying me now; I noticed my wit always increased in direct ratio to the rudeness that I received.

‘Chess, the odd game of Dominoes’

‘Chess?’ he spluttered.

‘Dominoes?’

He pointed to the wall, I saw a signed picture of tennis ace Steffi Graf, and a couple of footballers in German international shirts. I did not see one of Schumey. Thinking about it the frames did not look very straight. How I longed to be able to straighten them, sure it would not take me long.

‘We only have sports personalities here.’

I played my best card it wins every time.

'Mr Ecclestone has expressed interest in my welfare; his wife arranged my transportation here in his private aircraft.'

Should have said his big plane, similar to the ones that came every night and bombed Germany into a pile of rubble. You Nazi fascist, I stopped myself just in time.

'Herr Ecclestone. Oh I see'

They gave me the best room in the house, not that it was much. Bare walls and inedible food, then it really got tough when the treatment or should I say torture started. Every morning at 8 they would take me down to the room that I soon dubbed 'the torture chamber'. They kept me there till 6 at night. No lunch break by the way. I was literally hung from some hooks with half of my torso immersed in warm water. They would then make me do exercises and have physio etc. It was agony after a couple of days I was ready to quit – no make that kill myself. I was starving hungry and every bone in my body ached. I used to moan to Anne about how these Germans were persecuting me, but why, when the war was surely over?

I had time to think when I was in there, I thought a great deal about my time with Ronan and the involvement with Radio

Caroline. One of the records that was always playing in his crowded office was 'Bits and Pieces' by the Dave Clark Five, I'm in pieces bits and pieces.' How relevant to that time.

In the next room were some footballers; I think they played for Bayern Munich. Do not recall their names but they were famous internationals (Barcelona's superb player Lionel Messi ended up in the clinic for a while some years later). These two used to have a laugh at me though, inviting me for a kick about after my treatment. 'Bastards', as Slavica would say. I loved it when Arsenal won over there the year Bayern Munich became champions of Europe.

At the end of the day the woman, who was in my view persecuting me, said, 'You will feel better in the morning.'

Oh yeah, well I didn't for a while. My spirits improved though when the promoter of the Hungarian Grand Prix, Thomas Frank, drove hundreds of miles to deliver me some kosher food. Slowly I responded to treatment and at the end of the second week I was actually walking again. Bit like Douglas Bader when he got his new tin legs in that Kenneth More film *Reach for the Sky* but I was standing again.

Dr Dungel the owner of the clinic, who with his daughter had played a huge part in getting me to walk again, came up to me the day before I was due to leave as I was proudly wheeling my Zimmer frame down the corridor and said 'Wonderful news'. I thought he was referring to the fact I was fit to leave but in fact it turned out that he was delighted by the news that Michael Schumacher had won another race.

Speaking of Schumacher reminds me of the gag we played on Damon Hill when I came over to Hockenheim. Bernie and I offered to give him a lift to the track. At that time Damon was locked in a bitter struggle with Michael Schumacher for the World Championship.

This stunt involved Bernie and me pulling off the main road and tearing down a little country lane that lead to the forest. It might have been the Black Forest, it was that dark.

'What's up?' said Damon.

'I am afraid we are being followed.'

'By whom?'

I joined in now: 'Them – the terrorists.'

Damon seemed worried. 'Terrorists! What terrorists?'

‘The Bader Meinhoff mob’ said Bernie, watching me turning the wheel and looking into the rear mirror.

‘Could be the Red Brigade’ I added in a serious voice, craning my neck to look at some passing cars.

‘Yes I heard about them re-forming’ Bernie concurred.

Damon was puzzled ‘I thought they were all dead or in prison.’

‘New mob, splinter group, seems they are all die-hard Schumacher fans; see him as the new power in Germany.’

Damon was horrified ‘But Michael’s not political.’

Bernie countered ‘He isn’t but these guys are nutters. 'They take life seriously.’

‘Fundamentalists, they want to kidnap you. They see you as the threat’ I added.

‘Damon, you better get on the floor’ Bernie ordered.

So we drove on the track with the future World Champ face down at the back, covered by Bernie’s blanket, the one his dog slept on. Luckily we had the radio on, it covered the sound of our laughter.

Funny, Hill has been critical of Bernie in recent times saying that 'He was not interested in the sport. He's interested in the return it gives.'

I read this through gritted teeth and found his statement incomprehensible. If it weren't for Bernie Ecclestone motor racing would still be a minority sport. It was the love of motorcars that drove him to become a billionaire; it was the passion in his life. Nobody knew more about cars than him, still does. We used to play a game where we would walk down any street in the world and he could reel off the current value of any car parked there. Drivers like Hill and his ilk would never have made the money they did without Bernie's influence.

To celebrate my recovery, Slavica asked us to stay in Gstaad for Christmas that year at the magnificent family Villa La Leona. It was quite an honour as nobody got invites to the marvellous chalet. We did not wish to impose so we elected to stay at the Olden Hotel, which is owned by Bernie, it's in the centre of Gstaad opposite Cartier.

The girls were growing up fast. Petra was a massive fan of the Spice Girls who were going for World Domination around that time. I contacted the girls' management and obtained from them a huge amount of merchandise, photos, T-shirts, badges, autographs everything Spicy in fact. I turned up at Gstaad in a Santa suit with a sack full of Spice Girls memorabilia for her.

Later Tamara was to develop a crush on another Damon – Damon Albarn, leader of the band Blur, one of the pioneers of Britpop. By a coincidence their manager Chris Morrison used to work for me and I was able to arrange a visit for her to go back stage to one of their shows. There she met young Mr Albarn, a proper musician. Flaubert insisted that one should never meet your idols because their glitter comes off in your hands. Now I can vouch for the accuracy of this maxim and having got this far in the book you can see my point. (Bearing in mind that we have not even started on Formula 1 yet.)

Tamara was not disappointed with meeting so perfect a pop star, she even petitioned me to try and remove his then girlfriend from the equation. I could not get involved in such emotional scar tissue though, my researchers inform me that the love of Damon's life at that time was Justine Frischmann who now lives in California with her husband.

The Christmas's we spent with the family in Gstaad were wonderful. Memories we will always cherish. When I came back for a lengthy visit to London in the spring of 2013, Slavica came to visit me in my hotel. Due to a silly misunderstanding we had not met for several years. I took along the DVDs of the times we had spent together, we both sat there enthralled by it, tears running down our faces. We both smiled, nobody could smile like her. We knew the real truth about so many things. That is what made us smile it was our bond.

What happened to you, whatever happened to me?

Slavica made that Christmas by working so hard to keep everybody happy. Petra made a great snow dog but it melted. So did the marriage between Bernie and Slavica but not before he made a gigantic mistake. In the late 90's because Slavica was not domiciled in the country Bernie decided to transfer everything over to her to avoid death duties. To affect this he set up some irrevocable off-shore trusts. ***Irrevocable*** being the key word here. A solicitor close to Bernie came up with this idea. Despite his other advisors opposing this Bernie proceeded, this was his Achilles heel, thinking that no trust was truly irrevocable. Here we have that contradiction: the same thinking and mode of behaviour that set him apart and made him a billionaire could prove his undoing. Achilles' mother bathed him in the waters that protected him against anything but by holding him by his heel she left a spot that was unprotected. Look up 'irrevocable' in the dictionary you will not see a picture of Bernie.

Simply put, his ex-wife Slavica now controls the bulk of Bernie's fortune. When you read of Tamara Ecclestone spending £7m (or was it £12m?) on her wedding, remember it wasn't Bernie who paid for it. When you read of Petra living in a Gatsby-style mansion in Beverley Hills or a 32 million pound house in Belgravia, remember it wasn't Bernie who bought them. In all the years I've known Bernie, he has always loathed extravagance it's simply not his style.

Of course, both girls are the core of the celebrity tabloid papers and social commentators. Tamara is a successful entrepreneur now advised by someone who rejoices in the name of Scott Harvey Nicholls. She is endeavouring to become one of the leading Beauty experts in the world sparing no expense with products. They sell at the top end of the market in stores like Harrods and Harvey Nichols (no connection with our friend Scott).

I trust that her marriage to a young disgraced City Trader after a whirlwind romance will be a resounding success.

The problem is Tamara is now just a target for these people, just a top tabloid totty staple, the new Katie Price. The comments sections in the celebrity columns of the press are just full of vitriol against her,' famous by proxy', loathed by people who never even met her. Warhol's dictum that in the future everyone will be famous for 15 minutes did not take into account mind-boggling wealth.

Here are some of the nasty things I read on the net:

'Cheap and tacky' (Cleary forgetting the old Dolly Parton quip: 'Do you know how much it cost to look this cheap?')

'This is everything wrong with the world today.'

'Both too much in love with themselves for it to last.'

What an ugly thing to say.

I am sure Jay Rutland will make her an ideal husband and will be sure to keep her in the manner to which she is accustomed

There appears to be no end to Tamara's talents because the May edition of *Playboy* finds her strutting her stuff. Displaying the sort of poses that annoyed her mother so much when we sent Bernie similar pictures of Playboy models years ago. I was disappointed to hear of this; she hardly needed the money.

I read of her worries about being hounded by the media. Tamara did not have a lot of luck with men, Jay's predecessor, the heavily tattooed Omar Khyami, was branded a 'love-rat' by *The Sun* following their split after a sex tape was circulated showing him cheating on her. At the time of writing she was going through the courts trying to retrieve a £380,000 Lamborghini Aventador from him.

What happened to the little girl that used to run me to Knightsbridge in her little black Audi?

Petra leads a quieter more simple life, if you can lead a modest life in a 123-room mansion. Her child is the apple of her grandmother's eye and I am sure the little one could not have better role models than her grandparents.

Bernie "the strangler" Ecclestone

Christmas with Bernie

Bernie "Klammer" Ecclestone

Anne and I hit the slopes in Gstaad

Christmas Hugs, Bernie and Petra

Tamara says farewell to "Snow Dog"

Anne and me Gstaad 2000

Anne with Tamara and Petra at Chalet

Slavica and Tamara at Silverstone

Slavica, Tamara and Petra

Bernie briefing the local police for the Damon Joke

Mission Accomplished

Chapter 8 - With The Beatles

'I can't think about money. It rains in and rains out. I always wanted to be an eccentric millionaire'

John Lennon in an interview with Ray Connolly

November 1963 was one of the most pivotal months in the history of the 20th Century. In the history of John Bloom it was the month I tried to take over a crisis torn QPR (it's good to know some things don't change). For the Beatles it was the month that they played the Royal Variety Show at the Prince of Wales Theatre, just five nights before my party. That was the night John Lennon introduced 'Twist and Shout' with his memorable crack to the Royal Family about rattling their jewellery. Their success that night was so total that the *Evening Standard* announced that they had won over the 'grown-ups and the husbands'.

On Friday 22nd November 1963 their second album, 'With the Beatles' was released. It included another theme song of mine, 'Money', that's what I want.' On that day in Dallas Texas the President of the United States, John F. Kennedy was gunned down. Kennedy, the same person that obsessed Ronan O'Rahilly, and whose death in an oblique way paved the way for the Beatles to take over America and after that the world. Let's not blind you with history but soon the whole universe, was to be the Beatles.

The funny thing was that we very nearly did not become friends because at first they were refused admission to my party by a jobs worth porter who was on duty at Aldford House that night. In a very short while the fab four were to become the most famous faces in the world but that night the porter, an old codger called Arthur Dyer did not recognise them. Did I say four; actually there was only three than night. Paul McCartney had another appointment; I think her name was Jane Asher. The red-haired waif was his girlfriend at that point in time; she was just 17, you know what I mean.

Anyway, to Arthur these three young men looked a bit suspect with their long hair and Cuban heels. Sure they had suits on and collars and ties but they talked with northern accents. The little one even had a black shirt on, with a dark suit? This was strictly taboo in those days.

The trio introduced themselves by saying, 'We're the Beatles and we have come to see Mr Bloom.'

Arthur said 'They all say that. We get a lot of your types, all trying to crash Mr Bloom's parties.'

Eventually he rang through and they were ushered into the party. Within moments I witnessed up close what the papers were to dub 'Beatlemania', a disease, which for a while spread like wildfire around the globe.

Everyone in the room went hysterical; they became the sole focus of attention. It was extraordinary the effect they had on people of all ages and backgrounds. I was witnessing in microcosm their transition from teen idols to a worldwide phenomenon. Max Bygraves and Shirley Bassey, two of the biggest names in popular music entertainment were also present that night, but it was the Beatles that everyone wanted.

I thought they would soon go, with all the fuss around them, but to my surprise they were still there in the early hours, ridiculing my record collection of Johnny Mathis and classical LPs and sipping soft drinks. Presumably my party was not that bad because here we all are. We hit it off straight away. John was my favourite because of his sense of humour, but George was the sweetest and Ringo was well, Ringo. You got what you saw with him, what was written on the tin, a genuinely nice guy, laid back and easy going. I often wonder about why they seemed so relaxed that night, perhaps they knew that things were about to go stratospheric and they just wanted some normality. If being with John Bloom could be normal.

I had invited them because Leslie Conn (him again) had asked me a few weeks before if I had heard about this new group that everybody was talking about. To be honest I hardly listened to music I was so busy, there were no iPods, downloads etc in those days and my involvement with Radio Caroline was yet to commence. Of course I had heard the name on the news – but the truth was the pop milieu was being totally re-invented and John and his buddies were laying the foundations.

The connection to the Beatles was Dick James, Lesley's partner and the fellow that had set up Northern Songs, the Beatles' publishing company. The story went that he had set up the company after just one hearing of their first number one hit 'Please, Please Me'. A fat, jolly man, everybody liked Dick; he had been a singer himself in the 50's, his solitary hit the theme from an ancient black and white TV show called *Robin Hood*. Readers of a certain vintage will doubtless recall the catchy song: 'Robin Hood, Robin Hood riding through the glen...'

The young Beatles growing up in Liverpool must have watched the show and recalled the theme, whenever they saw Dick they would break into their own version of it (it was never released by them unfortunately). They were so funny, that was the thing I remember about them most. Particularly John Lennon. Virtually everything he said in those days was a joke. I have told you about my love of the 'Goons' and this was a direct link to it.

The official photographer was taking dozens of snaps of the boys and some featured me and them messing about with an old accordion that was lying around. It was going to be the first super-group of the 60's. 'Ladies and Gentlemen I give you 'Troubadour', John Bloom and his new backing group the Beatles'. I could have done my version of 'Kevin Barry' with them. Forget 'She Loves You' George suggested we do some busking one evening, John was worried about the crowd control though if we played at Piccadilly. If I knew what was around the corner in the next few years I might have taken it a bit more seriously.

About 2.30 in the morning John told me that they were in the *News of the World* and that he wanted to get a copy. Whatever happened to the old 'screws of the world'? If there had been mobiles then mine would have been the first one they would have hacked. In those days you could obtain a newly printed paper hot from the press in Fleet Street from the newspaper vendors. It was popular especially amongst football fans who wanted to read the scores and reports. Of course there was no teletext, Internet or 'Talk sport' to inform you how the Arsenal had fared. I offered to take them there in my new Rolls Royce Phantom V. My chauffeur had the night off, so I drove, a yawning Anne next to me in the front seat. Perhaps you have never been in a Rolls Royce but in the Phantom there was a partition between the driver and the back seat that was operated electrically. John amused himself throughout the journey by winding the window up and down, up and down.

‘Fancy buying one John?’ I enquired.

‘Nah, too big for me’ but later he admitted that once he made some money he probably would.

By Christmas of that year, the Beatles’ stranglehold on the UK charts had reached almost unbelievable proportions. On Christmas morning they held the top two slots with the singles ‘I want to hold your hand’ and ‘She loves you’. They also had the top two albums in the LP charts; the new album ‘With the Beatles’ sold so well it actually made the singles charts. This was at a time when records sold in huge quantities and the Beatles were the most powerful creative force in the business in terms of tonnage shifted. Soon John would have enough to buy anything he wanted, ‘Baby you’re a rich man.’ What did Tony Montana say in *Scarface* about wanting the world ‘and everything in it?’

John did buy a Rolls Royce eventually and in the crazy flower power summer of love in 1967 he arranged for it to be hand painted in best psychedelic style. It became the most famous Roller of all time. The chaps at Rolls Royce were not impressed, that was around the time the drummer in The Who was driving their finest models into swimming pools. I think some collector has the Lennon motor in America, worth millions. Bernie would love to have it in his collection of vintage cars at Biggin Hill.

The evening was not over yet. I dropped them back to their crash pad in Green Street just around the corner from where we lived. It was a mews flat rented for them by their manager Brian Epstein to save on hotel bills. They asked us back for coffee; Anne helped Ringo in the kitchen. George went to bed whilst John showed us the artwork for their new 'With the Beatles' album. It was the famous shot taken by Robert Freeman, with the half shadow headshots of them in the black Sportique polo necks. Very cool, very noir.

John Bloom missed an open goal that night – I should have got the boys to sign a copy, instead I was only interested in Anne's coffee. The lower the number of records the more they are worth. I understand that today there are only 35 LPs in the world that have been signed by all four Beatles. The famous white album was recorded at a time when they were no longer big mates and had no pictures of them. One copy went a couple of years back for nearly $25,000 and recently a signed 'Sgt Pepper 'LP sold at auction for ten times that.

The visits to each other's homes became a regular thing for a while. Anne and Ringo would make the coffee and George and

John would have a chat with me. Anne liked Ringo and he would tell her about his girlfriend, Maureen Cox a Liverpool hairdresser who he had been courting since the early days on Merseyside where they had played at the legendary Cavern club. They had met at the underground club after a lunchtime gig. Maureen came down to London one weekend shortly afterwards. Ringo brought her to our place to meet us and soon Maureen became a good friend of Anne.

One night the mop tops invited us to go with them to watch them play a concert at the Birmingham Hippodrome. I had to decline due to pressure of work; it turned out to be a crazy night because Beatle mania exploded into a vortex of noise and hysteria. Thousands of shrieking fans besieged the venue and the boys had to flee the building in a Black Maria van disguised as policemen. It would have been an amazing but possibly terrifying experience for us to be part of that madness. I remember reading that at the end of the evening the most lasting memory was of the pungent smell of urine with hundreds of female fans literally weeing themselves in excitement.

I felt bad about missing the show so Anne invited them around to dinner. George came with a girlfriend and John brought his then wife Cynthia, a pretty blonde in a blue crepe dress. Only a handful of people knew at that time that John was married as it threatened to have dire consequences for his career as a Beatle.

Cynthia told us that they had met at Liverpool Art College and married when the group was on the cusp of fame.

She struck up a friendship with Anne and asked her many questions about the best places to shop and the most fashionable restaurants. The young marrieds had only been in London since the summer and had to maintain a very low profile to avoid the attention of the press. I had the impression that they were still out-of-towners at that time. That old North–South divide, still there to this day.

George Harrison was on good form that night, beautifully dressed in a grey lounge suit with a thin velvet lapel (they were still well into the mod look then). The flower power gear bought in the strangely named 'Granny Takes a Trip' boutique was to come later. I noticed how much young Mr Harrison smoked, the lifetime reliance on nicotine was eventually to kill him.

The conversation turned to money and I tried to explain to them the workings of the stock exchange and share dealing. A good place for them to invest their money, I thought. John was the most business-minded and streetwise but I sensed he was becoming bored with the subject and we changed topics. I had seen the potential in them and had vague some ideas about getting involved with their business side of things but when I started asking John about their finances he cannily avoided the whole issue.

What struck me most about him were his vitality and the terribly British, deadpan humour he had. It was very self deprecating, ironic. Once we talked about education: neither of us had fitted in. Neither of us had gone to university; if we had had better educations neither of us would have been the people we were though.

John talked about their forthcoming Christmas shows at Hammersmith Odeon, with Rolf Harris as the compere. Later the Beatle talked about his manager Brian Epstein, I sensed some resentment against him, yet also some deep respect and affection.

'I think Brian should give all his money to the starving people in Africa'.

This pre-dated Bob Geldof by about 20 years, I was keen to make the acquaintance of Brian Epstein and a few weeks later had the first of several meetings with him. My mind was turning over the options; some merchandising deal perhaps? At that time he was late 20's, but looked older. He always looked old actually. We should have had a lot in common, both being Jewish, of similar age and with a shared love of good clothes and an eye for the main chance. Brian liked classic clothes and was always name checking Cary Grant.

Brian had run the family business in the heart of Liverpool, a large electrical store called NEMS. His particular interest was the basement record department in the store, regarded as the finest in the North. One day his curiosity was aroused by fans coming in and asking for records by this local group called the Beatles. The rest, as they say, is history...

What hardly anybody knew at the time, though, was that Brian was gay and that he had a personal interest in the group's success, that interest was John Lennon. In the early 60's homosexuality was still strictly taboo and was a crime punishable by imprisonment. A civil partnership was unthinkable back then. Brian was into what they called 'rough trade' and particularly vulnerable to blackmail and physical harm. I was told all of this by a family friend of the Epstein's when I visited Liverpool to attend a charity dinner in the Adelphi hotel. Good friend eh? Always somebody ready to dish the dirt and drip feed innuendo – I found that out early in life.

Originally I was going to be guest of honour, but once again work took priority and I had to decline. Then the deal I was working on crashed and I was invited along as a guest. Anne and I flew up to what was then known as Speke airport ... I think it is called John Lennon Airport now.

Brian Epstein was the new guest of honour and the place was packed with his relatives and friends. One of them, seated at our table, became very drunk as the evening wore on and started mouthing off about Brian. He was recounting lurid tales about Brian's sexual escapades and was very loquacious about the grief he had given his poor parents. Beneath that suave, sophisticated exterior was a troubled, highly disturbed individual who had been expelled from school, discharged from the Army early and whose acting career had flopped. We were both shocked to hear these revelations and were surprised at how out of touch the media were.

That was a funny trip because I met another of Brian's acts that night. This was Gerry Marsden from the Mersey beat group 'Gerry and the Pacemakers', the first UK band to have a hat-trick of number ones with their first three singles. Gerry was a true Scouser, born in Dingle and a boyhood friend of Lennon with that same irrepressible sense of fun. We spent the evening moving shoes from floor to floor in the hotel. An old custom in the hotels was for the guests to leave their shoes outside the rooms at night for some poor employee to clean and polish. Such a practice was too much of a temptation for jokers like Gerry Marsden. On tour sometimes I heard that the lead Pacemaker would fill the shoes up with jam. Rock 'n' Roll. Would not happen today would it? Imagine Tamara Ecclestone leaving her favourite Christian Louboutins in the corridor of that expensive place in Dubai.

I liked Brian but sensed that danger lay ahead for him particularly when I heard from John that his strategy was to crack America. I could only see problems for them in the USA, those Cuban heeled boots with the elastic sides would be walking on quicksand. British acts meant nothing out there; Sir Cliff Richard went to America and died the death. Ninth on the bill behind Bobby Vee, if I recall, it nearly shredded his whole career. The Mafia had control over most of show business; the country was still reeling from the death of President Kennedy. It was a non-starter as far as I could see, doomed to failure.

The boys themselves they just wanted to go over to New York and buy new records. Nobody in the camp saw it as anything more than a low-key promotional junket. Epstein's office was in Argyll Street right next to the Palladium, I wanted to go in there and talk him out of it all. Something stopped me, just as well really. Things would have turned out a lot different had he heeded my supposed words of wisdom. Way to go John.

We were all wrong – in early February 1964 the Beatles Pan Am jet landed in New York to scenes comparable to Charles Lindbergh's arrival on the other side of the drink after his solo flight. Everybody had miscalculated the situation. America needed something new to lift them out of the trough of deep depression that had settled on them after JFK had bought the farm. Everybody was bewildered by the rapid changes in society; it was just like some accident waiting to happen.

I never saw John again; nothing was ever the same after America. I thought my workload was impossible, but the lads got sucked into something that would actually eventually lead to either destroying them, or scarring them emotionally forever. Be careful for what you wish for. Perhaps that is motto of this book. That brief period described above involved a band of brothers who actually changed the world. Some people would include me in that. If Tolstoy had written it, it would have dismissed as being unbelievable.

A few weeks before the Beatles went to America Dick James sent a message to me via Leslie Conn that he might be interested in selling his shares in Northern Songs to me. Dick had 50 per cent of the Lennon–McCartney songs, 20 per cent each to John and Paul and the balance to Brian Epstein; it was an arrangement that to this day still rankles with McCartney, particularly as he never regained control of them. Dick was interested in doing a deal involving my company's shares that were riding high at that point. It was the deal of all time but as I explained, my mentor Sir Isaac Wolfson gave it the thumbs down.

I was worried about the Beatles, impending trip to America; a band called the Dave Clark Five had knocked them off the top of the UK charts with that 'Bits and Pieces 'song I was telling you about in the last chapter. In some parts of the media the Beatles were already being written off as last year's thing. All these things contributed to my decision. Excuses, excuses, put it down to experience. As Oscar Wilde reminds us, *'experience is the name everyone gives to their mistakes'.*

The last time I saw Brian Epstein was at a Foyles literary lunch, I forget why I was there as my first book was not even published. Perhaps this one will get me an invite. Brian was picking up an award for his book 'Cellarful of Noise'. Lennon always called it 'A cellarful of Boys'. Brian looked tired and pre-occupied, like he had no expectation for the future. He mumbled something about calling me but he never did. Brian Epstein died on August Bank holiday, 1967, found dead at his London home of a drug and alcohol overdose. The old 'Valley of the Dolls', but in reality it was the valley of death. He was only 32.

After his death rumours circulated about him being whacked out but I thought he just had died of drugs brought on by the terrible strain of his business worries and an unhappy personal life. It was sad that despite his vast contribution to the culture, not to say the economy, of this country he received no honour from the Queen. The Beatles were lost without him, and like all great love stories it ended in tears. Their friendships had long since evaporated and they were like characters in a Sartre play trapped in some living hell.

On Thursday 30th January 1969 they played their rooftop farewell concert at 3 Savile Row above their 'Apple' offices. 'Apple' was the name they gave to their ill-fated business venture. The weather was freezing and footage shows Lennon wearing a fur coat whilst Ringo was clad in some red PVC deal. It was a good-sized flat roof, accessible via the main staircase. I know this because I had been up there with the building's previous owner Sir Jack Hylton. Jack was a marvellous human being and a great friend of mine. I loved Savile Row, home of the bespoke suit. The collective noun for a group of tailors is a disguiser –Savile Row was the last stronghold of that. Number 3 was originally a Georgian townhouse and the period front rooms were unchanged since that era.

That house was the scene of some marvellous parties and social happenings. Jack was plagued by back trouble and he knew this brilliant osteopath called Steven Ward. I first met him at one of Jack's parties. I cannot remember if it was held in Saville Row or another of his favourite spots the Jack o'Clubs. What I do know is that Steven Ward was involved in the Profumo Affair that in 1963, with a backdrop of call girls, Soviet Spies and randy Cabinet ministers caused the biggest political scandal this country has ever known. In a way that also set the scene for the Beatles to become as prominent as they did the country had grown tired of the decadent old guard.

The time warp of 3 Savile Row had not been occupied for over a decade, last I heard of it.' Apple' had pretty turned rotten to the core and the whole thing just collapsed. I keep meaning to have a look at the old building but perhaps it's best to remember it as it was.

Time went by. My next connection with the Liverpool lads was when my daughter was in her teens and attending Queen's College. She would come home full of stories about this girl in her class called Lee Starkey. She had a fantastic personality by all accounts and had the whole school on a string, the name seemed familiar to me but I could not place it. One day our daughter asked Anne and I if we could drop her off at Lee's house where she had been invited for the evening. Imagine our surprise when Maureen answered the door. Then it clicked with me, Starkey was Ringo's real name. We had a pleasant time discussing those far off times and the boys' flat in Green Street. Ringo and Maureen had married in 1965 when she was only 18 and pregnant with Lee.

Lee became great friends with our daughter and asked if she could come 'on holiday' with us to our home in Majorca. I phoned up her father Ringo to ask permission. He was pleased to hear me at the other end of the phone and we had a great chat about our lives and times, some good, others not so good, Old friends catching up after several lifetimes. At that time he was living in Tittenhurst Park, a white Georgian mansion near Ascot racecourse, it was originally bought by John and his second wife Yoko Ono. John loved the 72-acre estate it was set in, he had written and recorded some of his greatest songs there, 'Jealous Guy' and 'Imagine'. You have probably seen the video of him in Tittenhurst's long white drawing room performing 'Imagine' at the white baby grand. I just find it unbearably sad, knowing John as I did and what was to happen to him.

The place meant so much to him that when he left for America he sold it to Ringo because he could not bear it to go to anybody else, outside the Beatles. He divorced Maureen in 1975 and had a succession of girlfriends including actresses Stephanie La Motta, Nancy Andrews and singer Lynsey de Paul. In 1981 he married Bond girl Barbara Bach, you may recall her sister the gorgeous Catherine who was Daisy in the *Dukes of Hazard*. Ringo was always the most grounded and affable of the Beatles.

Maureen took the split with Ringo really hard and at one point she was so depressed she drove a motorbike into a brick wall, badly injuring herself. But they make them tough as old boots in Liverpool and she picked herself up and got on with her life. She married again, a guy called Isaac, who happened to own the 'Hard Rock Cafe 'franchise. She still remained friends with Ringo, some people never truly split no matter what. He was at her bedside when she died of leukaemia in Seattle in the early 90's.

By the way, Lee had a great holiday with us; the high spot was going to a baby bullfight. Nothing could faze a Beatles daughter. I tried to impress her by laying on special VIP clearance at Palma Airport. I should have realised, of course, that this was normal service for the progeny of the drummer in the world's greatest group.

I used to see George at the Grand Prix when I started going again. He always said 'hallo' and would stop to talk, and ask about Anne. Like I told you, he was the sweetest of the group, history has proved he could be the equal of Lennon and McCartney as a songwriter, when they gave him a chance. When he passed on it was another sad, sad moment, like someone walking on my grave. Look out for the rare previously unpublished picture of him in the book. I could eBay it for a fortune but some things really are priceless they are so important to you. I still cherish the precious memories of those golden days.

Lastly, we come to John; they say you always remember where you were when you hear earth-shattering news. I was in Spain that December morning in 1980 when the news came through that

John had been shot by the deranged Mark Chapman, on his own door step. I never could figure why he was the other side of the security gate when he got out of the limo. They said it was a mild night in New York City...

The Beatles were the greatest pop band of all time.

I accept we look back on the 60's through rose tinted glasses, but it was a fabulous time, and for a brief moment the Beatles defied the system, and for a short time anything and everything was possible. We live in tawdry times now, the '*Hammer Horror*' story that masquerades as the news reminds us of that on a daily basis.

I was so lucky that, for all-too-brief a time, I was friends with the men that did make a difference, that did set a mark, against whom no other group could compare.

My Band

George's first visit to the flat

John, George and Ringo

John and Ringo

Max Bygraves, John and Ringo

Brian Epstein and Christine Foyle

Lee Starkey at the Baby Bullfight in Spain

Max Bygraves, Shirley Bassey Anne and I

Chapter 9 - Stephen Ward

'To the living one owes consideration

To the dead only the truth'

Lettres sur Œdipe –Voltaire

'He paid a lot of rent, drove a fancy car and liked good restaurants because that's how he met the people he wanted.

'Style' he would say 'it's all about style'. He was a very talented artist.'

Christine Keeler talking about Stephen Ward

Steven Ward is fashionable again. At the time of writing, Sir Andrew Lloyd Webber was composing a musical about him. He was an osteopath and treated me for chronic back pain. My love of powerboats had not helped the situation.

I met Steven through Jack Hylton who also called him in to help with his own back pain. He was a 68 year old man who ran about like a boy of 18.

I feel the same way at 81.

Steven was on the same table as Anne and I at one of Jack's parties. We found him a very sophisticated and pleasant man.

Steven Ward was a great osteopath, but he was perhaps an even better womaniser. My back sessions with Stephen were as much educational as they were therapeutic, he would often recant stories of his salacious escapades as he worked me, using the kinky details of his sexual encounters to distract me from the pain of working out kinks in my back, he was clever like that, or perhaps given his penchant for S&M, subconsciously he simply couldn't resist the combination of pleasure and pain.

The papers were full of the 50th Anniversary of the Profumo affair. I was on the outside of the scandal that rocked the very foundation of the country.

Steven was impeccably connected; he had certainly built up a marvellous practice with a dazzling database of clients, including Winston Churchill, Ava Gardner, Frank Sinatra and Liz Taylor.

He was a good-looking man with thick brown hair and a strong jaw line. He wore glasses as he was very short sighted but was nearly always photographed without them.

A real aristocrat, he always dressed casually when I saw him: cashmere jumper, silk cravats, and cavalry twills. Hackett would be his shop of choice today. He had a beat up Jaguar but it was fast. Deceptive, understated like the man himself.

Steven was the son of a Hertfordshire vicar and educated at a minor public school before studying medicine in the States. Before that he had spent some time as a translator in Germany. He lived in Hamburg, the City that the Beatles had spent their most impressionable years in and It was there that that he must have acquired his addiction to young girls and the darker side of life. At night he would frequent the red light district of the Reeperbahn and sampled its myriad temptations. He had found the wild side and walked on it for the rest of his life.

Stephen's easy manner and laid-back style soon helped him ingratiate himself into the upper reaches of society, he looked, and more importantly, spoke the part. To the manor born. He struck up a friendship with Lord Astor, a very wealthy aristocrat who owned a country estate called Cliveden on the banks of the Thames near Maidenhead. Cliveden was a beautiful place. Oswald Mosley, Max's dad, was a frequent visitor before the war, as was Von Ribbentrop, Hitler's British ambassador. Lord Astor let Steven live in the cottage on the grounds for a peppercorn rent of a pound a year. It was said that it was because Astor liked to have him around to attend to his back problems.

The truth was Steven was supplying an endless stream of young girls for the amusement of the rich and famous, who flocked there on weekends.

Steven invited Anne and I down there for a weekend, which we declined. I had no idea what really went on down there, but was not impressed with the aristocratic circle that frequented it. Some so fabulously wealthy they could not even begin to count it. I much preferred to be in the company of real people like Adam Faith or Bernie Ecclestone, speaking of which, Steven Ward was another person with his fair share of OCDs, like Bernie, he was fastidious about his appearance and hygiene. The osteopathic physician was also incredibly neat and tidy, though I'm not sure about his attitude to picture hanging.

It was just as well that we declined the invitation, because if I had been on record as going to Cliveden I would have doubtless been linked to the sensational events that went on there. They tried to pin everything else that went wrong in that decade on me. I was blissfully ignorant most of the time.

The Profumo affair and its fall-out could easily fill up the rest of this book. It was a story that had everything: politics, oodles of sex, espionage, courtroom drama, violence and death. Like we said of the Beatles story, you could not make it up.

Like the Beatles fairy story it gripped the nation and generated a rainforest of newsprint.

By that amazing year of 1963 the Conservative Party, led by Harold Macmillan had been in power for a dozen years and we were at the height of the Cold War. The previous autumn the world had come perilously close to being blown to pieces, with the Cuban Missile Crisis at its height. The golden boy of the Conservative Party and a man tipped to eventually be Harold's Macmillan's successor, John Profumo was discovered to have a mistress who was also sleeping with a top Russian secret agent. The girl's name was Christine Keeler, who for a while was to be the most famous woman in the world, the most famous femme fatale of from the 60's, making the journey from nonentity to notoriety. A line that once crossed, was impossible go back on. I walked it for long enough.

Profumo had met the impossibly beautiful Keeler in 1961 at Cliveden House; the 19-year-old was attending a party there hosted by Stephen Ward. Profumo was then the Secretary of State for War and married to Valerie Hobson, a famous actress from the previous decade, he first saw the young model nearly 30 years his junior, as she was climbing naked out of the swimming pool.

They started a short-lived affair, which received scant attention in the press, but when it was discovered that she was also sleeping with Yevgeny 'Eugene' Ivanov, a senior naval attaché to the Soviet embassy in London the scandal became front-page news around the world. Profumo then lied to Parliament in March 1963; he told MPs there was 'no impropriety whatsoever' in his relationship with Christine Keeler. Harold Wilson was the Labour leader then, and smelled a rat ... not to say blood. The rumour factory went into overdrive. Within three months Profumo admitted his deception and resigned his post.

The affair had come to light when a former lover of Keeler's, Johnny Edgecombe, had fired six shots into the door of Stephen Ward's flat in Wimpole Mews, Marylebone. Christine was staying there and Edgecombe fired at the lock in an attempt to gain entry. (Echoes of the Blade Runner athlete Oscar Pistorius who shot dead his lover Reeva Steenkamp through a locked door in February 2013). Keeler was involved in a tempestuous triangular relationship with Edgecombe and a vicious psycho basket case Jamaican drug dealer, Aloysius 'Lucky' Gordon. The self-styled 'blues singer' was a terrifying individual who Christine first met when she went to score drugs in Notting Hill. Johnny Edgecombe stood trial for knifing Gordon in a brawl over Keeler and when she failed to turn up in court the press went to town, splashing huge headlines like 'War Minister shock'. Talk about one drop of water making the cup spill over.

Johnny Edgecombe was cleared of the charges of slashing Lucky Gordon and the attempted murder of Christine Keeler, but drew seven years for possessing a firearm with intent to endanger life. The sentence was passed by Mr Justice Thesiger, though justice seemed in short supply then, as anyone and everyone connected with the scandal was ruthlessly taken out of the game, like chess pieces being taken off the board.

The establishment took their revenge on Stephen Ward, their principal patsy in this farrago of lies and double-dealing. In July of that year he was prosecuted for living off the immoral earnings of prostitution. It was one of the biggest carve-ups in history.

They wanted it to be all about sex, which according to the poet Phillip Larkin started that year. Ward was branded a pervert, a sex case that lived off the immoral earnings of Keeler and her stable mate Mandy Rice Davies. A ponce, a pimp, call him what you will. It steered the spotlight away from the inept, morally and spiritually bankrupt, Conservative government. It was a lynch mob camouflaging the truth.

Christine Keeler in her erudite book *The Truth at Last*, published four decades later, expounded the theory (without any supporting evidence) that Stephen was a Soviet spy who worked with the debonair Sir Anthony Blunt in a complex espionage ring. Blunt had been appointed Surveyor of the Queen's pictures. She reasoned that it was acceptable for Ward to be damned as a pimp rather than a spy. At that time the Russians had outsmarted the capitalists. They targeted the British Upper classes; the hated bourgeoisie. The KGB used people like Kim Philby, Burgess, MacLean, Blunt – all members of the upper class. They were all sacrificial lambs, they used them all to cause havoc but they did not count as anything at all to them. Would the public have been enthralled to think the Russians had been running MI5 for years back then?

Stephen Ward was committed for trial at the Old Bailey and charged under the Sexual Offences Act 1956. Both Keeler and Mandy Rice Davies were called as witnesses at the trial, which became perhaps the first real media circus that London had witnessed. There were doubts that the charges would stick but in the wave of hysteria that was surrounding the scandal the police tried to put a case together. Look how hard they were looking, Keeler had been put under terrible pressure, having been questioned on thirty-eight separate occasions. It was a show trial, a kangaroo court similar to what my mate Bernie Ecclestone was subjected to in Germany at the time I was writing this. I can speak from experience because as later in the book you can read (The Star Chamber) of my own ordeal of being tried in a Kafka-type court.

Defamation of reputation was the name of the game; just the hint of impropriety was enough to damage most careers beyond repair.

Keeler and Mandy Rice Davies testified against their former mentor Stephen. The jury was regaled with lurid tales of bacchanalian orgies, bucketing down champagne, S&M perversions and total licentiousness. Former policeman's daughter Mandy Rice Davies, in answer to Lord Astor's denial that she had sex with him at Cliveden, made one of the most famous remarks of the era when she said: 'He would say that, wouldn't he?'

This was why I liked Mandy; the media saw her and Christine as sisters in crime. The perception of the dynamic duo was they went together like foie gras and toast. In fact they were poles apart. If Christine was serious, an intense soul, then Mandy was the original 'party girl', always looking for a good time. As bubbly and effervescent as the vintage champagne she used to swig down like cherry coke. As Christine succinctly put it in her book: '*everything about her said "I want to marry a millionaire;" she might as well have carried a placard'.*

Blind ambition or was it blonde ambition, she had a much-publicised affair with the infamous Peter Rachman, which ended with his premature death. Look up 'slum landlord' in the dictionary and you'll see a picture of Peter.

I met Mandy some time later in Israel where she had a successful nightclub. I had sailed there in my yacht, as you do. I was enjoying the delights on offer, well as much as I could.

No one gave John Bloom anything in this world. I had to take it, fight for it, graft for it. I've had it and lost it, got it back and lost it again. Still getting it back, always will. I never felt bad about being hideously affluent, driving a Rolls Royce or having money. I've earned every penny. That's the great thing about money; nobody asked you where you got it. If you go in a show room to buy a top of the range limo, they are pleased to see you. You could have obtained it by selling the cheapest washing machines like John Bloom or by smashing glasses in faces like Reggie Kray.

It's true, Mandy Rice-Davies may have charged for her particular services in those days, but she had come a long way; she had married a wealthy businessman and now lived a quiet life. She had fulfilled her ambition and avoided the penury that haunted Christine's later life. She was still shapely and with the Monroe pout that had served her so well (the original blonde bombshell would be 87 this year had she survived). The world had eaten chunks of us but she had no rancour about the past. She told me she would never winter in England again. I had shipped over my latest car for the trip, a shiny red Lincoln Continental convertible, a real quality motor she must have seen me drive up in it.

We chatted about it before she went back to her friends. I was glad that she had survived with her dignity.

The case continued against Stephen Ward, it was like a Whitehall farce. Eggs were chucked at Christine when she arrived at the trial. I recall seeing pictures of the scrum outside the Old Bailey as the police battled to control the crowds and the media. Her eyes looked medicated to me. Stephen's barrister was a chap called James Burge whom they later based the 'Rumpole of the Bailey' TV character on. I doubt if even Rumpole himself could have helped Steven, the way the cards were stacked. The case against him was full of lies and circumstantial evidence. It was all to deflect attention away from the awkward questions about espionage and the rampant decadence in the upper classes, the agenda was to discredit Christine Keeler and convict Stephen Ward as a pimp.

The prosecuting counsel, Mervyn Griffith-Jones, made a harsh attack on Stephen's character in his closing speech on the penultimate day of the trial. It looked hopeless for him now. On the way home the taxi taking Stephen to Wimpole Mews stopped outside Harrods and his agent's son popped in to collect a prescription for Nembutal, sleeping pills. That night he overdosed on them and I remember seeing the photographs of him on a stretcher being taken to St Stephen's hospital in Chelsea, He was dying in agony but it took three days for him. The public trial of Steven Ward became his public execution.

He was still in the coma when the jury found him guilty of living on the immoral earnings of Christine and Mandy. The charges of pimping were rejected and the trial was adjourned but when Stephen died the trial was closed. Legal experts later said that the guilty verdict was a miscarriage because Keeler received more money from Stephen Ward then he did from her. The law's case was that Christine had paid for phone calls whilst living in Wimpole Mews using the money she made from her punters.

Stephen Ward died at the age of 51, a guy that could not apply the brakes. Only six people attended his funeral yet he must have provided 'entertainment' for half of London's debauched upper classes. We all belong to the same hypocrisy. We sent some flowers; next to it laid a wreath from 21 writers including Kenneth Tynan, the first man to say the 'F' word on TV and Joe Orton, the brilliant young playwright who was to die so violently soon after. On the card it read 'To Stephen Ward, a victim of British hypocrisy'.

The remains of Dr Steven Ward were cremated at Mortlake Crematorium, at the foot of Chiswick Bridge, near where the Boat Race ends.

The coroner's jury officially ruled his death as suicide by barbiturate poisoning. He left 12 notes one of them with the line 'sorry to disappoint the vultures'.

All the secrets died with him, including the persistent rumour that Ward's spy ring included a senior figure in M15. There was no Internet then of course and M15 had even more power than today, many covert acts went unpunished because they were simply not exposed.

Prime Minster Harold MacMillan resigned on the grounds of ill health shortly afterwards. The following year the Harold Wilson Government swept to power as the entire Conservative regime went. Christine Keeler was found guilty of perjury charges relating to the Johnny Edgecombe trial and sentenced to nine months, she served six. John Profumo lived to be 91. I heard his son on the radio recently pedalling some book he had written about his father and saying how strong his marriage was. Valcric Hobson stayed with him to the end. I always think about John Lydon's assertion that history is written by the victors.

My dealings with Stephen Ward were minimal but I am writing this chapter because the story deserves to be re-examined with the passage of time. He was a fine artist; he could sketch and do a picture of someone very quickly.

Amongst the rich and famous who sat for him were The Duke of Edinburgh, who I met several times at charity functions, the Duke and Duchess of Kent and the Earl of Snowdon. So when he painted a picture of yours truly I was in good company. Unfortunately the painting was later stolen from me, I would love to own it again.

It was my wife Anne who came up with the idea when she wanted to get me a birthday present. It was 1962 and the money was cascading in. Those were the days my friend, I thought they would never end I had everything. I suppose narcissism came into it, a picture of oneself hanging in a place of prominence, how grandiose.

Anne met Christine Keeler a couple of times at 17 Wimpole Mews, when she took photos of me around to Stephen whom had been recommended by my assistant Harvey Langer as a great portrait painter, Anne found Christine highly intelligent a point that many people missed.

She lay on the sofa with her meticulously painted face. I liked the film *Scandal,* starring the stunning Joanne Whalley-Kilmer as Christine (if they were to re-make it then the model Kelly Brock would be perfect in the lead role).

With the pressure she endured throughout that period it was amazing she stayed alive. Christine was brought up in the Buckinghamshire village of Wraysbury in a property that was two converted railway carriages without any hot water. At 17 she headed for the bright lights/ big City and got a job working as a topless showgirl in a Soho club called Murray's Cabaret club, Paul Raymond's revue bar was nearby. That was where she met Stephen Ward and soon moved in with him. The relationship was purely platonic she always insisted. Stephen was a ladics' man, although theories have been put forward that he was bi-sexual. Ward had a strong attraction to young working class women; his interest was not so much sexual as more as a Henry Higgins type figure, a modern day Pygmalion almost. He collected young women like butterflies, snaring them and them keeping them under his total control. Cultivating them for his own use.

The next chapter deals with the actor Terence Stamp who I used as a greeter in one of my clubs. Stamp made a film called *The Collector* from the creepy novel by John Fowles. It told about a disturbed young lepidopterist that wins the pools (it was the football pools in those days, not the lottery that people dreamed of winning) and uses the proceeds to kidnap a young girl in the hope of making her fall in love with him. A heavy subject for those care-free times, when most people were watching Sir Cliff Richard driving his bus around in *Summer Holiday*.

You see nothing changes; there is nothing new under the sun. Stalking is considered to be a 21st century crime but what was 'Lucky Gordon' other than a deranged stalker? His obsession with Keeler boarded on the psychotic and she was so terrified of him that she enlisted hard man Johnny Edgecombe to rid herself of him. This in turn triggered a series of events, which could be said to have finally brought down a government.

Ward preyed upon the young and lonely, the vulnerable but then so did Jimmy Saville who used to frequent the same club that I employed Terence Stamp in. What's the difference? Ward was driven by some hatred of the establishment possibly; the same establishment that he was part of and played so relentlessly.

I was delighted with the painting, so much so that I hung it in the boardroom of Rolls Razor. When things went awful though, the picture was stolen and went on the missing list. It turned up years later and was auctioned at Christies for £1188 last year. I would like to get back some day. A symbol of a strange time and the work of a man described in the Denning Report thus: 'Osteopath, artist, demon, socialite and pervert'.

Stephen Ward's Portrait

Roy Orbison and Sandy Shaw at the Crazy horse

Chapter 10 - I Love The Night Life

'I knew I was an East End spiv who got lucky, a chancer winging it.

When the sixties happened London burst into Technicolor, everything's been crap since'

Terence Stamp

'Nothing is so dangerous as being too modern. One is apt to grow old fashioned quite suddenly

An Ideal Husband Oscar Wilde - Lady Markby

I loved the nightlife so much I ran a string of clubs that for a while were amongst the most fashionable in London. They also brought me a whole load of trouble that could have ended up with me being killed, more of that in the next chapter though.

At that time I was unclear as to what direction to take in my little life at that point I desperately needed to be earning, and get the money pot full again. A lot of my problems were in relation to personal guarantees that I had a reckless habit for signing. I had signed more than Tom Cruise did autographs. My brother in law, now deceased gave me a large one to guarantee.

‘Where do I sign was my attitude?’

Guaranteed loans were a guaranteed headache to me. The point was I always honoured mine though it was to cost me so much. Two other high profile bankruptcies of that era were Carpet King Cyril Lord and that Pioneer of the aviation world, Freddie Laker, when their businesses went down the pan they just walked away leaving a trail of debtors. Cyril Lord was a personal friend of Harold Wilson and emerged unscathed from the collapse of his business, funny old game, finance.

One particular guarantee was to give me tremendous problems. It concerned an individual called Norman Jones who asked me to cover an overdraft of £36,000 with Barclays Bank. He had grandiose ideas about opening a club and had asked the bank for money to enable him to build one in the cellar of a flat near the Underground station at Baker Street. This was situated just a few yards down from Madame Tussauds, thinking back I wonder what establishment housed the bigger dummies...

My advisor the MP Reader Harris thought it was a sound idea so I guaranteed the money. Things were going badly for me with the Rolls Razor collapsing and a Board of Trade enquiry into the whole sorry mess looming, this little matter was soon forgotten in scheme of things. That is until after the collapse and Reader informed me that whole £36,000 had been used up and the club was only half finished. It was literally a hole in the ground and at time we were chucking money down it, a real money pit. The builder was owed an additional £25,000. I had a difficult decision to make, write the whole thing off as a loss and put it down to experience or carry on and try and salvage something from the rubble. In the end I turned it over to my wife Anne who took over the liabilities in exchange for shares in the place. That way we had control and Mr Jones had no say.

Anne was new to the nightclub business and mooted the idea of forming a management committee comprising Sandie Shaw's manager Eve Taylor, Billy Wright and Joy Beverley (the golden couple of the 60's). They were the real 'Posh & Becks' of the day and Terence Stamp and his model girlfriend Jean Shrimpton. That description does really do them justice because Terry and Jean were easily as glamorous. In the Bowie chapter I compared the Wrights to the Beckhams but a nearer approximation would be Stamp and the 'Shrimp'. I have every respect for David, who was a fine player, the game lost a great talent when he retired whilst writing this. However he continues to be a wonderful role model and his wife Victoria has shown the world just how good a fashion designer she is. But for looks and sheer star appeal Stamp and his partner were in the same league.

Terence was probably the best looking man to haunt the nightlife of London and when I knew him he was approaching his prime.

Another East End boy he was the eldest of five children raised in Bow. The original criteria for a true Cockney was to be born within the sound of Bow Bells, now any oaf with an estuary accent passes themselves off as a Cockney, or is the correct term 'Mockney'?

My close friend Peter Ustinov cast him in *Billy Budd* in 1962, the film that catapulted him to fame. Peter invited me down to Elstree studios one day to watch it being filmed. That is where I first met Terence, he seemed very pleasant but a bit over awed by everything. Like the Beatles in their early days at Green Street, scarcely believing what was happening to them, almost afraid to blink in case it all faded away before them.

I had heard stories about how unrelentingly boring filming was but had no idea how true that was. It took them over six hours to shoot a scene 10 minutes long. Lennon hated it too, always moaning about it. When we next met in 1965, Terence was in the big time, his agent was a guy called John Hayman who also looked after Liz Taylors career. I had flown to Amsterdam to have a spot of dinner with them. Jean Shrimpton who I was to meet later was the first super model. Even more stunning in real life than in her photographs, which to this day are seen as iconic images of all that was swinging about London. With the longest legs you had ever seen, long shiny hair cut by Vidal Sassoon into a fringe and with those doe eyes she was an absolute knock out.

Jean was working in Milan that night where she had been gracing the catwalks at some high fashion shows. I could see they were very much in love. She only ever referred to him as 'Stamp', which I found amusing and posh. A few months later they caused a sensation in Australia when Shrimpton turned up at their equivalent of the Derby wearing a white shift dress four inches above the knee. She was sans hat and gloves and wore Terence's wristwatch; to attend a social occasion of that importance and defy the dress code was unthinkable. Their pictures were splashed worldwide and the mini-skirt was born, a look that was widely copied by teenage girls everywhere.

Terence had not long come out of a relationship with another actress Julie Christie who was in Shrimpton's class for looks. Julie had won an Oscar for her part in a film called *Darling*, John Schlesinger's bleak study of self-advancement in swinging London. You may remember her better starring in *Doctor Zhivago* with Omar Sharif or in *Shampoo* with Warren Beatty. Speaking of Beatty I recalled once having an amazing diner with his older sister Shirley Maclaine in the Russian Tea Room in New York. Holding court that night was Peter Ustinov who kept us spellbound for nine hours with a steam of colourful stories. Ustinov was the best raconteur in the business. When he started on a roll I just shut up and listened, if you have persevered with the book so far you must agree I have a fund of anecdotes and tales but compared to Peter I felt like 'Tommy' the eponymous hero of Pete Townshend's rock opera – the deaf, dumb and blind boy. It was the timing of these tales that was so perfect; he recounted them with the skill of an old time music hall performer.

One of Townshend's contemporaries was the Kinks' Ray Davies, who it was always said, wrote the great London love song 'Waterloo Sunset' about 'Terry and Julie' – Stamp and Christie. I used to drive over Waterloo Bridge frequently then and that song would come to mind. In the summer of 2013 when this was being written the BFI (British Film Institute) were holding a retrospective of Stamp's films under Waterloo Bridge,

I do not think they showed the film Terence was shooting in Amsterdam at that time. It was called *Modesty Blaise* it was not considered to be his finest work. He was having problems with the Italian beauty Monica Vitti who was the female lead. A muse of the legendary Milanese director Michelangelo Antonioni the blonde Vitti was notoriously temperamental and on the first day of shooting had kept the crew waiting two hours because she objected to the costumes.

Terence had turned down the lead role in *Alfie* to do this movie and was regretting it already. Michael Caine accepted the role, which to many people is still his best film. What many people do not know is that Terence played 'Alfie' on Broadway, but when it flopped turned down the movie role. My dear friend Adam Faith toured in a production of Bill Naughton's play in the later years of his life, Adam was playing himself really in most of his work.

So what's it all about Terence asked? He was on good form though, we staggered through the 15-course Indonesian meal, which was called a Ristafel, and he picked up the bill. I liked the Dam if it got to warm for me in London perhaps I could gone over there. By end of the meal, The film star agreed to front the club which was good news. We had decided to call it the 'In Place' and it eventually opened in June 1965, when we finally got it off the ground not to say out of the ground. I was in America on business when the grand opening took place and Anne kept a discreet distance away not wishing to bring a lot of unwelcome attention to the place. John Bloom was still in the news as the Board of Trade hearing was still dragging on.

The guest list was a who's who of the rich and famous and nearly 500 of them, Rock Royalty in the form of Rolling Stones superstar Mick Jagger, king of the scene, he still is. The lead singer of the band had been in a three-year romance with Jean Shrimpton's sister Chrissie; she had a jolly hockey sticks accent. I used to see them in the club occasionally as loved up as Stamp and her more famous sister.

A couple of Beatles were there also, George was asking after me I heard later, Roy Orbison was there too, another nice man and brilliant singer. I think he wrote so many sad songs because he had such a tragic life, his first wife was killed in a motorbike smash, and two sons died in a fire. You couldn't write it.

The opening was a huge success but then how could it not be with the A-listers and everything free, the booze, the food. It was short lived though and by giving a place the moniker 'The In Place' I was asking for trouble. Oscar Wilde's quote headed this chapter and his maxim about the surest way to be out of fashion tomorrow was to lead it today was certainly true of the 'In Place'.

My concept was to make it the favourite bolthole of London's top names. A club where pop stars, actors, royals and entrepreneurs could come together let down their hair down and party the night away. Maybe for that one night it worked. John Bloom had invented his own aristocracy. I did not belong with the toffee-noses or the low life's so I said 'have this – it's much better' the problem was that there were only so many 'In' people. The 'In' place quickly became the 'Out' place. The 'in' door became the exit. The place was packed the first night when it was free. When the 'In Crowd' had to pay for the Veuve Clicquot, when they to pay their way and not get comped, it was a different story. Anne had also noticed that some of the committee were inviting their show biz pals in on freebies whilst members of 'Joe Public', the ones who were actually paying cash were being turned away for not being trendy enough. It was self-defeating. Studio 54 in New York in the 80's had this elitist door policy but we got there first.

The few times that they were there Terence and Shrimpton were absolute magic. They were at the centre of fashion and she was the love of his life, when they split I do not think he was ever the same again. His glittering career lost focus, he made some bad choices in films, turning down the lead in *Camelot* and concentrating on art house movies. This was whilst Caine was making films like the *Italian Job* and *Get Carter*. In a recent article in the *Evening Standard* Stamp talked sadly about the break up: 'It was my fault. She did not leave me for *'no reason'*. She left me because she saw I was a lunatic'.

A lot of us in that class of '65 became lunatics. I know I did for a while, but more of that later.

Broken hearted, Stamp withdrew to his beautiful flat in the Albany. He wrote movingly in his brilliant memoir about winter days when he lit the fire and stayed by it all day. Then at night, unable to sleep, he would take the night bus back to the East End. Eventually, heartbroken he quit London to decamp and find himself abroad. As his black cab travelled down Savile Row he looked up to see the Beatles playing together for the last time on the roof of number 3.

What really did it in for the 'In Place' was the loss of the late night drinks licence. It only really got going in the wee small hours of the morning, as Frank once sang. Being in showbiz most of our clients had their own shows to perform in or had all-day film schedules. They were looking for a place to unwind in, after what the Beatles called 'A Hard Day's Night', the name of their first movie, the one Lennon hated. An essential part of that unwinding process involved alcohol, the Beatles' drink of choice was whisky and coke (or Pepsi); most stars liked champagne. After a year the local residents, bandied together to successfully object to the renewal of our late-night drinks licence. Thanks a lot, they should have been glad that the neighbourhood now included the biggest names in entertainment and pop music, even if they were squabbling, swearing and sometimes even fighting on the pavements of Baker Street. Anyway bottom line comes the midnight hour (Wilson Pickett, who had a global hit with the song, was one of the many soul stars who graced the club. I think we got him for £15 per night ... I mean Simon Dee and Blackburn did not pull that down in a week) and we stopped serving alcohol. You heard about the pub with no beer well we were the club without alcohol; the trendiest discotheque in London was the Cinderella club.

I needed an alternative venue and rented the night club section of Billy Walker's 'Baked Potato' Piccadilly-based restaurant, the ex boxer who was shrewdly managed by his brother George. Some of you may recall Billy was a useful heavyweight in his time, shooting to fame when he knocked out a giant American in a televised Amateur contest. That was when a star-studded Great Britain team whitewashed the USA 10—0. Billy, despite being dubbed the 'Blonde Bomber' could never really build on that but earned and kept enough from the fight game to open a string of clubs and restaurants. Seems strange now but baked spuds were regarded as somewhat a delicacy then and people would actually go out for an evening and consume them.

We called the club 'Reflections' and when the 'In place' shut we would ferry the punters down to it by limo. Bernie was on the scene then and arranged for a huge Mercedes 600 to be the taxi. What a monster this was, it was massive and could have easily passed for one of those Third Reich staff cars you used to see in the war films. The punters were impressed particularly as it was common practice for some of the girls to come along for the ride. I dreamt this wheeze up myself but these days it is common practice for establishments like the 'Spearmint Rhino' to have these stretch limos.

You can catch them whizzing around the West End dropping of and picking up clients, cocooned in luxury. Interesting story coming up in the next chapter about Bernie and the 600 Merc.

I tried to appear blasé about it all, until I was approached by Dino Cellini about a running a Casino in my 'In Place' club. Dino was Meyer Lansky's right-hand man and running things for Meyer in London with the aid of some trickster lawyers.. Lansky was the most celebrated of the Mafia's financers. He came to London in the early 60's on a gambling junket but I never saw him. They had set up the 'Colony Club' in Berkley Square. I would take Anne there sometimes, the food was the best in London, and they served you all the time. All you had to do was lose a lot of money on the card tables. We used to see the famous actor George Raft in there. What an actor he was, he appeared in the original *Scarface* back in 1932 with Paul Munni. (You should check that out, he was the one that flipped the coin). There was a lot of speculation about him actually being a gangster. I suppose he was employed in a similar role to that of Stamp's i.e. as a greeter. Soon afterwards he fell foul of the internal unit of the American Internal Revenue and pleaded guilty in the Federal Court to tax evasion. In 1967 he was refused entry back into the country because of his perceived mob connections, and George the gangster's gangster died of leukaemia two years later.

Sometimes Anne used to sit next to Telly Savalas, the famous bald American actor. He was over in England making the epic war movie *The Dirty Dozen*. Telly was a charming fellow, a big gambler. Dino and his playmates wanted to have a casino in the club. The place was on two floors and his plan was to install the casino in the lower one, we had talks but I was wary and I think the Mafia thought that I was a bit too high profile and attracting enough unwelcome publicity for their purposes. All dealings were done on a cordial basis though, like my experiences with them in America.

There was too much competition around for us in the form of the famous clubs such as Scotch of St James's, The Bag of Nails and the Cromwellian. All had good reputations and were chock full of pop's biggest hitters. I was looking for a new angle and thought I found it with the 'Crazy Horse' theme. No, not the Red Indian chief who killed Colonel Custer but a club based on the famous French one. A very high-class cabaret club that pre-dated the lap bars that are so proliferate in London. This was a million miles away from them, very tasteful, wonderful lighting, sensuous dancers, avant-garde scenery, so discreet and classy – an exotic milieu.

I had visited it once and it turned my head around, full of the most amazing looking women you had ever seen, from all parts of the world, all nationalities, hues, the only common denominator was that they were all staggeringly beautiful. I had seen into the future and this was it.

We did our best to sign up the cream of the Crazy Horse line-up and bring them to London. Russian Roman would have been proud of my efforts to sign up the best talent available. He dealt in world-class footballers – we tried to deal in these world-class beauties, but it was not so easy. Sure London was swinging and they would be mixing with the rich and famous but try selling a wet Baker Street on a Monday night. Most of them were socially ascendant and in relationships with abnormally wealthy older men. We had no option but to start recruiting from the Homeland. There were some beauties there mind, but we could never capture that Continental vibe and the club struggled.

I brought Laurie Jay in to manage the Crazy Horse. When I put this chapter together I phoned Laurie for some background and we had a lovely chat about those days. Laurie was a drummer and worked with the Shadows for a while when Tony Meehan was ill. He was an original member of the Echoes, maybe not totally familiar to you but a group who worked with every big name of that era, from Dusty Springfield to Jerry Lee Lewis.

Ringo Starr actually replaced him for a short while when he left the group in 1962. Laurie went on to have a long career in show business managing amongst others Shirley Bassey. We got the late licence back eventually but the club continued to struggle to make a profit despite Laurie's management. Laurie managed the singer Billy Ocean whose big hit stateside was 'Red Light spells Danger'. Already there were a few red lights flashing in the life of John Bloom and I should have taken better notice of them.

Victor Lowndes another resident of Alford House, had approached me at the start of the decade about getting involved with the Playboy club on Park Lane. Hugh Hefner who ran the Playboy Empire was branching out into Europe and saw London as his beachhead; Victor was his chief executive and confidant. Sir Isaac Woolfson, the genius who told me not to buy into the Beatles songbook, had a similar low opinion about the Hef and his travelling circus. The fears and cant surrounding anything remotely salacious and the changes in sexual reform were still highly prevalent in Woolfson's generation. (He talked me out of taking over Ladbrokes the bookmakers too, when the late Cyril Stein approached me. Seems to me that in the worsening economic recession that still grips this country the only businesses that are opening new stores are the bookies and pawn/payday loan shops.)

Instead I invested in a club called El Toro, a glorified meat market in the Finchley Road, near Swiss Cottage. It was one of the first discotheques in London and my partner was a character called Barry Huntman.

This was late 50's, I was just starting to make money and yet to meet Anne. I used to drive past it on the way home when I moved to Cricklewood. I found that the club was very close to my factory. After a hard day on the coalface I would put in there to try and unwind. It had two attractions, a late licence very important that, and it was packed with young ladies, they called them 'Rank starlets'. Starlet was an interesting term in those days, along with 'show girl', 'party girl', 'dancer', 'model' all trotted out at Steven's show trial to besmirch Keeler and Rice-Davies. The evenings were like some endless 'Amy Winehouse look alike' contest, with their heavily lacquered beehives and lipstick the colour of Arsenal's shirts.

How many of these protégés were actually under contract to Rank is open to conjecture although a small number did go onto make films, if not exactly star in them. In my view the only connection with the Rank Organization is that were possibly employees at the Odeon cinema at Golders Green dispensing choc-ices and being usherettes, another profession that seems to have disappeared.

I spent too much time down there and became part of the broken furniture. It was a mood that prevailed in me of seamless but exhausting partying. Eventually it re-opened with some large neon sign proudly stating: 'Barry Huntman and John Bloom proudly present the new El Toro Club'

It was the first time I saw my name up in lights, I was yet to visit Las Vegas but that is how I imagined it to be, not that I learnt a lot about the night club business from the El Toro, but I did I did learn something about women.

I digress, I kept in touch with Victor Lowndes, Laurie introduced him to his wife the model Marilyn Cole, a staggeringly good looking woman who could have had top billing at the Crazy Horse Saloon, (the Paris one not mine). Cole combined the erotic romanticism of the Hollywood star Rita Hayworth and the sex appeal of a Christine Keeler. Marilyn was the only Brit to be voted 'Playmate of the Year'. The photographer Eric Bowman took a photograph of her that was used for Bryan Ferry and Roxy Music's most iconic album cover image on 'Stranded'. The cover of Marilyn in a red dress was a masterpiece of graphic art. Ferry always had a glamorous woman on a Roxy cover, they were an item them. The idea behind it being that the more stylish the woman the more status he had as a rock idol. Bowman later worked with the shoe designer Manolo Blahnik; Tamara Ecclestone used to buy his footwear by the truckload.

Chapter 11 - The Chaps

'You bought a lot of me Terry. For a smile and a nod, and a wave of the hand and a few quiet drinks in a quiet bar here and there. It was nice while it lasted. So long Amigo. I won't say goodbye. I said it to you when it meant something. I said it when it was sad and lonely and final.'

The Long Goodbye Raymond Chandler

The problem with having a club is you are always going to draw the attention of the criminal classes (or the Chaps, as the underworld referred to them as) who wanted their share of the action. I was blissfully unaware of such things and just jogged along. I always liked Humphrey Bogart in *Casablanca*, the guy who owned the club and played chess in the white double-breasted dinner jacket. He never drank in his own club, he just observed.

My uncle Alf ran the club most of the time when I was trying to keep my business and my sanity. It was called the 'Phone Booth' now that the 'Crazy Horse Saloon' was being put down as an ambitious but ultimately costly failure. The gimmick of the 'Phone booth' was strangely that it had a phone on the table. In the 21st century when everybody has a Smartphone, such an innovation would seem antiquated, but back then it was very popular. You could phone the DJ and request the new Beatles song or even use it to chat up that chunky blonde on the next table.

One evening a burly guy in a suit two sizes too small for him came in and asked to speak to the owner. He was fortyish, with a vivid scar under his eye, not unlike the one sported by Paul Munni in that George Raft film I was telling you about.

'I have come about the insurance.'

'Got some thanks' said Alf

'No, this is special insurance.'

'Special Insurance?'

The burly guy pointed to the windows.

'See all that plate glass, well this insurance covers you against bricks going through it, or even a car. Imagine the damage that would cause'

This puzzled Alf at first, Scarface continued.

'You don't understand do you?'

Something in his tone, struck a chord with little Alf, he finally cottoned on, realizing this was some hard core criminal and not the man from the Prudential.

'My nephew owns the club; I will speak to him about it.'

'I will be back tomorrow to collect the first premium, my name is Graham. It's a oner a month, cash.'

Spooked by now Alf rang me straight away.

'Johnny, Johnny you got to come over, some guy has just been in, wants a £100 tomorrow for insurance. It's some protection thing.'

He always called me Johnny, one of the few people in the world that ever did. I could tell he was upset and my heart sank when he told me the story. There was only one person who could sort this out for me. Actually there were two, Ronnie and Reggie – The Kray twins, the meanest, most celebrated gangsters that ever ran London Town.

The Krays had moved into the West End in the mid 50's when they had a share in a drinking club called the 'Stragglers'. It was situated in Cambridge Circus, opposite where Les Mis has been running all these years.

The first I heard of them was when Reg got into a row with an African gentleman in a drinking club in Tottenham Court road. He hit him over the head with a truncheon till it broke then Ron stabbed him, no charges were ever brought.

In the early 60's they started leaning on Peter Rachman, he had paid the twins £5k to avoid trouble in Notting Hill where Rachman was himself leaning on his slow paying tenants. The book is studded with 'look in the dictionary/see a picture of' but in the *Oxford English Dictionary* there is a word Rachmanism, which is defined as the extortion or exploitation by a landlord of tenants of a slum.

I could never understand how Rachman was so intimidated by the Krays, in the last chapter I described the squad of Lebanese loons he employed to mind Christine and Mandy. Terence Stamp and Michael Caine had the problem. The guy who worked the door of the Discotheque was a completely out of control. He was German called Norbert Rondel, when he was not splitting heads in Wardour Street he was a pro wrestler called the 'Polish Eagle'. That was his alter ego; don't know where the Polish bit came from.

It was in the Discotheque that Reggie grabbed Mandy Rice-Davies's arm and ordered her to get him a drink. Mandy told him in no uncertain terms that she did not work there.

‘Now you do, get the drink’ growled Reggie.

Mandy refused again and got the ‘Polish Eagle’ to have a word, but when he recognised who it was he returned ashen faced he told Mandy to apologise and fetch Reggie’s drink sharpish. (He would say that, wouldn’t he)? Mandy was a feisty lady and still refused, the Krays were about to unleash hell when Rachman appeared on the scene and gave Reggie a sizeable cheque to placate him.

Rachman also gave Ronnie a club in Knightsbridge called ‘Esmeralda’s Barn’ this was in 1960 when Reggie was imprisoned for 18 months for issuing protection-related threats. The club was the twins’ HQ, they loved it, giving them a foothold in the West End and raising their profile even higher. That is where I was headed that night, I do not know why they called it ‘Esmeralda’s Barn’, it was a curious name I googled it, but there is no explanation. It was close to Harrods and near where the Candy boys have erected sumptuous luxury apartments.

I was on nodding terms with the Krays. I had seen them at some charity events and they had acknowledged me; we did not socialise but there were no problems between us. Just as well, I think they saw me as some sort of renegade, not so much a kindred spirit but an outsider like them.

They were both there when I entered; Reggie was sitting in one of those big wicker chairs that were fashionable then. I noticed Ronnie's shiny cuff links as we shook hands. His hands had that long tapered quality of a surgeon. They gave me a seat and a cold drink.

'Got a problem?' Ronnie enquired.

'Yes…sort of. Guy came in my club tonight and said we needed more insurance. I wondered if he was anything to do with your organisation'.

'John, why we do anything like that' Reg spoke for the first time. He said my name softly like he had known me since we were kids. That was what so scary about the real heavies, that calmness.

'Who was he? What was he like? Did you get his name?' Ronnie was becoming interested, his face was flushed.

'Said his name was Graham, 40's, scar under his eye'. I touched a place on my face.

Reg nodded.

'I think he is on the firm' said Ronnie.

'Yeah, think so' Reggie was smiling now. He was wearing a red tie and a pale blue shirt with white cuffs.

'Listen John we will sort it. No problem. Don't worry'

I thought I would quit whilst I was ahead; I made a show of noticing the antique clock above the bar and told them I had to go.

'I know you're busy, I did not want to trouble you, just thought you boys could help. You know everything that is going on.'

'We do that, don't we Ron'. Reggie stood up,

'*Nice to see you John, anytime we can be of assistance, you know where we are'* Ronnie was saying.

The next evening a chastened Graham walked into the Phone Booth and asked for Alf. He then told him that he did not need any insurance. In fact Graham even went so far as to that that should we encounter any problems of any nature then we should contact him immediately. He never came back. Some years later I heard that Graham had been shot and stabbed to death in some Soho alley.

It was the first time I had encountered such a thing as protection and thanks to the Krays I avoided paying out any.

This incident was a lesson to me; I could not rid myself of a nagging worry that seemed to invade my metabolism. So I decided to beef up security by recruiting an ex-convict by the name of Norman Johnstone. He had just come off the moor after serving a life sentence I never knew the circumstances. His taciturn manner seldom drew any attention to him but he could look after himself. Norman knew everything that was going on in the London underworld and was warning me about problems that some of the other clubs had been having with fires, fights and staff problems. The name Joe Wilkins kept coming up in this connection, Norman suggested that I get in touch with him and have a general chat. He had a contact number for him and when I rang it a woman's voice answered. She told me that he was not available but that I should leave my number, which I did.

I thought no more about it. A couple of nights later I was at home thinking about money and how much I needed some. Anne had made me a tasty sandwich; I took a bite just as I heard the phone ring.

'John Bloom?'

'The one and only.'

'People told me you were a clever man.'

I was rising to the bait.

'Not to say good looking and funny.'

It was Joe Wilkins, returning my call. We agreed to meet for a coffee.

Joe was at best a sociopath, up to his elbows in blood. The common denominator amongst his type was the total disregard for the fate of their victims and the pain caused to their family and friends. Wilkins possessed no curiosity, anger or conscience. He started out as a used-car salesman, like another associate of mine, and then he became involved in the lucrative one-armed-bandit business. Protection was his racket when I first met him.

When we had our coffee he turned up well dressed in a blue suit and dotted tie. I was prepared for anything really but was surprised how big he was 6ft 4 and rising, he was very tall for his height I once remarked to Anne. Joe categorically denied having anything to do with the club fires and said to me that he would never have anything to do with such a thing, we got on well, you do at the start. The outcome was that he asked me down to his Dorking farm one weekend for tea, I accepted immediately and a few days later drove down there in my latest motor, A Jensen Interceptor, sky Blue like Man City's shirts.

Joe was living the life of a country squire, another to the Manor Born. When I pulled into his driveway a man approached us on a huge black horse that blocked our path. I had never seen such a creature, it was massive, and they measure horses in hands, don't they? Well this one was so large; he had more hands than in my old mate Max Bygraves' hit song. The equine made the late Henry Cecil's wonder horse Frankel look like my daughter's My Little Pony, the one the FBI roughed up. Pearl later told me it that it was 18 hands and was called guess what 'Blackie'. This first horseman of the apocalypse (how appropriate) turned out to be Joe on horseback, He was so tall but on this thing he looked gigantic. He was a good-looking man who always wore those horn-rimmed specs sported by Caine in the 'Ipcress file'. Today he was in the country tweeds and wore brown leather riding boots, a legitimate gangster, and the real thing, that is what was in it for him. Wilkins wanted the world to see him as another hard grafting London lad that had done all right for himself. There were plenty of us around then.

'Follow me' he snapped so we drove on down the drive till we came to this place which looked like it had just came out of the front page of *Country Life*, it must have been a large farmhouse or something, to call it a cottage did not do it any favours. But then Steven Ward's cottage at Cliveden where Keeler met Profumo was big.

It was a very tranquil scene, his daughter was on her very own 'my little pony' and she was practicing jumping over those tiny fences like they have in the Horse of the Year show. The idyllic scene was completed by the presence of Jo's wife Pearl. She was lovely, an ex dancer in the Marilyn Cole, Shrimpton league, eminently capable of gracing one of Mr Ferry's record covers.

I phoned Pearl Read recently when I was putting the Wilkins saga together. I wanted some stories of Joe and even a picture; at one time I knew she had the most marvellous collection of them. After my Anne she was probably the most photogenic woman I had ever seen. This is coming from a man who has dined with the Shrimp and little Lesley Hornsby, better known as Twiggy. I still see her on the M& S ads and marvel at her bone structure. Pearl still modelled in her bra at the age of 56 in Age Concern's advertising poster campaign around the turn of the last century.

She was pleased to hear from me but did not want to talk about Joe, he was insanely jealous of her and I know for a fact he vented his terrible temper on her. The scars of which still haunt her to this day. She had destroyed the collection of photographs she had of them. That day Joe was the perfect country gent and it was a delight to be in his company. It was like *Downton Abbey*, not that I have ever watched it. Pearl laid on high tea which would have graced the first day of Royal Ascot, beautiful sandwiches, smoked salmon or cream cheese and chives on brown bread. Free range egg and cress on white. Vanilla and sultana scones with clotted cream and strawberry preserve. English strawberries and pouring cream all washed down with Earl Grey tea. I was seriously impressed.

Jo got into a long monologue about how violent London had become, all the different factions that were vying for control of its nightlife. In his view most of them were no-marks calling themselves gangsters. It would be Interesting to hear his views on the East Europeans and Somali gangs that operate over here now.

'Why don't we merge?' he suggested.

Don't forget how young I was then, the first Englishman to make a million before he was thirty. I was impressionable. I looked up to mentors and believed that everything they said was true. Sir Isaac Wolfson had talked me out of millions with his ill advice, in a similar way I bought into Wilkins's act. So I helped green light it and soon we were in business together, it should have been a good experience for me ... should have been. The company that ran the whole caboodle was called G&W automatics. We had 'the 800 club' in Leicester Square. This had been previously known as 'the 400 club' (it was half the fun) and was fashionable amongst Guard officers and their ilk. At the height of its fame Princess Margaret frequented it. We arranged to ferry clients from the Crazy Horse when the bar shut to the 800 club.

My first inkling of trouble came when two of the staff of the 800 club were charged with rolling punters in the alleyways leading to Leicester Square tube. These unfortunates had had a few already by the time they had left the Crazy Horse and were topped up at the 800. Wilkins was charged with trying to pervert the course of justice at the trial of the club staff by giving false evidence. He was acquitted as was the 800 club staff. Somewhere at the back of my mind a red light was flashing.

I later heard that he had squared a lot of cab drivers to drop unsuspecting punters and tourists off at the club. *'Here we are then?'*

'But I wanted to go to Windsor Castle!'

Most clubs had arrangements with the drivers over such transactions and would either give them a few quid or comp them at the club. Joe was no different and the cabbies did not want to upset him.

When he went on one, he was just terrifying, a one-man war machine. I knew one of the doormen quite well, the usual stereotype, shaven head, completely bald with the little Chicano beard. He told me that one Friday the 800 was packed full with jolly jocks down in London for the England v Scotland game at Wembley.

They do not have them anymore because it's too much trouble. Imagine the carnage when about 50,000 Scotland fans descended on London to cheer on their favourites. They just took over every bar in London. In the end even the tubes went on strike because of their behaviour. Most of them just wanted to drink themselves stupid and have a good time but there was always an element that was looking for it. Joe was always at the front line though, looking back.

It started over nothing really, as these things do. One of the jocks got a bit touchy-feely with one of the waitresses and a row developed. Joe just walked into the middle of them and hit the biggest of them, red haired feller wearing a kilt. What a dig he had on him, no back lift. Bang! The guy in the kilt went down like Muhammad Ali had clipped him. Then Joe started on the rest. Just lashing out wildly. His eyes were bad; sometimes I could not see them for want of looking, just these two pieces of glass staring back at you. The lenses were so thick. Anyone in his range took a whack, the jocks got out of there double quick. They were a handy mob though, the London football clubs had a lot of serious gangs between them, The Head-hunters, ICF and Millwall's crew but they all went AWOL when the Scots were town. This was different though, the man in specs was for real and they went up the stairs three at a time as Joe heaved a table of glasses after them.

When he calmed down a bit later he was all sweetness and light, sitting quietly chatting away. The trouble was drink triggered him, made him so aggressive. He was paranoid at the best of times but alcohol sent him over the edge. His lieutenant was a guy called Wally Birch, slim with dark hair. Before I teamed up with him Wilkins had a string of failed clubs behind him. One in particular called Winston's caused him a lot of problems. The previous owner Bruce Brace maintained that Wilkins had terrorised him into giving the establishment to him. Wilkins was arrested in Dorking and along with Birch was charged with licensing offences. Both were acquitted.

It was in Winston's that it was alleged that Wilkins pulled a gun on Terry Downes after an altercation. Downes was ex-middle weight champion of the world, and was one of the finest fighters London ever produced. His fight with Paul Pender was regarded as one of the most brutal held in this country. For once Joe had picked on the wrong person and Terry just snatched the gun out of his hand before cursing him. The boxer had a string of clubs himself, I used to see him in one called 'Downs's' in Kilburn, Cricklewood bordered on it, bed-sitter land, near my factory. Terry used to wear this cream suit, once somebody bumped into him in the toilet and he threatened to cane the life out of him. He used to nod over at me and say 'Hello John'. But then he called everybody John.

Bernie Ecclestone fronted it out with Joe Wilkins, one of the few people to have done it at that time. Do you recall the Big Merc that I was telling you about that used to ferry the punters from the Crazy Horse to the 800 club, well we had bought it from one of Bernie's finance companies and needless to say Joe did not keep up on the instalments. He knocked everybody he could, never paid a soul, and never even bought a drink. Well Bernie decided to re-possess the Merc and breezed into Joe's office at Curzon Street. A hoodlum blocked his path and tried to stop him gain entry. Bernie refused to be deterred and told the heavy that he was here to see Mr Wilkins on an important matter. Eventually he was shown into to see Joe, Wally Birch was there also, *'I have come about the car, you failed to keep up on the payments so I am here to collect it'* said Bernie.

'Oh yeah' Joe replied languidly, *'Bit little ain't you for a big car like that, why don't I get you a cushion.'*

'My feet can touch the pedals' replied Bernie, adrenalin shooting through him.

Joe only had three states of mind, pissed off, hostile (that was when the red lights flashed) or some manic happy, excitable mood. He must have been in the latter that day because if it had been the second one then Formula 1 today would probably be a lot different.

'You better take it then'. He tossed him the keys and never looked at him again. Wally saw him off the premises. This sums up Bernie Ecclestone, no matter what the dangers or odds if he wanted something he just went for it, full tilt.

I got the impression Wilkins used Wally to spy on me. After a while I became increasingly disturbed by his behaviour. It's hard to describe but he became obsessed with me, not in a sexual, emotional way but just really odd. Like he wanted to be me, he seemed jealous of my ability to talk to anybody whether it be the Duke of Edinburgh or the guy on the door at the Discotheque. Looking at how many crime books there are on the market I was surprised that nobody ever wrote one on him. Certainly books have been written about characters with half his charisma and who did far less than him, not that any of it was good. He pops up in several tomes on the 60's crime scene. (Funny you could say the 60's was a golden age for gangsters just as it was for music, fashion and film) much is made about his great personality. There's always someone with a faster gun than you though; as Jesse James found out. Peter Ustinov could outshine me in any social situation; Terry Downes was too strong for Joe Wilkins. Elvis outshone Tom Jones.

We all went on a cruise, the inaugural one of the *QE2* from Southampton to New York. (You know me and a cruise).

Gracie Fields was aboard, not doing the cabaret; first night out she was in the lounge. I started singing 'Now is the hour'. (Least it was not 'Sally-pride of our alley'). The Captain learnt of my presence on his boat and Anne and I got an invite to his table, which if you do not know the social etiquette was a real result. John Bloom, entrepreneur, youngest millionaire, etc, etc was welcome whereas Joe Wilkins, professional criminal with interests in vice and extortion was not included. He went bonkers. What was going on? Why wasn't he invited? He became very agitated.

The next night a terrible storm hit us, it was like *The Poseidon Adventure*, at any moment I expected the ship to flip over. Joe was real seasick; he retired to his bed as the ship bobbed up and down in the mountainous seas. Me I loved it, I went up to the dining room and started eating gateaux and all those other sickly delights, like the world was going to end. Looking out at the waves perhaps it was.

Eventually Joe staggered into the dining room, green to the gills, he looked liked the Incredible Hulk.

'All right Joe, like a slice of cream cake, nice milky tea perhaps?'

The hardest gangster in London looked even queasier as I beamed across to him pointing at the pastries suggesting that he tucked in. He had gone from white to grey to green.

Eventually the storm blew over, (as they do) and the next morning the ship was sailing along on what appeared to be glass. Joe still looked sicker than Hitler on VE night; he got worse when John Bloom won the ship's table tennis competition. (About the only sport I was any good at.)

All these things just built up, I spent a lot of time on that holiday plotting in my mind how I could get away from this lunatic. One night in the Rainbow Grill he caught me talking to one of the waitresses. He looked so angry

'*Get rid of that bitch, I need to speak with you'*.

He had this crackpot scene about taking over some more clubs in London and wiping out the opposition of those remaining. It was said in such a matter-of-fact style it chilled me to the bone. That's when I seriously made my mind up to dissolve our arrangement. A weird surge of foreboding filled me I could see the bodies stacking up as he ruthlessly eliminated all the competition. Making a big decision I told Anne that maybe she could speak to Pearl or even Joe about splitting.

It would sound better coming from her, much better I reasoned.

'No you do it'. Anne refused point blank.

Should not be too hard I thought, after all I had out-foxed Bernard Levin on national television and Joe was not in his league for brainpower. Mind you old Bernard would not have fared so well in a row with some drunken jocks, I'll Just tell him straight out.

That is what I did, I told him straight out, maybe we should go our own ways, ideological differences but we would still be mates, blah, blah, blah... Joe had the emotional thick skin of a herd of rhinos; he did not care what other people thought of him. He was a real loner, operated on his own. The difference between him and the Krays was that they were of course twins and always together. That night I went to see them in Esmeralda's Barn they were also surrounded by hangers-on, sycophants, lieutenants, aides, and villains. Joe was like Clint Eastwood in *The Outlaw Josey Wales* when he went out on his own on horseback to confront the Indians, a one-man army, travelling light, hit and run.

'Ok' he shrugged and that was it.

I sent Anne dashing around to Pearls to get her to sign the deal; she had joint signing powers then.

I had to strike whilst the iron was hot; so to speak. Before he changed his unbalanced mind and hit me with a hot iron or something. It was years later that I found out that when Joe returned home she told him that she had met Anne and dissolved our partnership. Joe's mood had changed and he beat her up badly, furious that she signed away our deal.

That was far from the end of it. The police visited soon afterwards, not your average coppers but a special unit working out of Tintagel House. They called themselves 'The Untouchables', based on that film with Sean Connery about the police unit that finally brought down Al Capone. Police corruption was rife in that decade but these fellows were above all that. They painted me a bleak picture of former associates of Wilkins that they found hanging from meat hooks. I knew they were trying to scare me with this stuff, they offered me complete protection. We were even offered some witness protection deal, I took the Fifth Amendment. Arsene Wenger, Arsenal coach was always renowned for his failure to see any controversial incidents involving his players. 'I did not see' was his mantra. I did an Arsene over Wilkins, I did not see anything going on with him that was in my view illegal.

I owed Joe nothing, if it had suited him he could have killed me without a moment's hesitation but I had my own set of values.

I refused to give him up or co-operate, I was still waging my own war with the system. I started this chapter with a quote from Chandler's sublime novel *The Long Goodbye* written when his wife was dying and before his final slide into the alcoholism, which ruined his constitution and talent. In a nutshell the complex plot is about the fallacy of friendship. Perhaps for a brief time we were friends but at the end as Chandler put it so well, 'that was two other guys'.

Joe and Birch started to run escort services, which in those times was another word for prostitution. At one stage he had over 200 girls on his books and the business had a huge turnover. In 1972 whilst waiting trial for conspiracy both he and Birch were shot in the offices of their escort agency. Joe took a bullet in the lung but survived. Pearl was always of the opinion that the word had come down from the twins, now both serving life sentences. Wally Birch survived too; he had history with the Krays going back years. In their youth they had been charged with GBH following a bicycle chain attack on him outside a dance hall.

I had an associate called Bruce Wells, who was the host of the Crazy Horse Saloon and an ex silver medal boxing champion. He had warned me about Wilkins when I opened the 'In place', he was another one that had a history with Wilkins. One night he was having a quiet drink in the 'Phone Booth' when an unknown assailant hit him hard on the back of the head with a bottle.

Bruce never did explain the reason behind the assault, not that it matters, the point is that Wilkins didn't care how tough you were, he was no afraid to attack anyone that got in his way.

Walking to Marble Arch synagogue on the Day of Atonement I was ambushed by some guy who pushed me to the floor and started kicking me repeatedly. Later I found out he was a professional hired by Wilkins.

Anne jumped on his back to try and stop the beating; she was a better bodyguard than Kevin Costner. The guy just carried on with her as a piggyback, he eventually ran off when brave Anne ripped off his Balaclava. As we arrived back home battered and bruised the police unit from Tintagel House were there. They told me Wilkins was out to get me as I knew too much about him, which I felt I did not. They could have used the balaclava as evidence today and got some DNA but there was no CSI then.

Not many chuckles then, Joe wrote to me from Brixton where he was serving two years for conspiracy. By the time he came out I was in America, another good reason for going there, at least I was good terms with their 'Chaps'.

When he got out he went back to the escort business. I had lost contact with him by now. His empire had quickly fallen apart.

The Inland Revenue hit him with a huge tax bill and he lost the clubs blaming me of course. He was then accused of some scam involving the switching of a bag of currency at Heathrow but walked on that one. Then he got clobbered for living off immoral earnings (that old chestnut; where do I remember that from?) and drew three and half. They even lumped Pearl in on that but she was given a conditional discharge.

They eventually divorced, it was now the late 80's, and his next escapade was when he was caught soaking up the rays on a boat carrying £1.5 m of cannabis. The boat was called the 'Danny Boy' and Joey boy started singing like a canary, naming 'Mad' Frankie Fraser as a key member of the Costa del Sol drugs business. Way to go Frankie, the gangland enforcer was 89 and in a London care home when I wrote this. It was reported that he had been issued with an Asbo following rows with fellow residents.

Wilkins also claimed that he was an undercover agent working for the Spanish police but despite all this he was sentenced to 10 years. Charles Kray, the twin's brother once told me that he thought if Joe had diverted his energies and brainpower away from crime he could have done very well. From now on it reads like a Nick Love/Danny Dyer gangster film.

Shortly before his imprisonment Joe married again, he was sent to Ford Open. I could never figure how a criminal of his notoriety ended up in an open prison. Anyway, I know that after while Joe absconded on the basis that he was worried about his new bride and the effect drawing ten years would have on their relationship. The same caring husband that used to batter Pearl about the place. Recaptured he was sent to another open prison Highpoint in East Anglia. The highpoint for him then was when he went on an unaccompanied trip to the dentist. That is right, unaccompanied. There must have been too many people in the waiting room because he turned up in Spain.

Over there he worked as an informant (that's another word for grass). It was said that he had been given a 'helping hand' to flee from England to set up a cover. The police were obsessed with catching all the Chaps that were living in luxury over there on their ill-gotten gains. The scam was for Joe to introduce undercover police officers posing as businessmen to criminals and to get them to invest their filthy lucre into various money-laundering schemes. It worked for a while but a Judge ruled that the sting called Operation Cotton was illegal and the case against 10 men collapsed.

Joe was then rumoured to have been involved in the 'Death on the Rock 'affair when three IRA men were shot down by the SAS in Gibraltar.

Things were getting very hot for him and it was not just all that sunshine. Further rumours abounded about him when he was introduced to one of the Brinks Mat gang who was on holiday. (There was the small matter of the £28 million worth of gold bullion stolen from a Brinks-Mat warehouse at Heathrow in 1983.) Wilkins was touting a scheme in which the remaining gold could be exchanged for cocaine by dealing with the Colombian cartels. Kenneth Noye, currently serving a life sentence for murder, was alleged to have been involved in the laundering of the proceeds of the robbery.

Joe still found time to dupe a lottery winner out of his winnings. Tom Papworth, a middle-aged ambulance driver won £6.5m by selecting the correct Lotto numbers and headed for the Costa del Sol for a new life in the sun. He ran into Joe, now calling himself John Fay, and the two became friends.

In 2000 Wilkins was badly beaten outside his property, he was trying to get into his Rolls Royce Corniche when he discovered that the locks were super glued. Before he knew what was happening he was set upon by 4 men who beat him savagely with an iron bar. I am not sure that he ever recovered fully from that, neighbours told me that he could never walk properly. He died in 2004 in Estepona; several myths arose around the circumstances of his death.

My research indicated that he had stomach cancer and by the end he was incapable of moving and had lost control of his bodily functions. I never went to the funeral but to paraphrase Groucho Marx I approved of it.

Chapter 12 - The Burning Of The Midnight Lamp

'Man, he's an alien, no doubt about it man. A UFO dropped him off and said 'Jimi, show us how's it's done', we'll pick you up in twenty-eight years, all right? He went 'All right'.

Bill Hicks, Talking about Jimi Hendrix

'The story of life is quicker than the wink of an eye.

The story of love is hello and goodbye - until we meet again'

Jimi Hendrix (From a poem found at the time of his death)

I was never a great music fan, as the Beatles will tell you, but so many of the biggest names in the business had dealings with me that I felt I had to tell you a little something about them. In an interview shortly before he was gunned down John Lennon said that he wanted to write a book about all the crazy times he had in the 60's when they were the biggest things to hit London since the bubonic plague. The Beatle was an avid reader and had become besotted by David Niven's *The Moon's a Balloon* book, a collection of anecdotes and brilliant little stories about his days in Hollywood.

I should have talked to David about his book that night me, Bernie and Adam Faith met him in the casino. They must have been partying a lot when they decided to let Ringo sing. 'We all live in a yellow submarine'.

There are not many of us original renegades left who witnessed these things. Anyway maybe John's book would have included stuff like this, my agile memory permitting. For example on any given night the 'Phone Booth ' was packed with star names Bill Wyman, Dusty Springfield, Tom Jones, even Jimmy Saville came in. I always thought he was strange, there were many rumours about him then but people thought he was more of an eccentric than the monster that he turned out to be. Many of stars came to see some of the black acts that were just starting to appear in London for the first time. Amongst the acts that played in my club were Marvin Gaye and Stevie Wonder, both kings of Tamla Motown.

The reason I managed to secure these legends at a very low cost was through a man called Roy Tempest who promoted them. Roy had a connection with Berry Gordy the man who founded Tamla Motown in Detroit. Gordy was a formidable character that ran Motown with a rod of iron, utterly ruthless; he was like an assault tank in business. Gordy had the idea of grooming the Negro acts to appeal to the white audiences and saw the burgeoning English market as the ideal area to test them out.

Marvin Gaye played one evening in the club for me. When I walked into his dressing room Marvin just nodded back, he never showed a flicker of emotion. Like Bowie I really had no idea who he was and what a legend he was to become. The singer's duality, his deep religious nature and his struggle with secular stardom marked his whole career. My business instinct told me that there was not a lot of staying power in a guy like Marvin. I was in Spain when I read of his almost biblical end, murdered by his father.

Stevie Wonder was a much easier person to deal with, despite his disability, always smiling and joking. Roy Tempest worked him very hard, often booking him into three shows a night, on a ceaseless treadmill of constant touring. Playing an early set in my club, and then piling him and his gear into a transit van and driving him to the California Ballroom at Dunstable, then back to town to play at the Scotch of St James. That was the late-night venue for the big stars to congregate in and unwind by watching acts like Stevie. The club had these bagpipes on the walls, plaid table cloths and the pretty waitresses wore these tartan waistcoats.

I used to joke with Roy about how hard they pushed the young prodigy and Roy would recount the story of how one night he played the same venue twice.

This was on stages upstairs and down, but not before they had put him in the van and driven around the block for a short time. What a talent Stevie had, and he was also an exciting performer to watch on stage.

Roy was instrumental in setting up the first 'tribute' acts, the Drifters group had so many factions and splinter groups that it became a bit of a joke in the business because there were so many versions touring. I read that in their long history they have had 60 vocalists. Today you have all these imitators re-hashing and re-treading, the bigger the group the more the imitators.

Perhaps the greatest musician I had dealings with, was the gargantuan legend that was Jimi Hendrix. After just a few short years since he had exploded on the scene Hendrix was to die after a hedonistic period of drugs and mass adulation.

Comedian Bill Hicks' tribute to him always struck a chord with me. Hicks also died tragically young at age of 32 from cancer. Another maverick and provocateur that waged war on the system, Bill was the first comic to be censored at the Ed Sullivan Theatre, where Elvis Presley was famously censored in 1956.

I was there the night Hendrix was discovered by a guy called Chas Chandler who I managed at the time.

Well over 6ft tall, Chas had a full face with sparkling blue eyes and a Beatles haircut. Chas was a founder member of a group called the Animals who in the 60's were very big. They had a number one hit on both sides of the drink with 'House of the Rising Sun' one of the longest singles to achieve hit status. I think it clocked in at around 7 minutes or something unheard of then.

They had other hits such as 'We gotta get out of this place' and my favourite, 'Bring it on Home to me', a Sam Cooke song. I was in America when I heard about Sam's mysterious death in a hotel, shot dead by the manageress. There was a lot of death around music then, it was a dangerous time for many.

The Animals were managed by Mike Jeffrey, another larger than life character who came from South London. His office was on Gerrard Street, it had the sign 'Anim' above it. He owned clubs in Newcastle and Majorca and approached me about a deal. I gave him a half share in my club called Golf in Cala Mayor. In return he gave me a half share in the Animals, who he had made a fortune from managing.

I found him to be a mysterious character, rumours were rife about him, and some even suggested that he was a spy. He spoke fluent Russian and had spent some time in Egypt, the original International man of mystery. Alan Price had left the band by that time but the dominant figure in it was the vocalist Eric Burdon, he was a great singer with a really powerful bluesy voice. Chas was the bass guitarist, a big guy who was looking to expand his horizons and get into management. My favourite was Hilton Valentine, who ended up working for me, a very nice, modest fellow and most unlike a pop star.

One night we were New York and Chas and I decided to go out and sample the nightlife. Chas loved the Blues and heard about some Negro guy that was an amazing guitarist. He was playing the clubs in Greenwich Village that specialised in that type of music. I was not a great blues fan, but it was a night out and I had heard a lot about the thriving arts community.

We ended up in a little place the Cafe Au Go Go on Bleecker Street in the heart of Greenwich Village. Once again, as seemed to be the norm for these places, the noise was simply overpowering. What added to my discomfiture was that we appeared to be the only white folks in the place. It was not a hostile vibe but I just felt out of place and hankered to get back to the comfort zone of my hotel. Just then this tall figure strolled onto stage; he had this crazy dandelion hair and was wearing blue jeans, a black waistcoat thing over a colourful shirt with some little figures on it. The crowd had obviously been waiting for him and cranked up the volume when he appeared.

The first thing I noticed was that he played left-handed and upside down on a white Stratocaster guitar. It was an amazing show Chas was speechless. Afterwards we met him back stage, somebody had told Jimi that one of the Animals and an English millionaire had come all the way from London to see him. Jimi was calling himself Jimmy James then, he seemed very humble, a sweet guy. The place was made of red bricks and my memory of him was sitting against the wall, nodding quietly. Chas told him about how good he was and how he would like to take him to London and they could do all these marvellous things.

On the way back to our hotel I told Chas that he better move quickly to sign him up, the one thing that the last few years had taught me was that speed was everything in making these deals. Chas met him again soon after in the Cafe Au Go Go. This time he took Mike Jeffrey along him to assess Jimi's star potential – though Stevie Wonder could have seen it. There was no love lost between Chas and Mike, the Animals were always bitching about how Jeffrey had short changed them. Their beef was that Jeffrey had always put himself first to the detriment of their careers. In fact Chas was on the verge of quitting the group, despite being a wonderful musician he had tired of life in the Animals. Chas figured there was money to be made in producing records and even talked of going into management if he could find the right talent.

So many big groups split in those times, the public would seem very surprised but the truth was most of the members were on very low money and could make more going solo or making new more lucrative contracts than the ones they were locked into. John Lennon told me that when they first came down to London Brian Epstein paid the Fab Four a wage of £50 a week. Jeffrey looked and talked the part, but Hendrix was suss enough not to sign with them straight away. Chas was suss enough to realise that he needed Jeffrey's business acumen at that stage, Soon Jeffrey was opening an account in the name of Jimi Hendrix in a Bahamian tax shelter known as Yameta. Chas bought him out of an existing recording contract he had with a little company called Sue. They were supposed to take more but Chas was delighted when they accepted his first meagre offer, He learnt fast but then he had a good teacher.

They even arranged a passport for Jimi and in September 1966 James Marshall Hendrix arrived in London on a Pan Am flight from John F. Kennedy airport, the reverse journey from what the Beatles had made a few years earlier. The difference was that when they arrived in America the word was all ready out and Beatle mania started, Hendrix took a little longer. Chas wanted him to play in one of my clubs but with all his amps and gear I did not think we had the room.

Terence Stamp's brother Chris, was co-manager of The Who and had just formed Track Records who were quick to offer him a deal; soon he was on his way.

The remaining members of the Who are touring, still playing their opera 'Quadrophenia', when they played the O2 in the summer of 2013 they had a video film playing behind them. The film could have been a trailer of this book with footage of Radio Caroline, (they played the Who incessantly) and some clips of Christine Keeler and Mandy Rice Davies.

Jimi died of barbiturate-related asphyxia in a London hotel in September 1970. The last few months he had appeared burnt out and deeply troubled. Sometimes people accomplish what they want to do and that's it. Jimi did it quicker than most. Mike Jeffery died three years later in an air crash over France. Mike had been travelling in an Iberia DC-9 that literally disintegrated in mid air when it collided with a Spantax CV-990. Bodies and debris were scattered for miles. The Animals manager was only identified by the jewellery he always wore. The crash was the subject of a lot of theories; the Spantax landed with no loss of life, there was the usual unfounded accusations of pilot error, unwatched radar etc. I know for a fact that often he transported large amounts of cash on those commutes between London and Majorca. He used to tell me that he always liked buying property, as 'an accountant could not make off with it'.

Chas Chandler died at 57 in 1996 in a Newcastle hospital where he was having tests relating to an aortic aneurysm. I saw Eric Burdon on that Jools Holland music show one night recently; completely white haired but his voice as strong as those nights I used to hear him rehearsing. The legacy of Hendrix lives on.

When I had my successful chain of medieval restaurants 1520 AD in America Hilton Valentine walked in one day to my flag ship restaurant in California late 1977 and asked me for a job.

'I don't need any guitarists, Hilton,' I joked back.

'What about just working in the restaurant.'

Times were very difficult for him them, Eric had quit the band to form his successful new group 'War' and for a while the Animals were defunct. The Geordie needed to be earning so I gave him an assistant manager's job and he did very well, especially with the wenches. The punters loved him too especially when he told them some of anecdotes about life on the road with the band. He ended staying with me for several years before drifting back to music. There were several re-incarnations of the Animals over the years though not as many as the Drifters. Last I heard of Hilton he was still playing the clubs with a band called Skiffledog, another survivor of those mad times.

The 1520 AD restaurant was another idea of mine that turned out to be highly successful, and if anything ahead of its time. The first one opened in London in St Martin's Lane which involved the clients being served an eight-course banquet by these pretty waitresses, or as they were known in those days 'wenches'. Long flowing skirts and low cut tops were the order of the day. We spiced it up in other ways by employing dwarves, wrestlers and minstrels.

One more Animals story: I promoted a concert in Essex, and they were headlining the bill along with' The Pretty Things'. Another of the most outrageous groups of that era, they were definitely not pretty. When the first came onto the scene in the early 60's they had really long hair and I mean long, seen by many as degenerates out to destroy Western civilisation. Their singer Dick Taylor had the longest hair, the drummer called himself 'Twink' and was mental, and they were really crazy. I got these guys to do the posters, the artwork was strikingly bizarre. They splattered these things all over London. The overheads were really staggering; at the end of the evening after we had paid off the groups, the security, the lighting crew etc I was presented with my share of the proceeds – £8. It was not worth a lot even back then, it could not even buy a programme at a gig today. They were charging £15 at the Who concert.

The management game changed completely when the managers started to work for the record companies directly and merely reported to the groups. I opted out of it.

Another mate of mine was Eric Clapton, the greatest guitarist this country has produced. I met him in the 60's when he was in band called Cream, perhaps the first heavy metal group, what a din they could produce. Clapton idolised Hendrix who he always said was the better guitarist. The day before Hendrix died Eric had bought him a left-handed Stratocaster guitar as a birthday present. The Cream group included drummer Ginger Baker, another giant of a man with wild red hair. In the 90's Eric became very interested in motor racing and I used to see him at the Grand Prix. Somewhere in the book there is a great picture of him with Bernie clowning around before the start of a race.

I liked jazz and used to go to Ronnie Scott's on Firth Street with a guy called John Hawksworth who was in Ted Heath's band. Ronnie's in those days was a club for musician's rather than the tourist spot is has become today. There was none of that behind the rope/VIP/celebrity nonsense we have today – you were either part of the scene or out of it. A famous trumpet player called Eddie Calvert played there a few times. Eddie was great musician and he had some big hits before the Beatles came along and blew all that instrumental stuff away.

Eddie hated the Labour government that was in power then and quit England to live in South Africa, where he was to die of a heart attack.

Another friend of mine from that era was a great singer by the name of Valentine. Not Hilton but Dickie. My friend Laurie Jay (you will recall he ran the Crazy Horse Saloon for me) who has been in the music business for nearly 60 years) thought that Dickie was the greatest singer that this country has ever produced. Even placing him in front of Matt Monro, the former bus driver who Sinatra rated so highly. Dickie and his first wife Elizabeth became very good friends and we socialised a great deal in the early days of our marriage. He had the first Christmas number one with a song specially tailored for that season called 'Christmas Alphabet'. He was another artist whose recording career waned when the beat boom came but he was still was very popular with his live performances. Driving back from a show late one foggy night he lost control of his car and was tragically killed. Dickie is almost forgotten now but not by those who had the pleasure of knowing him and witnessed his great talent. A headline splashing the news of Dickie's demise was included in the Who film I was telling you about.

My memory of Ronnie Scott was not so much as his prowess as a musician but his amusing repertoire of jokes and asides.

Sometimes he would finish playing and then say 'I would play some more songs but I do not know any more'. As is also the soundtrack of London today, the sound of sirens could be heard in the distance most nights at the club. It was very late at night and the sound was either of an ambulance or a police car speeding to some emergency. Ronnie would put down his saxophone, cock his ear and say *'Hold on I think they are playing our song'.*

Ronnie would also pick on members of the audience. As my fame grew he drew more and more attention to me. One night he saw me down in the audience and said *'Ladies and Gentlemen we have John Bloom in tonight. John is one of the finest businessmen in the country. (pause) Course in the City he is not so hot...'*

Laurie Jay, you may like to know played with the Shadows in the early 60's for a while when drummer Tony Meehan fell ill. They were not only Sir Cliff Richard's backing band but had many hits in their own name including the number one song 'Apache'. The Shads were a great influence on the Beatles; Epstein modelled his band on them at the start copying their smart suited appearance and tight little dance routine.

Tony Meehan was out for a couple of months and Laurie played drums behind the bespectacled Hank Marvin, rated another great guitarist and role model to both Lennon and Eric Clapton. When Tony finally quit the Shadows, along with fellow bassist Jet

Harris to form a duo Jay was in the frame to join the Shadows on a full time basis. The problem was he was in Sweden touring with Shirley Bassey, who he ended up managing and was not contactable. No Internet or mobiles then. A mate of Laurie's, Brian Bennett ended up getting the gig and stayed with them for years. Tony Meehan and Jet Harris had a number 1 hit with a song called 'Diamonds', their future looked bright but Jet Harris was another loose cannon and was very badly hurt in a car smash that was to derail both of their careers. Jet Harris ended up bankrupt selling cockles on a Jersey beach before dying of cancer, a classic example of riches to rags; I used to see Harris a lot in the clubs.

Another attempt at management by me ended up with me looking after a band called Los Bravos who had a huge hit with a song called 'Black is Black' in 1966. It was a number 2 in the UK and reached number 4 in the States. They were the first Spanish group to have an international hit but the problem was they spoke very poor English and failed to capitalise on their success becoming one hit wonders. After 9/11 an American media conglomerate distributed to over 1,000 radio stations a memo listing over 150 songs with what they deemed 'questionable lyrics' guess what was one of them?.

Another interesting musical connection was with a fellow called John Bindon, John was about as musical as I was but ended up working for Led Zeppelin as a roadie and minder. I was going to include him in the 'Chaps' but space did not permit me. John was one of the hardest men in London and had connections with both the Kray and Richardson protection gangs, though nothing was ever confirmed. Bindon was also a character actor and appeared in many films and TV programmes such as *Quadrophenia*, *Get Carter*, *The Sweeney* and *Hazell*, which was co-written by former Spurs and England coach Terry Venables. Bindon was just playing himself really; he acted all his life in fact. Check out the Mick Jagger film *Performance,* which features Bindon, the first 30 minutes of which depicts the most accurate portrait of a protection gang committed to celluloid.

John was a very affable guy and I would see him in the Curzon Club with his girl friend Vicky Hodge. Vicky was not only the first topless model on Page 3 but was also the daughter of a baronet. John was a real ladies man and amongst his conquests was Christine Keeler – just cannot keep her out of it. David Bowie's first wife Angie also had an affair with John. Bindon moved in very high circles and was one of the set that partied with Princess Margaret on the island of Mustique.

Difficult to say this but John was a chap that nature had endowed very well and his party piece was to balance five half pints on that particular part of his anatomy. Sounds unbelievable I know but I actually saw the photos, to be truthful I had them in my possession. Do not ask me why or how. Anyhow a safety deposit box housed these works of art and guess what it got rifled. Of course the tabloids got hold of the story (though not the pictures) and wrote it up like the biggest heist since Alfie Biggs and the chaps stopped the Mail Train.' Bloom Box rifled!' it screamed. Imagining I had a box full of Kruggerands or bearer bonds. The pictures never did turn up, perhaps someone did a deal or it was suppressed by MI5. I never did find out the truth. Like Stephen Ward's death though it was another cover up made to look like something else.

They made a good film about it, *The Bank Job*, try and catch it one night. Here are some samples of the Headlines -

Daily Mirror 26/09/1971 *'John Bloom in riddle of lost £100,000'*

Evening News 26/09/1971 *'Lost £100,000 isn't mine Bloom'*

'Bloom laughed when asked by the host of the Ricky Lash show which was broadcast live from Palma Mallorca if it was £10,000 or £100,000?

'It's not mine' was referring to the robbery at Lloyds Bank in Baker Street.

Bloom interrupted the host with frequent quips, especially after the host suggested that there was not any cash or jewellery

'Just four of your old washing machines'

Bloom quipped that 'They must be worth a fortune!'

Bloom had a soft drink in his hand when I interviewed him later,

'Do I look like a bloke who has lost a £100,000?'

Bloom laughed 'It's all a mystery to me. I suppose Fleet Street want to keep it going for a couple of days. It's a good story isn't it?'

Bloom planned to leave early today on his super yacht 1520 AD from the quayside on Paeso Maritimo where it's moored near his promenade flat.

It was reported that a safe deposit box held in the name of Mr Bloom containing £70,000 in jewellery and £30,000 in cash had been amongst the boxes that had been broken into'

Amusing eh? I do not think they realised how much room 4 washing machines would have taken up.

Bindon nearly kicked a guy to death in America when he tried to pull a knife on the Zepp's guitar hero Jimmy Page but he got off. They had hired him after losing the takings of one of their night's gigs. It was for a Madison Square Garden show and at time the biggest cash robbery in America. Their manager, a fat man called Peter Grant only let the Zep play if it was cash up front. The original, show me the money', Grant was a terrifying individual – he made Mike Jeffrey seem like Hugh Grant. Peter used to work the door at the 2i's Coffee bar where the Shadows' governor Cliff Richard and Adam Faith started off. Adam had seen him in action, tossing troublemakers into the gutter as if they were sacks of rubbish.

John Bindon died in 2006 of an Aids-related illness.

Like Joe Wilkins his end was shrouded in mystery. Sometimes people would rather let it be known that their relatives died of cancer or even an overdose than something connected with Aids. In 1978 he had survived a terrible battle in a place called the Ranelagh Yacht club. (I had never visited there in any of my craft, not even sure if they were any boats moored up). John was accused of the murder of a gangster called John Darke but was acquitted after a high profile case at the Old Bailey,

Funny – started off with Hendrix then Dickie Valentine, but ended up with John Bindon known as 'Biffo' to his friends. You could never get far away from some villainy in those days.

Dickie Valentine

Joe and Pearl Wilkins aboard the QE II

Eric Clapton

Eric and Bernie (not to be confused with Eric and Ernie)

Chapter 13 - Who The Hell Is George?

'If I had been born ugly, you would have never heard of Pele' - George Best

'I like men who have known the best and the worst, whose life has been anything but a smooth trip, storms have battered them, they have lain, sometimes for months on end, becalmed. There is a residue even if they fail. It has not been all tinkling; there have been grand chords.'

'Burning the days' - James Salter

George Best was the best player I ever saw – end of conversation. George Best was the best player the UK ever produced – end of conversation. George Best was the best bird puller of all time – end of conversation. The George Best that my family and I knew so well was one of the nicest people that walked the planet.

Over the years the public's perception of George changed a little, instead of the beautiful young man that was *'the Beatle footballer'*, we are presented with the image of the little old man carrying a carrier bag of booze. The former wonder boy had turned yellow with drink, dying, slowly and painfully in front of us. Piers Morgan's wife even wrote a harrowing book about the last few agonising years of his life when she travelled around with him working for a national paper. Best's once Michelangelo body now fatally polluted by alcohol, his walk once so airy, now a sequence of lurches. Today the media just wants to get into underwear of public figures. George was as 60's as Carnaby Street, Ronan's Radio Caroline, flower power and Jean Shrimpton's mini skirt. I want to roll back the years and tell you about the real George. They say football skill relates inversely to age, the older a man gets the better a player he was when you saw him as a young man. I do not know about that, but George was something else.

I first met him on the beach in Majorca in one of those golden summers of the late 60's. I was on holiday and loved the place so much was thinking of buying a property there, which I eventually did. I had this marvellous boat that ran on massive jets as opposed to the usual engine and propeller deal. It had been designed by a genius called Pina Farrina and I had obtained it from the former head of Aston Martin David Brown. I literally used to point it at the crowded beach and land up on it, you could go anywhere with the boat. Its top speed was over 40 knots and was like one of those landing craft in *Saving Private Ryan.* A fabulous craft, it was years ahead of its time.

The unfortunates sunning themselves on the beach used to scatter when they saw it coming thinking they were going to get injured.

I sent my faithful dog, a wonderful St Bernard called 'Lucky'; we had him for years, down the retractable ramp at the back of the craft. The intrepid Lucky went ahead of me. The canine was usually wet and would spray anybody near him with water. Me – I loved an entrance. Binoculars came out of their beach bags and sunglasses were put on perhaps George had spied me doing this act. In those times there was no EU regulations and red tape, you could just park up on the beach. Now the schooners are moored a long way out, just used as floating base camps.

Majorca in those early days was very exclusive and many of the top footballers holidayed there. It was a special favourite of the Manchester United boys, and I used to see another of their superstars Dennis Law down on the beach but even though he was a great player it was George that drew all the attention. He was like a Beatle, in that everybody knew him, he cut across every age and even people that did not like football knew of him. Perhaps he was the fifth Beatle; his haircut was a copy of Ringo's, as he was the first footballer that made the transition from the back page to the front. I was the first businessman to make the journey from the financial/city page to the front pages so we always had that press thing in common.

He spoke through half closed eyes. That sensuous, hypnotic mouth unpeeled to reveal the neat white teeth.

'Hi I'm George, seen you in the papers.'

'Hi I am John, seen you in the papers.'

We both laughed and savoured the moment, perhaps at that time we were the two most famous faces in the country, the most written about, (that is if you leave the Beatles out of it). The pair of us owned the beach as we strutted over the hot sand. He was creeping towards mid twenties then and was the current European Footballer of the year having recently helped Manchester United become the first English club to annexe the European Cup. That is when it was a real competition when only the champions of each country could enter, not the top four.

We had a brief chat about the forthcoming season then he was gone. Later on I saw him with a throng of young people further down the beach; most of them were female, Nordic with shameless very blonde hair and china-doll like cheekbones. At that point it was the best time of all to be young, great looking and fancy-free. Little did I know that he was already riding the rapids of a very fast and extremely treacherous river?

The next time our paths crossed was around 1975 in Marbella. Best had left United and was on his nomadic travels from club to club, he had friends in the place and spent a lot of time there living in the Skol hotel.

Today the whole of that coastline is highly developed but then it was not so built up and most mornings my wife would meet him on the way to breakfast in one of the little places by the beach. He had spent the evening drinking in the Marbella club or another favourite haunt of his was a place called 'Frank's Bar'. Frank it was rumoured had unsettling connections with some heavy-duty East End gangsters and had fled London to set up a bar. He made a great success of it and ended up becoming a respected pillar of the community.

George loved those sorts of places, today the clubs in that part of the world are crowded with the Euro trash, Russian looters and South American dealers but then it was a mixture of retired criminals, ex-pats and even the local fisherman. He never talked about football if he could help it. There must have been a million conversations with people reminding him of the time he left Chelsea Captain Ron Harris lying in the mud at old Trafford that night he slalomed through their whole defence to score a wonder goal or the day he scored six times at Northampton. The only time he spoke about to me about it was when he said at his zenith with United he used to spend an hour a day jumping over a 3ft bench. This was to avoid the knee-high tackles that would have shattered his career. George was playing against the assassins that every club employed in those days like Tommy Smith, Norman Hunter and my club Arsenal's Peter Storey.

That is why he was such a great player because these chaps would be outlawed today yet Best faced them every week. Nobody ever nailed him as he was that quick, tough, and so well balanced. Unfortunately that balance did not apply to his personal life and the opponent that beat him was himself.

My favourite football story of George Best concerned the guy called Storey. This was when I went to Arsenal to see Manchester United at their old stadium Highbury. I was still incredibly busy with my business problems but always tried to see George play when he was in town; marking him that day was the hapless Storey. Peter was a real tough nut, an uncompromising defender who cut down opponents ruthlessly. Off the field he could have been one of the 'chaps' as he served time after his football career for selling dodgy cars and running a brothel. Best had teased and tormented him all game and at one point the Arsenal keeper Bob Wilson gave a short clearance to Peter. He started dribbling up field but suddenly George appeared. He was in Blue that day as Arsenal were at home and United had to change their strip. The defender panicked and swivelled round to pass back to Wilson, It shows how long ago it was as the back pass was not outlawed then. The problem was Bob was out of position and the ball ended up in the net for an own goal. George had scored without touching the ball; the point was that that such was his reputation even arguably the toughest man in football was terrified of him.

He drinking increased in Spain, the climate was conducive to that culture, you could stay up all night drinking and watch the beautiful creamy sun rise in the morning, bathing the whole beach in pink. That was the best time of the day to me. I was up early most days walking Lucky along the beach and would spot George going home. He would wave back.

Anne told me that an amusing story once that she saw George on the beach one day in the company of two young ladies with thick Manchester accents. Anne said hello and went down to her spot on the beach under an umbrella where she could relax in the shade. The girls stayed with the Belfast Boy throughout the day in the blazing Spanish sunshine, they had no sun tan oil or skin protection with them but were afraid to leave his side in case their place next to the Adonis was taken by some of the sun goddesses that had parked themselves around the trio's sun beds. The poor creatures were literally like lobsters by the time Anne had finished her stint on the beach.

In Marbella he was a frequent visitor to my home, though never on a Friday night no just because of my religious beliefs but also because George had a golden rule in that he never went out on a Friday night. Even at the end when he had finished playing he used to stay in on a Friday night. I always enjoyed his company, especially his razor sharp wit. *'I guess we have both messed up our knighthoods* 'He used to joke.

We both shared the same contempt for authority, his frustrations in big time football had led to resentment against the whole system, sometimes he would ask about my business dealings but like Lennon he had very little interest in money or finance.

He would often play backgammon with my wife or sometimes just play kick about with my kids. I think he just craved domesticity and being around a family. I never saw him drink that much as he was always relaxed. Anne used to see him in a place called Cozzi's Bar which was his particular favourite, owned by his great friend Paul Cozzi, either drinking wine or his other tipple, vodka. Vodka was the poison of choice of hard drinkers like the hell raising actors Richard Burton and Richard Harris. George told me that when he was at United he started drinking vodka and lemonade because it did not look like anything alcoholic and if anyone grassed him up he could plead that he was just drinking lemonade. The picture of him in the t-shirt taken in our living room best describes what George was going through at that stage: 'Who the hell is George?'

His friends said he wore it a lot. It must have been a subliminal cry for help as fame was slowly crushing the life out of him. He was the Gemini man, born on 22nd May 1946. I wanted to call the chapter that until Anne came up with the photograph from her photo album. Gemini was his star sign; the best footballers were Gemini's. Maradona, Eric Cantona (one of the few United players in their star studded history to ever come close to Best in terms of skill and popularity), Beckham and Ronaldinho are the others that spring to mind) Gemini – those born under this sign have the good characteristics of wit and versatility, but they also bear a darker, immutable side.

George was in conflict with his own penchant for hedonism, yet as just explained he nurtured a longing for the stability of family life. A battle between being a self centred, narcissistic, womanising drunk and the over-sensitive, brilliant sportsman and genuinely decent human being. He was careering on though like a train without brakes.

George told me he liked London and was considering an offer from Fulham; he later signed a deal for them and for a short while played some of the best football of his career for them. Rodney Marsh, another maverick, played alongside him. I missed our chats but was happy to see George in his element again.

We later renewed our friendship in LA. This would have been 1976, a well remembered summer. I had the highly successful chain of 1520AD restaurants and I was still on the long road clawing back the fortune I had lost in the 60's, George was playing for Los Angles Aztecs and thriving in the relative anonymity scored 15 goals in just over 20 games.

I saw a lot of similarities with him and David Beckham who also ended up playing in Los Angles for the MLS side LA Galaxy towards the end of his career.

The girls still craved George, and he married a bunny girl called Angie Macdonald James, but the achingly eager women were always around. I have been around famous people most of my life, from Terence Stamp in the 60's to racing driver Jenson Button today. Matinee idols like Bryan Ferry to hunks like John Bindon. Let us not forget the original boy band the Beatles. Best had the most charisma though, the most animal magnetism with his jet-black Provencal hair and perfect skin burnished by sun and salt. The only man I saw with similar power over women was my great friend the actor Michael Landon, who I told you about earlier. One night Michael, a huge sports fan, took me to see the Muhammad Ali v. Ken Norton fight. This was the second fight, not the one where Norton, a very under rated fighter, broke Ali's jaw. Ali won that night on a split decision; many said that was the night his fabulous career started to decline. Well, when we arrived at the ringside I never saw such a furore as caused by Michael's appearance. With his high cheekbones and dazzling smile Landon had been a household name for 20 years but even I was surprised at the reaction he provoked.

Particularly from the many beautiful women present at the fight, some of them even tried to slip him a note with their phone numbers on, the girl thing was just a side effect to both Best and Landon.

George would teach my son Darren football on the beach, lucky boy. It must have been like a teenager going along for his first driving lesson and finding Michael Schumacher at the controls. I could watch George practise for hours; his head would tilt slightly to one side as he juggled the ball for ages. He was never happier than when he was playing football even if it was just a kicking a ball around. Perhaps in his mind he was my son's age again – juggling a tennis ball on the streets of the Creagh housing estate in East Belfast. There was a record I used to hear in America called the 'Boys of Summer', one of the Eagles did it. I always think of George as the 'Boy of Summer' down on Huntington Beach in Orange County.

When he went to school the next day my son's class mates would ask him what he did on the weekend and he would say: 'George Best came over and taught me to play football.'

I do not know what their reaction was of course. I was not a bad player when I was young, bit of a goal hanger to be honest. To my schoolmates I was known as the 'offside king' Many a tense playground match had been settled by a cool young John Bloom slotting the ball home from close range after a terrific scrimmage. I always fancied myself in that Jimmy Greaves role of just lurking in the penalty area and waiting for a chance to strike. I got pretty good at working out where the ball would end up and the most efficient way of dispatching it between the jumpers that served as goal posts. Pity my games teachers did not see things the same way and encourage me more. My failure ever to head the ball did not help my cause though. I had to seek out other ways of earning a crust.

George invited us to a game the Aztecs played at the Rose Bowl, a huge stadium that had the capacity of 80,000. It must have been about a 10th full; the atmosphere was like a reserve game at Arsenal that I used to sneak into at Highbury 30 years before. I just thought George was wasting his time playing to empty houses, a bit like George Harrison's suggestion that we should all busk together down Oxford Street. What is this guy doing here I thought to myself? I think boredom was setting in around then.

One night I raised the matter with him and suggested that he should be playing in New York for the famous Cosmos side. Pele, some people's idea of the greatest player of all time, was starring for them along with some other fine players including Franz Beckenbauer and the Italian George Chingalia. I thought it would be a great move for George if he were to hitch his wagon to the Cosmos' star.

The mouth watering prospect of those two linking up would have been sensational, any comparison was sacrilegious. That is when he said his much quoted remark: *'you would have never have heard of Pele – if I had been born ugly.'*

He told me in a slow and deliberate voice that he was happy where he was playing; he loved living in California with the beach life and the beach girls on tap. Everything he ever said was cloaked in civility.

'But the night life George, Studio 54 Steve Rubell would welcome you with open arms-every night.'

I was reminding him about what for a while, was the best known club in the world, a disco planet with stars like Mick Jagger, Andy Warhol and Liza Minelli packing it out, This was pre-aids before Rubell lost his hair and ended up inside for tax evasion.

'Nah – too late.'

Sometimes I thought that when I was in his company I had a better time than he did. Deep down there was a gloom, a Celtic melancholy. For the first time since I had known him I noticed something not quite right with him. It was almost imperceptible, but fraction by fraction fame, or was it life itself, was wearing him down?

I thought of my conversation with John Lennon when I was telling him that after you attained a certain position the only place was down. Perhaps he knew there was not much football left in him. George's sorry spiral of decline from being England's most famous footballer to England's most famous drunk, was proof of that – but John was dead by then.

We went our own ways, though we had talked about running a club together. George had a place called 'Slack Alice' back in Manchester in the early days and sometimes talked about running a club again. Nothing ever came of it though, we were supposed to meet up in London when I had made a brief trip there but that was the week that he crashed his car into a lamp post outside Harrods after a long bender in Jermyn Street. He required 55 stitches to sew up his face. George was like the elusive butterfly in that song: he arrived and was gone before you really had a chance to appreciate him.

Sometimes I think about the terrible consequences of fame – the point where people get so famous there is no one else on their level, no one else they meet was on that plane of hyper-existence. That was what George saw in me that day on the beach in Majorca. I was the youngest ever millionaire in this country, George was reputed to be earning a £1,000 a week when he was 20, an unbelievable figure for those times. But it was never about the money for either of us.

The problem for George was because he was the first superstar footballer, he had no map to follow, no script to learn from. The ex United star was sailing alone in unchartered waters. He frittered away his time and talent; spiralling debts forced him to work the after-dinner circuit. I read that he was selling that 1968 European Footballer of the Year award just to raise funds. It was just a small metal football on a plinth but I knew how much it meant to him. I would have liked to have bought it and kept it somewhere for him but somebody beat me to it. If it had not been inscribed with George's name then it would have ended up in an Oxfam shop.

The world was never the same for me and Anne when George died, never so innocent, never so pleasant. Sometimes when you read of his exploits it was hard to defend his behaviour. It was never hard to tell people what a great player he was though and how easy it was to love him as a friend.

Ian Ure

George is an impossible act to follow but a couple of stories related to the beautiful game that I shall conclude with. In the early 60's Arsenal desperately needed a centre half and was linked with this player called Ian Ure who was reckoned to be the finest centre half in the land and the best thing to come out of Scotland since its whisky.

In those days Scotland was like a nursery for the big English clubs to snap up their star players. Over the years that supply line of great talent had dried up and the dearth of young talent has seen Scotland plummet down the world rankings.

Ure was playing for Dundee who had a fine team managed by Bill Shankly's brother, that included Alan Gilzean, a bald-headed forward who had went onto do great things at Tottenham where he partnered Jimmy Greaves. They won the Scottish title in 1961-2 and the following year reached the semi final of the European Cup. An amazing feat, Ure had been their mainstay but he had been in dispute with his club and refused to sign a new contract. The problem was in those days the minimum wage was in effect. A bit like the Resale Price Maintenance law that I will be telling you about soon. I was a big Arsenal fan and wanted to see my club have the best players. I approached the Arsenal board about injecting some money into the club and maybe taking a seat on the Board of Ds. I was rejected, their faces frozen in horror, the same old boys' network. Bloom was considered 'new money'; nouveau riche and not welcome in this bastion of old money, old Etonians and old ideas.

Fast forward more than a half a century and the same battle rages. Oligarch Alisher Usmanov is the richest man in the country and owns a major stake in Arsenal but is not on the board.

By time this book is published than a lot of this will be old news but at the time of writing Alisher was, according to the *Sunday Times* Rich List worth £13.3 billion. So fabulously wealthy he could not even begin to count it. The notoriously patrician Arsenal board headed by Old Etonian Peter Hill-Wood have so far steadfastly refused to allow Usmanov onto the board.

Sounds familiar. I was desperate to get Ian Ure into an Arsenal shirt and wrote to him offering a job at Rolls Razor, This was just as a sales advisor and he would only have to attend the occasional board meeting and pop into see me once a week. In return he would earn in excess of a £100 a week and be free to fulfil all the duties that Arsenal Football Club would require him to do., Sounded a good deal; it sounded plausible that I could make him Arsenal's centre half. Ian travelled down to London and we met up I showed him around the factory and told him of my scheme. Never sure if he fully understood the deal or the terminology, he seemed a bit suspicious of the whole thing but he shook my hand and told me he would seriously consider my proposals.

A few days later I read that he has signed for Arsenal, details of the deal were not really reported and perhaps my proposal had triggered them into doing something. I like to think that anyway. I would also like to tell you that Ian Ure was a huge success and his signing was the catalyst for greater things but I am afraid not.

Ian never really settled in London and was never the dominant player he was expected to be. Injuries hampered his progress though he played over 200 times for the Gunners. He was very prone to mistakes and is remembered for a particularly horrendous one in Arsenal's shock 1-3 League Cup final defeat to Swindon. That was the game that traumatised a young Nick Hornby so much he was compelled to write *Fever Pitch* about the agonies of being a Gooner. Glad I got to play a part in the history of the club.

Curt Flood

In the early 70's I met a guy in Majorca called Curt Flood. He was a major league baseball player but had fallen foul of the system when he had tried to challenge the contract ruling. At that stage he was out of the game and fighting a brave battle, the fact that he was a person of colour did not help his case. He had precious little money but was spending the summer on the island because he heard it was cheap. In a nutshell Flood had starred for the St Louis Cardinals but objected when the traded him to the Philadelphia Furies. Curt considered the team to be in decline and also did not fancy playing in front of their partisan fans many of whom he considered to be racist. He wrote a moving letter to the Baseball commissioner a fellow who rejoiced in the name of Bowie Kuhn; from which I quote.

'I do not feel that I am a piece of property to be bought and sold irrespective of my wishes. I believe that any system that produces that result violates my rights as a citizen and is inconsistent with the laws of the United States'

Curt was influenced by the black power salutes given in the 1968 Olympic Games; he compared the existing laws to 'slavery'. Bowie Kuhn rejected Curt's plea for free agency but he took it to the Supreme Court alleging violation of federal anti-trust laws. They kicked it out but as a result of the controversy caused by the case within a short time players won the right to veto any trade. This was known as the 'Curt Flood' rule.

I used to meet Curt frequently for a cup of coffee and he would tell me stories of the old prejudices he encountered in the game. Eventually he opened a bar in Palma before returning to America to work in the game he changed single-handed.

I was very sorry to learn of his death from throat cancer in 1997, the same year his contribution was acknowledged in Congress.

QPR ! Ha-ha-ha

In November 1963 I tried to take over Queens Park Rangers who were stumbling about in the then third division. (For youngsters that was the league below the Championship and where Swindon was playing when they beat Arsenal at Wembley). The previous year I had joined the club as a director and now I had an idea to turn them into a big club. I had always seen them as a club with great potential that to this day has never really been fulfilled. Great location, huge potential support but I was always disappointed how they had failed to capitalise on the situation. Their potential is even higher now I think with the opening of the exclusive Westfield shopping mall.

My plan was to overthrow the board, make myself Chairman and implement my own ideas. I was prepared to put in £150,000 a fortune then. (Tottenham Hotspur, known as the Bank of England club because of their wealth and power in the transfer market, were buying the best players in those days for about £50,000 each, the fee for Ian Ure's transfer from Dundee to Arsenal was £62,000). The previous season QPR had moved their ground to the White City stadium but the idea had not really worked (the supporters said that the pitch was too far away) and they had moved back to the crumbling Loftus Road ground. They were about to sell their star player, a guy called Mark Lazarus of all things. I tried to buy up more shares and put adverts in the evening papers, London had two papers back then, the Standard and the Evening News and I got a few more shares. I thought then that although it would be hard for me to achieve my end of owning QPR and making it another Arsenal FC, it still looked possible based on the supporters and small shareholders reaction. But a combination of the old pals act and the Watford chairman (joining forces with the old guard) buying spare unissued shares meant that I failed in my bid to obtain the club and achieve my dream. It was clear that at that time the established order did not want people like me buying football clubs. Fifty years on entrepreneurs / new money are the only people buying football clubs.

The tabloids had a field day; it was the first time that I had tasted defeat and they trotted out their usual glib headlines, Perhaps I should have seen it as a portent.

Who The Hell Is George?

The Infamous "Jet-Boat"

Football practice with George

George with kids in Marbella

Anne and "Lucky"

Michael and Lynn Landon in Beverley Hills

Chapter 14 - Face Off

'No I did not sell you anything my dear

You are a scarecrow looking for a bonfire to sleep on'

Mark Eitzel

'Every battle is won before it is fought'

Sun Tzu *The Art of War*

That month of November 1963 was momentous in the history of John Bloom. I met David Bowie, nearly bought QPR, Kennedy died and I blew Bernie Levin out of the water.

Let me tell you all about the critic Bernie Levin; now you will doubtless agree that I am opinionated, but this guy was in a league of his own. He was an intellectual and famous for his confrontations on television when he would grill some unfortunate about some subject about which he had a particular bee in his bonnet. Levin's style was highly charged: he was aggressive, seeking to browbeat his opponent with his supposed superior intelligence and detailed information on the subject.

I was by the pool in the South of France when the phone rang and it was fellow called Ned Sherrin asking me to appear on their satirical programme *That Was The Week That Was*. The agenda was for me to be interviewed by Mr Bernard Levin about Saving Stamps.

Many of you probably do not even know what they are but at one time they were a sensation. They had started off at the end of the 19th Century in America, and were a sales gimmick. The customer would spend money on a product and would also receive these stamps, especially designed, to encourage reward shopping. The drawback was that the stamps were originally for a very small denomination under 3p (or sixpence as it was known then) so you had to stick a great many stamps into a book to fill it up. The idea lives on though because many firms use loyalty cards and at the checkouts today customers are routinely asked for their point/advantage cards. This is so they can clock them up and hopefully keep coming into the store and spend.

That particular programme was one of the most controversial of all time and made its host David Frost a household name. Its format was simple: it was shown late on a Saturday night and took an irreverent look at what had gone on in the previous week. Levin hated TV, as a young man writing for the *Manchester Guardian* in 1956 he attacked the new ITV channel calling it *'ordinary trash'* and most programmes *'not fit to be fed to the cat'*.

TW3, as it was known, was the brainchild of Sherrin. He created a magazine programme that was a mixture of comedy, debate, satire and music. Its female star was Millicent Martin, already an established singer. Its strength was the vast range of contributors which included the cream of the best writers of the day amongst them Keith Waterhouse and Willis Hall. They were the team who were responsible for one of the 60's best films, *Billy Liar* which starred Tom Courtney and Stamp's ex – Julie Christie. Other writers on the show included the novelist John Braine (*Room at the Top*), Malcolm Bradbury (*The Glittering Prizes*), Dennis Potter (*The Singing Detective*) and playwright Peter Shaffer. It really was a hot house of talent and also included actors of the calibre of Kenneth Cope (*Randall and Hopkirk Deceased* and *Corrie*), Roy Kinnear and a cocky young upstart called Michael Crawford.

The idea was to convince the audience that all the performers on the show were 'bright young things just down from university'. At the start of the decade the boom in satire had been started by the undergraduates Alan Bennett, Jonathan Miller, Peter Cook, Dudley Moore and David Frost with their 'Beyond the Fringe' revue show, first shown at the Edinburgh Festival. However on TW3 David Frost was the only one with the degree and had never been on television before, I met him some years later and the laid back, friendly, casual style had been replaced by a far more serious character. The pressure of an impossible workload was taking its grim toll. I should know because at that point I had more on my plate than Billy Bunter and to paraphrase the Beatles every day was a 'Hard Day's night'.

The show I was invited on was in the second series of TW3; it was facing that difficult second album syndrome, as they say in the music business. When it had ended its first run in April 1963 the show's audience peaked at 12m, a huge figure for a TV programme that started at nearly 11pm and ran for two hours. When it returned in September of that year the Profumo/Ward/Keeler scandal had exploded like an atom bomb. Frost had constantly harangued the government and it had launched the ex-Methodist Minister's son on the way to stardom. Frost lives in Chelsea now, married to Lady Carina Fitzalan-Howard and conservative estimates of his wealth are put it in the region of £200m.

I saw him playing football for the showbiz team several times; I was a loyal supporter of theirs for many years. Unlike a lot of these celebrities who make a point of telling us that 'they could've been contenders ' as a footballer David was in fact a very good goalkeeper, he was actually offered terms by Nottingham Forrest but opted to go to Uni. I suppose he made the right decision but it would have been interesting to see how he would have fared with Brian Clough as his manager.

When Macmillan's regime came to an end the satirists lost their biggest target. They had pushed the envelope a bit too far though, mocking religion and the monarchy. The new series was being heavily criticised for being stale and devoid of ideas. Rumours were rife that TW3 was about to be cancelled. It now relied heavily on Levin to keep it afloat, a bit like Van Persie and Manchester United.

In December 1962 Levin had interviewed the hotelier Charles Forte and denounced his company as 'Lazy, inefficient, dishonest, dirty, complacent, exorbitant – but disgusting just about sums it up'. That was just for starters – he went on to savage the catering at London Airport, and dubbed it 'A national disgrace'. Shortly afterwards he had some farmers on the show and opened with 'Good evening peasants'. Another incident involving Mr Levin happened in April 1963 when someone stepped out of the audience and cracked a right hander into his face. It was not Charles Forte but an irate chap whose actress wife had been on the receiving end of one of Bernie's caustic reviews. You Tube it, the fellow's name was Desmond Leslie and the actress was called Agenes Bernelle. Bernard was such a savage theatre critic he earned the sobriquet 'The Kosher Butcher'. Mrs Levin's little boy Bernard became one of those 'love to hate' figures people tuned in to watch.

They loathed the personality, but in a strange, perverse way were attracted to watch it, Joe Wilkins territory possibly. One thing was certain – the age of chivalry had passed.

Of course I knew nothing about any of this intrigue, as I was never in on a Saturday night and had not even seen the show. I had heard about it and read of the outrage it had caused. Ned Sherrin tried to set me up and was prepared to chuck what he thought was another unsuspecting victim into the lion's den, 'Trial by television', with John Bloom in the dock. I told my chums I was going to be on the most controversial show on television and that they should make a point of watching me on it. No videos or on demand play backs in those times. Their reaction to the news was one of horror. Lew Grade said to me with his voice full of compassion.

'*You have bitten off more than you can chew now John'.*

Funny I loved it when people said that to me: bitten ... chew? Do not understand. Jack Hylton was the most upset; he was really worried for me. Of all the people chronicled here Jack was the nicest, a lovely, lovely man. I have told you before about what a wonderful mentor he was to me in business and the sound advice he imparted, but I really must emphasise what a great human being he was. A former band leader he formed his own company called Jack Hilton Television Productions and helped many huge names in their careers including Shirley Bassey, Morecombe and Wise and the doomed talent that was Tony Hancock. Jack also helped the campest man in show business, Liberace, who Michael Douglas made a film about in 2013. When he spoke everybody listened, even Frank Sinatra took notice when he offered him some guidance. Jack had witnessed the public execution on television by Levin of the hairdresser Teasie Weasie Raymond. Teasie to his pals was perhaps the first celebrity hairdresser, another flamboyantly camp figure who even owned Grand National winners. His real name was Raymond Bessone he was born in Wardour Street. At the height of his career he ran a Mayfair Salon and the top actresses of the day would fly him to America to style their hair. Bernie had no time for such fripperies as hair dressing and scored an early knock out, I remember old Jack shaking his head and advising me to fail to appear.

For once I did not heed Jack's advice but decided to go ahead with the show, my ego perhaps. I read somewhere that the ego is the most dangerous threat to a human being as all our actions stem from it, of course others maintain that desire is the cause of suffering. Perhaps the megalomania was even more rampant, after all I was the golden boy and I could take anybody on.

I knew I had to prepare for this one though, like Rocky in his training camp putting in the legwork hour after hour, day after day.

I figured Levin would attack on two fronts, the first being me and my personal life, the second would be on trading stamps. Jack warned me that a common tactic Levin might employ was for the host to launch into a personal attack to try and make me lose my temper and control. The alternative was for him to go for the trading stamps angle. I used the services of a firm called Tellex Monitors to provide me with reports of programmes on television and the radio regarding stamp trading. Tellex were part of the Press Association and did a great job coming up with the data. I then memorised key points and asked members of my staff to come with questions relating to stamps.

Let me tell you a little bit about stamp trading. I had recently gone into them in a big way as I saw it as a great way around retail price maintenance (see next chapter for my battle against RPM). I was trying to undercut the other trading stamp companies in the market place and was even contemplating giving cash in return for one of my complete books. Do not want to clutter the book with stats or out dated price structures but as an example of the war that was going on I was offering a vacuum cleaner for nine books compared to 25 identical value books from another company.

Punch

10, Bouverie Street, London, E.C.4.

Cutting from issue dated....12 FEB 1964

BLOOM FOR PRIME MINISTER!

JOHN BLOOM'S move to turn his trading stamps into miniature self-portraits reopens the question of whether Mr. Bloom is selling washing-machines, or vice versa.

'John Bloom's move to turn his trading stamps into miniature self-portraits reopens the question of whether Mr Bloom is selling washing-machines or vice versa.'

I phoned the BBC and told them that as a condition of me being on the Frost show I would like to see some clips of previous interviews conducted by Bernard Levin. On 15th November 1963 I went to the BBC theatre to see some footage they had provided. This was the day before I was scheduled to be on the programme. Within a week though John F. Kennedy was to be slain in Dallas.

I doubt if I would have been on the show had my spot with Bernard been a week later. A special tribute to President Kennedy was shown on the night of his assassination, which Paul Foot of *Private Eye* described as 'sickeningly sycophantic'.

The BBC technicians showed me the Teasie Weasie and Randolph Churchill interviews. I noticed straight away that neither victim was allowed to get a word in edgeways and that at end of two minutes they were not allowed to put up any defence. Levin's tactic was, as ex Spurs hard man Graham Roberts once said, 'Get your retaliation in first'.

I had a plan forming in my head as I took my time sampling each moment of the interviews. Levin went into attack mode straightaway, he was unrelenting and his arguments had obviously been well researched. I asked my people to come up with all the background they could on Levin. His full name was Henry Bernard Levin, his father was of Jewish Bessarabian descent. He had fled from Tsarist Russia and ended up in London and like my father was a tailor, but the difference was mine stuck around to help me all his life; Bernard's father abandoned him when he was three. Understandably Bernard had a tough childhood being brought up by his mother and grandparents. Levin admitted himself that he had been emotionally impaired by this situation. The old pair told him stories about life in Russia, which gave the youngster a burning belief in the freedom of the individual. This stayed with him throughout his life and was the hallmark of his work. The more I read of him the more of a maverick he appeared to be. Despite being a brilliant child prodigy he was turned down by Cambridge where he was, in his own words, 'not considered Oxbridge material'. Bernard was no quitter though and won a place at the London School of Economics. There his developed his Marxist views, he had a red flag he waved a lot but he also honed his writing skills to near perfection. At the time we did the interview he was writing five columns a week for the *Daily Mail*. Later, in the 1970's he fell out with them and joined *The Times* where he continued his guerrilla war of words against the world. By anybody's standards he was a superb journalist and a highly clever man.

The theatre reviews were brilliant, in the class of Dorothy Parker. She was my favourite all-time wit and the writer who coined the 'ran the gamut of emotion from A to B' quip. Levin's disdain was on every page, one review spent hundreds of words describing the scenery with no mention of the play, and he finished it up by wishing his readers a happy Christmas.

The next day I turned up at the studio where Anne was in the audience. I was wearing one of my best suits, not sure who made it; it was not especially trendy but very well cut. I was wearing a white shirt with a pin through round collar.

Funny they were back in fashion the summer I wrote this, that Gatsby summer; the film had some of those mod fashions in it. Not practical on a really hot day though, having a stiff collar.

Here is a transcript of what happened on the show.

Bernard Levin

(Dressed in a dark suit, white shirt, dark tie and white pocket hanky. His hair wavy, he was 35 then not much older than me but he looked ten years older like Einstein or one of those brainy guys)

Mr John Bloom. I am going to talk to you and you to me tonight about Trading Stamps. Which I am an opponent of and you are a defender. And indeed I understand that you are contemplating using them in your own business.

My point is trading stamps are in fact a gigantic confidence trick (repeats confidence trick). In the first place we are told when you get them trading stamps are free gifts. Those are the words used. I don't believe this for one moment. Not only the things you sell have to be paid for by the shopper in higher prices but also the cost of administrating the scheme, the promotion, the stamps, the distribution, the warehouses and the transport have to come out of it.

I say if they want to compete let them compete in the best manner of all, which I do not see you doing, by cutting prices.

(Concludes) *That is my main take on Trading Stamps what is your defence of it?*

John

(Wriggles in seat, very confident)

Well Mr Levin. First of all you said in America costs have gone up. They have gone up by approximately 1.6 per cent. The values of the goods that have been given away in America are 2.5 per cent. Therefore whatever happens the public are 0.9 per cent. better off.

That is if your argument is right so far.

Secondly in America 45 per cent of the supermarkets give away trading stamps. 55 per cent don't.

Now it's up to the public to make up their minds as far as I am concerned

You a few months ago, in a programme here on 12th January I believe it was, said

'The public are not stupid. The British housewife can make up her own mind'.

I have built up a successful business by letting the public make up their minds. In this case they can do this. In the particular example of the grocery trade everybody cuts prices and gives away trading stamps, everybody does this.

Trading stamps are a way around RPM.

Levin

(Growing angry, the comic undertones becoming apparent to us all)

You might as well say have no laws for confidence tricksters.

John

But look

Levin

(Mutters something inaudible)

John

(Seizing the imitative, the cameras have swivelled now and the film is being shot from his angle)

Let's be quite clear about this. The stamp trader charges the public 1.08 per cent

The value is 2.5 per cent

Levin

Nothing of the Kind! Nothing of the kind.

John

Prove it!

Levin

(muttering)

In actual fact you are paying at least as high as the market price

John

Never. The cost to the bulk supermarket chains is 1.8 per cent

The actual cost

Levin

Where do you make your figures up from?

John

I don't make my figures up. Certainly not! Before I came on here to be alleged annihilated by you I checked the figures with all the people concerned.

(Levin seems a bit stunned and the audience start getting excited and clapping John.)

For instance I am not allowed to talk about my old company but I am not advertising.

If we go into trading stamps we will charge the retailer 1.8 per cent and give the public 3 per cent. They are gaining 1.2 per cent

Levin

There are always exceptional firms we are looking at the general companies

John

You said in your programme of the 12th January the public are not idiots. Are you changing your mind now?

(The audience sensing blood starts clapping and cheering)

Levin

You might as well say Mr Bloom

GONG IS SOUNDED WHICH SIGNALS THE END OF THE INTERVIEW

Fades to sound of cheering,

If it had been a boxing contest I think the referee would have stopped the fight. To save Bernard Levin from further punishment. The bell (or in this case the gong) literally came just in time for him. I noticed that his style was a mixture of wit, sharpness and a streak of school boyish sarcasm. I knew if I had let him settle into his stride he would have just steamrolled over me. At the start of the interview he rested his hands on his knees but later he crossed his arms in front of him, strange body language. The fact that it was live worked against him that night because it added to the tension. Today it would have been pre-recorded and heavily edited.

It was interesting that when the cameras were off us his face shrank visibly and he just slunk away. He never offered to shake my hand or even spoke another word to me. It was the first time he had suffered defeat.

Andre Agassi, the tennis ace made the point in his marvellous memoir *Open* that 'a win does not feel as good as a loss feels as bad'. I felt good though, that slot had been a two and half minute advert for John Bloom on the BBC! Marvellous publicity for me, it could not have gone any better. You could not have bought advertising space like that.

'The British housewife can make up her own mind. The public are not idiots' became the buzz words. I started to use it in all my adverts- with a little picture of John Bloom on the box, smiling out from the screen,

More claims of megalomania were thrown at me, they hated my star to shine. Was I the scarecrow waiting to jump on the bonfire or was it Bernard Levin? There was this starlet in the 30's who failed to make it in Hollywood and made a huge bonfire of her torn up press photographs, ignited it, then committed suicide by jumping on it. Tom Wolfe writes about *The Bonfire of Vanities*, thinking back though I was unbeatable for a short while. My life has always been a film, a drama, but that was a great scene.

David Frost came across at the end of show and congratulated me like I had scored the winner at Wembley, when the gong sounded I saw him in the background his face twitching. Perhaps he had been waiting for Bernard to fail or somebody shut him up.

You never know what goes on behind the scenes; I did sense a sinking-ship atmosphere. My new pal David introduced me to the illustrious regulars on the show, which included Lance Percival, Willy Ruston and Al Mancini. I became very friendly with Al and he did a marvellous turn at my wedding anniversary bash at the Jack o'Clubs the following Spring. You remember David Bowie did the cabaret that night? Al was a terrific guy; he was born in Ohio but was staying in London for a few years. Ned Sherrin used his considerable talents as a writer and actor on TW3 to brilliant effect. If the name is not immediately recognisable to you then you may recall him better as 'Tassos Bravos' in the *Dirty Dozen*.

Al eventually went back to live in America where he had a long career featuring in the smash TV show *All in the Family* and movies like the Michael Douglas hit *Falling Down*. Poor Al died of Alzheimer's disease in 2007. Three years earlier the same disease had claimed Bernard Levin.

Ned Sherrin wrote to me the next day and thanked me for my performance against Bernard, which he claimed, had been the best encounter on the show. Gardener Harry Wheatcroft sent me some roses and the founder of the Green Shield stamp company sent me a telegram. People did things like that then. TW3 got cancelled a few weeks later and an epoch ended.

Chapter 15 - RPM (Everybody Hurts)

'Most personalities have been obliged to be rebels'

Oscar Wilde

'Here as elsewhere in twentieth-century cultural history, images of autonomy obscured its eclipse.'

Richard Wightman Fox and T. J. Jackson Lears; introduction

The Culture of Consumption (1983)

Resale Price Maintenance hurt everybody (with apologies to Michael Stipe, who used to front the band REM). It was a complicated issue, the mechanism by which manufacturers could dictate the price at which their products were sold to the public. The political parties had thought long and hard about abolishing it but were afraid of upsetting the shopkeepers who were under the impression that RPM protected them from the supermarkets and big stores. That was the situation.

First let us take the story on a bit. At the end of Chapter 4 I had met the Irishman Mick Cosgrave, at first our friendship was based on sport, as so many are when you are young. We played table tennis together and he would always give me a sound thrashing.

Mick should have stuck to table tennis, I was a good player but Mick was incredible. However, we both needed money so Mick and I came up with this idea of selling paraffin door to door. Our target base of clients was West Indian families who felt the harsh English winters severely and needed a cheap source of heating. Many of these families lived in cramped poor conditions and their only source of heating was through those old paraffin heaters, as they had no fireplaces and electric fires were very expensive to run. They also gave out very little heat – if you sat in front of it your legs got burned but your back was cold. We worked the East End but it was the same story across town, where Peter Rachman started exploiting and terrorising the West Indian community.

Mick and me bought a big 50 gallon tank, put it on the back of a lorry that I had acquired, filled it with Fina Green paraffin and we were up and running. '*This time next year we would be millionaires*'. It took me a little longer. An interesting story behind the lorry by the way, I had started up a small haulage business with a chum but it soon went bust and I inherited the lorry after paying off the creditors. It was massive; I think it was ex-Army, and I parked it outside my front door but it so big it covered several other front doors. We had to winch the tank onto the back, took ages. Tank was the right word for it because it resembled a Sherman tank. It was awkward to drive also, especially when the roads were icy and slippery.

The hours were punishing and it really was hard work, at lot of it at night. That was when the menfolk were home from work and would pay us. I used to lug the heavy cans of paraffin up huge staircases, it was a miracle I did not give myself a hernia. To make the sales and smooth things along with the customers I started giving away freebies, cheap biros, badges and little dolls for the children. I bought all this stuff from a big warehouse in Houndsditch; the big red building is famous for being a clothes outlet now. The freebies went down very well, aided by our sales patter and jokey manner. Keep them happy was always one of my golden rules.

'Buy 5 gallons of paraffin and get a dolly for the kids.'

If they bought 20 gallons they would get a giant teddy, he was as nearly as big as me. The kids would come to the windows and look down at this crazy pair with a big old ted assisting them. We were always shouting about and making our presence known. Soon we had a large round and lots of friends in the community who looked forward to us coming round every week. The problem was sometimes I spilt more paraffin on myself than I sold. The smell of it was over powering and though I scrubbed myself night and morning it was always on me. The dry cleaning bills were staggering; my social life was non-existent because I was working such long hours, combined with the over powering smell of eau de Fina Green was a real turn off to prospective girlfriends. We both thought there had to be an easier way of making a crust so we got out of the paraffin business and moved into washing machines.

A clean break really, Mick had been a former salesman of the machines and had a mate called Jim Elvins who was buying them cheap in Holland and selling them door to door. As simple as that, so we bought two of his machines for £29 and that was how it all started. A guy called Dannie Ginsburg who was now distributing the Dutch washing machines in the UK, told me he had the market already sewn up. He went on about how we were wasting our time and would never make any money out of it etc, etc. Funny I love people telling me things like that; a few years later I was hearing similar talk about what mincemeat Bernard Levin would make of me on live television.

I knew nothing about the business; when a girlfriend's mother started quizzing me about the drying aspect of the process I had no answer. I was so naive about washing machines; my mother had taken care of all that sort of thing. It had simply not occurred to me that, having washed the clothes, the housewife would then have to dry them.

Speaking of my mother it was in April of 1958 that she died. It was a terrible blow to me, devastating, and I'm not sure if I was ever the same after it, my life certainly was not.

I was at home when she fell over and broke her leg. Septicemia set in and she died within a couple days. Women were always the dominant force in my life, my mother, my sister, my wife. I have had close mates all my life but it was always women that I listened to. Women, I love them – got all their albums.

I threw myself into work; I had to do something just to keep my mind busy. I was heartbroken but tried to suppress it. When Sir Henry Cecil died of cancer in June 2013 I saw his widow being interviewed on the Channel Four Racing show. Lady Cecil was breaking down with emotion after one of her late husband's horses had won at Royal Ascot. Displaying great courage and fortitude Henry's widow made the point that they had only got through a very difficult period by keeping busy. Looking back I could understand exactly what she meant.

The period of mourning lasted a week and I did not shave, at the end of it I had a healthy growth. No designer stubble in those days, I thought the beard made me look older and maybe people would take me more seriously in business affairs. I kept it and my image for that period in time was set.

I realised that we had to come up with a better washing machine if we were to be serious competitors. We were selling on a credit basis as opposed to hire purchase and using a firm called Belmont Finance.

The difference was that in a credit sale the customer only had to put down a small deposit, say £4 on a £50 machine but had to pay the balance up in just nine months. With HP the customer had to put down a large deposit but had years to clear the balance. The downside for us was that if the customers failed to keep up their payments then the Belmont Finance Corporation came onto us for the debt. Let us not forget we were selling to people often at the end of the market who could not have afforded the more expensive machines. Sometimes they could not even afford to buy ours. Vicious circle: the less you have the more you have to pay out.

I contacted the Dutch chamber of commerce for a list of companies who sold washing machines. My Uncle Alfie, you will recall him from the nightclub business days and his dealings with our erstwhile friend Wilkins, had lent me a £1,000 to start the company. I had a nightmare trip to Holland taking the ferry and booking steerage class, it was all I could afford, and I had to share a cabin with three other people. It was like a scene from that Marx Bros movie. Then as we were entering the Hook of Holland a huge storm hit us. My roommates spent the rest of the journey chucking up. The storm raged for hours; it was similar to the one that had done for the Spanish Armada.

In Holland I hired a cheap car and started trekking around the lowlands. The first few companies were not interested in a small time operator like me and told me so. I was on the point of going home when I struck lucky. Stay up all night to be lucky as the man sang. The Klean Washing Machine Company did a twin tub for £40, we were in business, (Has a ring to it, Klean Machine, the Beatles used it as a lyric in 'Penny Lane' but I never challenged them on it.) Now I had to gamble, big time, in September of that year I decided to advertise nationally. I spent £424 on a back-page advert in the *Daily Mirror*; it was the best £424 I ever spent in my life.

I received 8,000 replies and it all spiralled from there. I had an office at Number 1 Old Street near the heart of the City; it was just crammed with the coupons that had been sent back by prospective clients. Of those we had a strike rate of anything between 50–70 per cent. I started hiring old school mates to help process them, my father gave up his tailor's job to help out. I think that is how all that rain forest thing happened; there was so much paper everywhere. Just could not move.

The world was changing; since the war it had been a sellers' market: there was a shortage of goods but gradually production outstripped demand. Selling was now the key, the more aggressive the better. More women were working outside the home and consequently had less time for domestic chores.

The average family budget for consumer goods was just over a £1 a week so the purchase of a pre-Bloom washing machine would blow the year's budget.

Things just escalated, and another enormous stroke of luck helped me grow even quicker. To save on storage costs I was having the Dutch washing machines flown over by a charter company called the Channel Air Bridge. Due to some clerical/admin slip up they did not invoice me properly. When I gave them a cheque they did not present it. I was soon wise to this and pumped the money that would have gone to the charter company into my business instead.

The *Sunday Times* did a feature in their colour supplement on me in March 1964; in the interview with a lady called Margaret Laing I told her that 'If that mistake had not been made, there would be no business today'

The article pitched my debt to Channel Air Bridge as £19,000; in my first book 'It's no sin to make a profit' a figure of £11,300 was quoted. Looking back, I think it was nearer £23,000. By September 1959 I was living at 60 Park Lane, apartment 5 with a gold Chevy Impala outside and things were good, very good. One morning, really early there was a knock on the door and my girlfriend at that time opened it. Two guys charged in; one told me that he was proprietor of the charter company and we owed that huge sum to him. Freddie Laker was the proprietor, another name that ranked alongside mine in business terms during that crazy period. Another guy that did change people's lives, another guy that crashed and burnt (bad pun considering that he was in the airline business). Yet like Cyril Lord the carpet king he was never hounded or investigated for years like John Bloom. Why is this? I still ask myself this question even though it was so long ago. Pure Chekhov because of the absurd tragic-comic nature of the situation.

David Lynch the film maker had a famous dictum: 'you can go up in flames ...

You can go down in flames ... but you have to be in flames.'

Freddie Laker and I both went down in flames but that came later. At this point we were both soaring. Freddie introduced the other chap as his accountant, whose mistake had lead to this unfortunate situation. Calling on all my powers of persuasion, I talked him into not closing us down. I pointed out that if we stopped selling now he would not see his money. I promised to pay him back £500 a week and he accepted on the spot. Within a year I had cleared the debt.

I became a good friend of Freddie's and never forgot the favour he did for me then. I worked with him when I went into the holiday business and later when I lived in Majorca I used to see him a lot tinkering with his boat.

Mick Cosgrove was getting out of his depth by now. We had been through a lot together, all those freezing nights shifting paraffin in dodgy neighbourhoods and the excitement of seeing those mail sacks arriving when the coupons were flooding in. It was like the tickertape when Charles Lindbergh arrived back home from flying the Atlantic. I told him I had been paid a visit by the heavies and he became very upset. He disappeared to the nearest pub and downed a few drinks to steady his nerves. 'What have you done now, John?' he kept saying. At the start his idea of making big money was £50 a week, I had other ideas, I sensed for a long time that he was unhappy as the company grew and the atmosphere we were moving into was becoming rarefied. With the Laker problem simmering Mick knew it was a bad time for me but he badly wanted to jump ship. That night he asked me to buy him out. I always liked Mick and respected his decision. I paid him off with £2,000. He had serious doubts that I could discharge my liability to Laker and did not want to get caught in the crossfire. He was wrong.

There was no stopping me now. I was King Kong tearing down skyscrapers.

Soon I had 400 salesmen working for me; they were all self employed and lived entirely on their commission. In those days they earned £2 for the 39 guinea model and £3.50 for the 59 guinea model. I knew them all by name and their strengths and weaknesses; I made it my business to. It was all about charisma, and the best example today is José Mourinho, now back at Chelsea. If you want people to follow you and put themselves out for you must get them to like you first or at least respect your methods. I used to interview a lot of the salesmen myself; one day a guy came in for a job that I recognised from my RAF days. He was an officer that had helped make my life a misery at Compton Bassett. He did not recognise me in my Italian suit and beard, I doubt if he even knew my name when I was under his command. Anyway I went through the motions with him and got him to fill in all the forms and answer numerous questions. Didn't give him the job though, whoever said that revenge is a dish best served cold sure had it right. To this day he probably wonders how he flunked the interview.

We moved the operation from London out to Romford, a strangely named place called Gallows corner. It was beautifully positioned on the Southend arterial road and we had plenty of space. I was starting to draw attention from the press and whenever anyone from the media popped in for an interview we made sure that the place looked a hive of activity and industry.

Not that anybody had to *make* them look busy, because we were. I was courting publicity, little realising the huge monster that I was grabbing by the tail.

My plan now was cut the overheads by manufacturing the machines in Britain. To gain respectability I wanted to take over a stagnant company in the engineering industry. To this end my connections had led me to a company called Rolls Razor, who made safety razors. They were making losses and were struggling to survive. After some lengthy and secret negotiations a deal was done and we merged with them and an agreement was made to make 25,000 twin-tub washing machines.

I was heavily criticised for my irresponsibility in business methods but at this stage it made sense. In 1962 I formed an alliance with the Colston Company. I saw dishwashers as the next big thing. A few months later I took over the Prestcold Refrigerator business and slashed the price of fridges in half. My game plan was simple: cut out the middleman, sell direct by the coupons. How could it fail?

What I did not take too much notice of was the trouble I would cause and the fact that it was now a war situation with my competitors. In October 1962 the Retail Trade Retailers association launched a £100,000 fighting fund to campaign against direct selling.

One of my biggest competitors Hotpoint chucked £10k into the kitty and soon the other competitors were lining up to swell the fund.

The campaign was a total flop, a dismal failure – well what could they do, tell people to buy more expensive goods – yeah right. Thus the washing machine 'war' was started. It was anything but good clean fun though as it soon escalated into a dirty tricks campaign against John Bloom with thousands of snide coupons with false leads being sent in an attempt to swamp me.

There was also an independent group of retailers who formed in London. They called themselves the Appliance Trade Association or some nonsense. They were asking for subs every week from the independent dealers and £100 a month (not a small amount back then) from the manufacturers themselves. They had a crackpot scheme about a huge frontal assault against my company in the national press. It never really materialised, though, and only amounted to a couple of adverts in the Croydon local papers the *Advertiser* and the *Times*.

It was a propaganda war if anything; the manufacturers issued grandiose statements that: 'it was in the public interest that they should know more about the advantages of buying from a shop and the dangers of buying on the doorstep'.

Funny, in the 21st century all we have seen is more and more shops closing on the high street due to the recession and the fact that people are buying on the net. Even in those far off days there was talk of computers taking over and life being so different, but nobody really believed it was possible.

Another dirty trick involved was approaching some of my key staff, inviting them out for drinks on the pretence of business and then trying to pump them for future strategies. They need not have bothered because the majority (that is a key word here) were very loyal to me and besides all the strategies were in my head. I thought on my feet and reacted to whatever happened at the time. The banks talked of five-year plans; I did not have a plan for the next five minutes if truth were known.

A few rival cut-price machines were put on the market to try to undercut me but in fact they were merely following suit. They proved to be flops; I had shaken them out of their complacency. The price of a washing machine had fallen by £30 since Mick Cosgrave and I started selling them.

My biggest target, though, was retail price maintenance. Buy a washing machine and I will give you a fridge. One of my competitors brought out a heater so I started making them and gave them away with the washing machines. Then I started opening the discount stores.

When I visited them in the USA I had the idea of opening a discount store over here. In the economic wasteland of the second decade of the 21st century, what is the store that everyone heads to if they want a cheap razor or hair dryer? Even a kettle. Argos of course, got it in one. The cheapest outlet in most cases. What is Argos but a discount store? Argos grew out of the ashes of the green shield stamp empire.

By this time my advisors were the toffs at Kleinworth Benson who warned me about getting involved in any direct battle over RPM.

'You can go to jail for this, it is a very serious matter.'

'For what, selling a kettle at a lower price.'

I felt particularly strongly about this. I was the best salesman in the world at that time and now they were trying to stop me selling. How could selling something cheaper be illegal? To my mind it was crazy. Surely if you inflated a price and tried to get someone to buy a heater worth £15 for double that was fraudulent. Morphy Richards obtained an injunction to stop me selling a kettle at a price below the fixed retail price. Surely a case of the kettle calling the pot black?

I opened a shop in East Ham, modelled on the Corvette discount store that I had seen in America that sold everything from clothes to work tools. The old maxim 'pile em high, sell them cheap' was the order of the day. I was sensing tremendous animosity from the City. Really that was the point that it started to go wrong for me as the City had decided that I was too much hassle, a thorn in their side that had to be removed, quickly. It was as deadly a combination as did for Steven Ward, my misplaced confidence in the future and the establishment's view that I had to go.

After the Bernard Levin incident I was now one of the most famous faces in the country, and some market research firm came up with the ridiculous stat that if shown a picture of me then over 75 per cent of the country would have identified me. At that moment the press were courting me, and the fight against RPM made me very popular. I was the little man who stood up for the little man. I was carried along with it. Who wouldn't have been?

I read that in Roman times Caesar employed a man to whisper in his ear 'You are only a man', that's when Caesar was being feted by the crowd after another victory over the Germans or gladiators. I should have employed someone like that, but instead of keeping my feet on the ground I was being rushed headlong into a nightmare. What was worse was the people around me were pouring poison into my ears.

Chapter 16 - John Bloom Conman

'Accounts of the mechanics of sharping, and especially of simple confidence tricks, often seem absurd because they fail to convey the psychological adroitness that is the real core of the business. What the sharp most hoped to see in his prey's face was not stupidity but loneliness.'

The Victorian Underworld - Kellow Chesney

'Money is a bitch that never sleeps.'

Gordon Gekko (Michael Douglas) *Wall Street*

'Never take financial advice from anyone in a tie.'

Nassim Nicholas Taleb

Now there was a plot against Caesar. Aiming to depose me, the conspirators were my supposedly trusty lieutenants Leslie Goldbert, director in charge of buying, and the Jacobs brothers, Jack and Irving. I had surrounded myself with young inexperienced staff. I made a quote once about 'not wishing to be surrounded by 'fuddie duddies'. My big mistake? I never took into account their gluttonous appetites for power and wealth.

My loyal colleague Jeffrey Lewis advised me of the treachery that was going on in the court of Rolls Razor. I was away on business when Jeffrey received a call summoning him to a clandestine meeting. When Jeffrey enquired as to what it was about they told him he would find out when he got there. Present were the trio that I had dubbed the 'three musketeers' in my earlier tome. They made a big fuss about Jeffrey having no voting power in any executive decisions but informed him that he had been asked along because of his close connections with me and his intrinsic knowledge of the working of the company. Flushed with confidence they were very blunt and said cold-bloodedly: '*John has already outlived his use to the company*'.

They had formed this quorum and sought to vote me off as managing director in a sustained and well co-ordinated attack. I think they expected John Bloom to collect some knighthood for services rendered (some chance) and sail off into the sunset. Jeffrey was promised that he would soon move on up because he was honest. Clearly a quality that these gentlemen placed great store on. He scoffed at the very notion of a coup and turned them down flat stating that he wanted nothing to do with any of it. He added that I had been too good a friend and employer for him to ever work anything against me, and that he would always remain loyal no matter what the circumstances. To this day he still remains an old and truly valued friend.

This makes a mockery of another of the negative press reports that I received at the time stating that one of the contributory factors in my decline was my inability to make any lasting friendships in business.

The backdrop to this coup d'état was that things were badly wrong as my grip on the market weakened and the competition intensified. I had sold 200,000 washing machines in 1963 and was convinced that I could double that figure the next year. Why not? I had done it before in the previous years. Robert Heller, editor of *Management Today* did a piece on me once. A sort of financial Aesop's fable in which he stated: *'Bloom lived in dreamland; however, he overloaded both a weak organisation and weak finances.'*

Hindsight being a wonderful thing, I should have known that a phenomenal rate of growth could not be sustained year after year. In 1964 everything had been geared to sell 32,000 machines a month, in May of that year I sold 6,500. I was over extended and weakening public confidence was pushing me closer to the edge and now there were warring factions in the company.

Rumours were rife that Bloom, the golden boy, had quit the UK because of the fallout from a court case that I had been dragged into. I will explain the full story about that later. The glib huckster John Bloom was already being written off in certain sections of the press; my monumental business climb about to end in a long fall. I phoned my contacts in the financial press and they confirmed that there had been a commotion caused by rumours being put about. I decided to re-arrange the board and added my brother-in-laws to the structure in order to realign the balance of power. They subsequently resigned when the situation started to spiral out of control.

I turned up at the meeting straight from my sailing holiday; all I was wearing was the all-white strip, like Real Madrid of, shirt, trousers and shoes. All white was the dress code for Tamara's wedding; it went out about the time *Miami Vice* stopped showing on TV. My casual style was not in keeping with the tone of the meeting. I told Jack Jacobs unceremoniously, straight out: *'You are no longer a director. I would have fired you if I could.'*

'You will live to regret it' he snarled back.

I did not live to regret it, I was sick of the financial and emotional manoeuvring from a man who had started off selling machines for me door to door. I had jump-started his career but now he was the main threat to the stability of the company. Jacob's volatile ego had turned him into a bullying arrogant monster. The game plan was easy to spot: divide and separate me from the main board whilst discrediting me at every chance, '*Credit*' being the key word here.

I was also on the board at QPR and Jacobs tried to muscle in on that scene by disturbing negotiations I had in place with players. QPR were in a bad state and I was trying to inject much-needed talent into the club. Speaking of talent, Tallent Engineering in Durham was also the name of the company that had replaced Pressed Steel in supplying us.

July 17th 1964; the worst day of my life. I was in Bulgaria on a business trip in connection with the holiday travel firm that I had created. I was promoting holidays there and saw Bulgaria as the new Majorca. I was offering two weeks holiday in Bulgaria for £30. Sounds unbelievable today, it was another crazy adventure. I will tell you all about some other time in volume two of my life and times.

A postal strike hammered some huge nails into the Rolls coffin. The Beatles had a song called 'Please Mr Postman' on the 'With the Beatles' album, when I heard it I thought it was about those days. An urgent telex was sent to me from England that arrived too late to answer. As a result the company went into liquidation. I had been betrayed. The decision had been taken by the Jacob Brothers, Leslie Goldbart and Aaron Wright. They had abandoned the ship; I was staying on board despite the fact that it was holed beneath the water line.

Despite concerted efforts I could not find the reason why that decision had been taken, and the circumstances were highly mysterious. The day before we had gone into liquidation all Rolls debts to Tallent Engineering had been settled. It later came out that Jack Jacobs had accepted a personal payment from Tallent to the tune of £6000, I had also noticed over the months that Goldbart had been cosying up to Tallent though no evidence of any financial benefits was ever uncovered, the relationship was in hindsight more than suspicious given the situation that would ultimately unfold. Now it all became crystal clear, that uncanny sense of timing. Curious eh? As Sam Goldwyn used to say, we have all passed a lot of water since those days.

That vortex of treachery and deceit sucked down Rolls Razor. I tried to find out what happened to the conspirators and discovered that Irving Jacobs died and his brother is blind. Leslie Goldbart is still around, the last time I heard from him was when he tried to put a claim into me in respect of the losses he incurred on the shares. He had the cheek to phone me up from his mansion in Bishops Avenue (Mittal. the richest man in England at one time, lives there now) moaning about how he had lost so much and how he was in danger of losing his home. He had come a long way from his council flat where he first worked as a tailor.

Patrick Hutber reviewed my first book *It's no Sin to Make a Profit* and he wrote of this period in these terms: *'Some of the men around him would make you shudder, one in particular is the only man I have ever met who was evil in the way Iago was evil.'*

No prizes for guessing whom he was referring to.

Then the letters started pouring in as my long night of the soul started. The tabloids hosannas had stopped though. I was no longer Britain's brightest business luminary. When I was at my lowest ebb I built a funeral pyre of my letters and burnt most of them. Anne stopped me and I kept some in my archives, many of them charred.

The great Russian writer Gogol spent 18 years of his life writing the definitive novel. Millions of words during the course of which he went mad and beset by hallucinations, he burnt it. His wife rescued a small portion of the manuscript, which became the masterpiece *Dead Souls*. Perhaps these letters were my *Dead Souls*. I wanted to cleanse myself of it all, the debt, the strain, and the sheer enormity of the documentation. When collating the research for this chapter I sat down and started reading them, and within a short while the tears were streaming down my face. John Bloom is a tough old guy, you've probably realised this by now.

Tony Hancock once said that the major requirement in show business was resilience. Poor Tony was another of those fragile talents that died at his own hand but he knew what was needed.

I was more revolutionary in my mentality than most, the archetypal outlaw fighting against the system and never stopping defending and helping the poor. The problem was I courted controversy at every turn.

Here is a brief sample of those marvellous communications all dated Summer '64

Max Bygraves (Leatherhead Surrey)

'Big Business has many hazards and you found one – don't let it get too bad. You are extremely young and have a lovely wife and a few quid, don't sit around moping – smile. There are so many more tragedies that could have been far worse – this is nothing, a flea bite. Just pride is hurt-forget it. Life's full of good things-honestly no bull!'

Derek J. Hulland (Crewe)

'Sorry to hear of your misfortunes, but a man of ideas just cannot stay down for long.'

J. D. B. Willments (Cheltenham)

'It appears to me that the only two things you are guilty of is looking after your sales staff and letting the consumers have a good article at a reasonable price.

May you rise again?'

Mrs Stella Hilton (Bristol) signed just a housewife

'Sorry about your recent bad luck in business, it seems a shame as your prices were within the reach of average persons. Does it mean one won't be able to get a rolls washer now? My sister in law has a de luxe model and says it's fabulous'

Margaret Chapman (Littlehampton)

'Regardless of what has happened you tried to help the housewife by cutting out the middleman. I bought two of your machines and was satisfied and delighted with the gifts'

The Old Bradians Association (Ilford) Vice president Bud Flanagan OBE

'The Old Bradians Association have asked me to write to say how sorry they are to hear of your present difficulties; but wish to thank you most sincerely for your past support'

Monty Fresco (*Daily Sketch*) The most famous press photographer of the 60's, the original paparazzi.

'I want to apologise for making myself a nuisance when you had so much trouble on your plate. I am a press man and my constant requests for pictures were part of my job. I trust you will come bouncing back in your inimitable way. Remember, you still have one fan in me!'

H. R. Owen Ltd (Official Rolls Royce and Bentley retailers, 17 Berkley St W10)

'I was sorry to learn of the winding up of Rolls Razor. I hope that shortly the papers will once again be full of your success.'

Arun Base (Calcutta)

'Though I am on the other side of the earth, I wanted to write to you let you know how sorry I was at the news; I wanted to repeat to you the time old saying 'Failures are the pillars of success.'

I sincerely feel that men like you, Mr Bloom, will meet difficulties, and always beat them. This passing failure will inspire you to invent something new.'

R. J. Dodd (Whitehaven)

'I sincerely admire a man who can start with nothing and then come up so fast his name is a household word. I am extremely sorry that your company crashed and set the 'establishment' free again.

Sue Chapman (London SW10)

'I hold £6,000 of stock in the company. I bear you no personal animus for the present crisis, a view shared by many shareholders.

By forcing many firms to cut their profits, which were excessive, in the home appliance field, you must have raised ire in some quarters and perhaps you did not realise the dangers you ran from firms which I am sure were gunning for you'

I received hundreds of Post Office Telegrams from my legion of apostles

One marked 'ordinary housewife Belfast'

'We believe in you I have bought 10 shares. God Bless'

Adam Faith (Esher)

'Don't worry I am still your friend even though you are poor'

(Adam was now several years into fame and untold riches but never forgot his friends or his sense of humour)

A Letter from Charles St George (London E3)

'This must be a terribly worrying time for you. I do hope that you will be able to sort out your difficulties, which do not seem to be insurmountable. I thought I would let you know that should you need any help from me-in any way whatsoever-you need not hesitate to ask for it'

(Charles St George was another caring, compassionate person. A loyal friend in times of need he despised injustice with a passion. Charles was a great chum of the famous jockey Lester Piggott and Sir Charles two year old Lupescu, trained by the late Sir Henry Cecil, was the first horse ridden by Lester when he returned to the saddle after a 5-year hiatus. That included a year spent in jail for tax evasion)

W.C. Allen (a fellow traveller) Dagenham

'May I express my sorrow at the decision taken in your absence to place certain of your companies into voluntary liquidation and to express my personal hope that you will decide to continue the fight.'

G. M. Ropson (Derby)

'A complete stranger wants to say 'Keep your chin up'

Jim Walker (Salford)

'I am taking the liberty of writing after reading of recent shocks. You do not know me, I have never bought your goods and this is not a begging or whining letter.

But I have admired your success from humble beginnings and against terrific odds especially from established 'big fellows' of wealth and power who hated you for daring to compete against them. Along with some 'friends' now joining the wolf pack as you stumble.

You have given plenty their chance in life John now you know the true from the frail. '

Rafiquddim Ahmed B.A. (Liverpool)

'Though an unknown person I was extremely worried about you. I know for certain that you are a victim of circumstances and you are paying the fault of trusting your friends and associates. I would with pleasure give you as much as I could to manage by December.'

I could fill the rest of the book up with these absolutely amazing letters. Nearly 50 years later they still carry such impact. I was only going to print a couple but where do you stop? Amongst these above are ones from household names like Max Bygraves and the amusing telegram from Adam Faith. Charles St George was one of the wealthiest men in the country offering support along with the guy from Liverpool. One of my advertisements had me as head of the 'Give the housewife Something Special Movement' and I guess I was for a while. Getting cards and letters from people I don't even know. I want to finish this selection with these two letters that stand out.

Gertrude R. Burge (Ealing Common)

'Should you need someone to do some secretarial work for you at no fees I will gladly help out? My weekends and evenings are my own and I know you must still need someone to type the letters, which concern the winding up of your affairs.

The failure of your company smacks to me of jealousy and resentment of your success at such a young age and although it sounds hollow on paper I would like to say you have my sympathy. As I am old enough to be your mother, one can say these things. '

J R Dashwood (Twickenham)

'Pressure has been brought to bear to block effectively the provision of further finance, and possibly even the extension of existing credit facilities, so far as normal sources of short-term credit are concerned.

Sir Charles Colston is reported as stating that 'The Company is a good one and only needs sufficient cash to rejuvenate it'. If, unlike other most regrettable press reports, this statement is accurate, there seems no reason to doubt that the provision of bridging finance is commercially viable, provided the issue is decided on an objective financial basis, free of all prejudice.

It struck me that your difficulties may have been aggravated by a fear on the part of the financial institutions that their assistance might result in the loss of important customers, such as those industrial groups with huge accounts-and a large vested interest in your downfall.

Your television appearances convinced me of your integrity. In remarkably short time, your socially admirable achievements have become economic history'.

I rest my case J. R Dashwoods brilliant letter really is my case for the defence. I have nothing further add to add.

Something that I also wanted to put the record straight about was 'John Bloom Con-man'. Somebody put something on Yahoo with that tag. That was how this chapter came about, my rebuttal of those charges. This lady Susie S answered the question with another brilliant piece almost in the class of our friend J.R Dashwood. (Forgive the start where it lapses in some Irvine Welsh faux Scot speak)

'He wisna a con man he was smart.'

Rolls came into being in the late 1950's after the entrepreneur John Bloom bought the brand name of Rolls Razor to market a range of inexpensive twin-tub washing machines. Colston were formed around the time by Sir Charles Colston, formerly the UK director of Hoover, to market a compact dishwasher of his design. The companies amalgamated in 1962 but had gone bankrupt by 1964. Manufacture continued with machines built by the engineering company Tallent(who built the company's dishwashers) who rebranded them as such briefly but by 1965 were marketed as Colstons before the appliance division of Tallent was taken over by Italian firm Ariston in 1979.'

Somebody called Ragwort joined in the debate and added this:

'John Bloom was no con man. He was just a salesman who was angry with big company's price fixing (no longer legal). He purchased washing machines from Holland and sold them door to door at a fraction of the price that big companies with household names were selling their own makes. He made such a dent in their business that they ganged up on him and put him out of business. Never the less he broke the back of price fixing.'

I think those replies put an end to that line of attack. I quote from one last piece you may like to contemplate:

'For a large part of the 60's John bloom was cast as little more than a crook; an east end wide boy businessman who got rich quick than crashed spectacularly. But history has shown Bloom in a rather more sympathetic light   a man who broke open the price fixing cartels and complacency of British business. For good or bad Bloom ushered in the era of consumer goods affordable for working people.

John Bloom is the main reason why there is a washing machine in almost every British home.

In between he did just as Rockefeller and other 'robber barons' did. He chased profits by cutting costs and undercutting the price of his competitors. In doing so he ushered in an age of abundance in his industry'

This was quoted from a massive textbook called *Rediscovering the Fire; Basic economic lessons from the Soviet experiment*. You can get it on Amazon if you are interested.

Following the Collapse of Rolls Razor the press had a field day, I was hounded day and night, there was a public outcry and questions were being asked in the House of Commons. How this could happen? Who was to blame? The Sharks were circling and they smelled blood. One Labour MP in particular the Rt.Hon. John Lewis was demanding the Government instigate a Board of Trade Enquiry into the affairs of Rolls Razor, it should be pointed out this was the same MP John Lewis who had approached me the previous year, suggesting it would in the best interest of the Company to appoint a Labour MP to the Board of Rolls Razor, which at the time was heavily entrenched in the Conservative camp. Mr Lewis had offered to fill this position for a nominal salary of just £10,000 per year. I had turned him down flat.

Inevitably, the Government were left with no choice but to instigate the enquiry which was duly announced during a House of Commons debate that took place on 23 July 1964.

In spite of assurances given at the time by former Prime minister Edward Heath, still just a MP at that time and the President of The Board of Trade, in which he stated 'When the report is received, I will see whether it is possible to give it the speediest possible publication' The board of trade enquiry report has never been published in full. In fact upon completion in 1965 the full 431 page was deemed so sensitive that was immediately sealed by the Government for 80 years and remains closed from public domain until 2046.

Subsequent leaks of the report as well as number of articles, some published as recently as 2011, have drawn varied and often biased conclusions of the facts and proceedings that took place. In light of this I believe it is only fair I offer some further insight to the whole fiasco. The claims that allege I made profits in the region of £30 Million from insider trading are quite frankly laughable, in first instance the profits I made from rolls razor were actually in the region of £2 million, approximately half of which was tied up in the yacht and plane I personally had purchased but placed at the companys' disposal, and in the second instance 'insider trading' was not a crime at that time and in fact was common occurrence throughout the stock market.

Another laughable allegation was that I took large undisclosed interest-free loans from the company; this is complete and utter nonsense.

I never borrowed money from the company I had no need too. When I needed funds I simply sold some shares, in case people forget Rolls Razor was one of the most traded company's on the stock exchange for over 18 months, shares went from 2p to over £2 so raising funding was never an issue prior to the collapse and certainly was never taken from the company in the form of any loans.

In my previous book *'It's not a sin to make a profit'* I covered many of the details of the civil proceedings, however under the advice of council, many details and the nature of the Board of Trades' enquiry were reluctantly omitted. To go into the full details of the proceedings would warrant an entirely separate volume of this book so for time being at least, I will limit my comments to just a few key points of note.

I had planned for a skirmish but it became a war, I was a target because of my unceasing championship of lower prices. I was still facing bruising criticism from the press and misunderstanding from a lot of my peers. To the public though I was not a rebel, but a revolutionary. Someone once described me as a 'freedom fighter'. Economic freedom maybe.

The hearing took place in Gutter Lane. How appropriate, not so long ago I had been sailing around the Med in my boat now I was in the gutter.

Lots of people thought that I had never left it. The meeting consisted of two inspectors and two chief aides. Behind the scenes they had fourteen Chartered accountants and seven assistants examining every scrap of paper relating to Rolls. Do not forget in those days there were no micro-fiches or document readers. Just the smell of the dust was enough to trigger a sneezing fit.

To say the enquiry was an impartial and objective investigation in to the collapse of Rolls Razor would simply be untrue, in reality it was nothing short of a farce. Morris Finer QC was appointed to lead the enquiry this came as quite a surprise to me, as I had already approached him to retain his services for my defense. Any notion I may have had that the enquiry was going to be impartial was quickly dismissed from the outset.

Finer informed me that from the time of the start of the enquiry until the end under no circumstances was I allowed to communicate with any persons associated with or in regard to the enquiry, and specifically I was to have no communication whatsoever with any of the 53 people that were to be called as witnesses, this by default included being denied the opportunity to cross examine any of them.

Over the course of the enquiry I was asked to respond to 8500 questions, during this time no notes were permitted to be taken, no opportunity was afforded to me or my defense review any of the witness statements or evidence submitted, and no right to object given, in short I was denied any chance to offer a defense or even an explanation of the wrong-doing I was being accused of. The enquiry sat for a total of 54 days, I appeared for just 12 of them over a period of 11 months. It took almost another 2 years for the Enquiry to submit its report to the Director of Public Prosecution

After 2 years of deliberation and further investigation by Scotland Yard's fraud squad, (during which, in spite of their sterling efforts in inspecting every ledger, invoice, purchase order and petty cash slip ever produced by Rolls Razor, they were unable to reveal any evidence of fraud) the DPP decided that, based upon the conclusions of the Board of Trade Enquiry they would proceed with 2 indictments against me listing 7 charges of fraud in total. Of course during the time it had taken for the DPP to reach this decision a raft of civil actions had been launched, it was the legal equivalent of a bar fight with everyone suing everyone.

Immediately following the conclusion of committal proceedings, a civil case between the liquidators of Rolls Razor and myself took place. The prosecutions case was primarily based upon the findings and conclusions of the board of trade enquiry. Shortly following the start of the case, four of the five claims made against me were quickly overturned by the Judge, Mr. Justice

Fisher, the fifth claim was upheld. I may not have won that battle but in fighting it, it had won me the war. The decisions to overturn the findings of the Enquiry all but the destroyed the DPP's Criminal case against me, and allowed me the opportunity for ***a secret plea bargain***, which at that time was unheard of. This precedent paved the way for the use '*open*' plea bargains that are common place today. So as the Criminal case took place inside the court, negotiations got under way in counsels chamber and the gardens at Lincolns Inn. It was made clear to me in no uncertain terms, that the negotiations were to remain secret; at no time were they to be discussed in open court in spite of the Judge and both parties having implicit knowledge that the negotiations were taking place. ***We were sworn to secrecy.***

This was new ground we were breaking, the negotiations were lengthy and often heated with neither side willing to concede, at times it was more like a Turkish bazaar than a legal negotiation. I believe the turning point came when realising the weakness in their case against me, the prosecution made an application to introduce additional charges to the indictment. The introduction of further charges at this stage in the proceedings seemed ludicrous, especially given that the prosecution had already had 5 years in which to prepare their case against me, it merely highlighted the trial for the witch-hunt that it really was, a point that was brilliantly summarised to the court by my QC Michael

Sherrard who said *'one does not like to use the words "witch-hunt" but one of the charges now brought against Mr. Bloom seems to say "You may not be a witch but we have found in your kitchen some twigs which may be made into a broomstick so we will charge you being in illicit possession of them"'*. However in spite of our strong objections Judge Gillis allowed the application to stand, supporting the prosecution as he had done and indeed continued to do so, throughout the entire trial.

Realising the weakness of their position but determined not to accept defeat, the prosecution played their final hand, they informed us that if I did not plead guilty to at least some of the charges, they would proceed to trial and take their chances with a Jury in the hope that the difficulties in understanding the legal and financial complexities of the case and large sums of money involved and the fact I had already been tried, convicted and executed in the press would prejudice them against me.

Faced with a trial that was likely to take several years and the uncertainty of a prejudiced Jury a deal was reluctantly struck. I would plead guilty to two minor charges, the sentencing for which would be financial rather than custodial. Judge Gillis was quietly informed of the agreement that had been made and trial was drawn to a close. The prosecution managed get in one final blow, in that by pleading guilty I was be treated as a convicted felon and in accordance with Home office protocol would taken to Wandsworth Prison and stripped of my civvies and incarcerated overnight pending Judge Gillis's summing up the following day.

The tension in the court was high as Judge Gillis began his summing up, I suppose I was the only person in the room that was not tense, already knowing the outcome, though I have to admit I was a little nervous following the previous days events the thought of a last minute double-cross did enter my mind. I need not have worried I was fined £30,000 pounds for the 2 minor counts of producing fraudulent documents and barred from holding office in a public company for 5 years, but I was free to go, finally it was over.

It is worth noting that in the subsequent trial of my co-directors Reader Harris and Malcolm Cass who faced exactly the same charges I had that pleaded guilty to, both were acquitted. The presiding Judge Justice McKenna, forcibly made the point that those principally responsible for drafting the documents were Mr. Brooks of Kleinwort Benson and Mr. Norton of Norton Rose and that the drafting of such documents was a job for professionals, that is Merchant Bankers and Lawyers who were the experts and knew the requirements, it was not the sort of knowledge usually possessed by their clients that is the companies that employed their services.

It remains a complete mystery to me how the Jacob Brothers and Leslie Goldbert the 'three musketeers' who were responsible for starting the whole debacle, were never brought to trial or asked to answer for their actions in any way, in particular Jack Jacobs who had admitted during the enquiry to accepting a £6000 cash payment from Tallent Engineering, whose outstanding account incidentally, was paid in full the day before they placed Rolls Razor in to liquidation. And though severely criticised during many of the proceedings, Price waterhouse (whose audit notes were proven to have been considerably altered prior to submission to the Board of Enquiry) together with Kleinwort Benson and Norton Rose namely the institutions that had so poorly advised us, were never officially accused of any wrong doing and no charges were ever brought against them.

The committal trial had been the longest in British history. One hundred and fifteen days. The entire saga had lasted 6 years, the cost to the taxpayer was in excess of half a million pounds.

It was best summed up by a quote in the Sunday Telegraph by Peter Gladstone

" never has so much been spent, for so long, to expose so little guilt"

Several months later Robert Maxwell faced a similar court and approached me for information and background on it. Our paths had crossed in the South of France when I met him in the casinos. We were not friends but like the gunslingers of the Wild West our reputations preceded us. Captain Bob as the *Private Eye* magazine dubbed him had this infuriating habit of taking my chips from the gaming table making out they were his. If he was on black and red won he would seize a red chip. It really was a metaphor for how he lived his life. He rang me one day out of the blue, making out we were lifelong buddies and how I should come for lunch one day and catch up on things.

So there I was in the dining room of his Fitzroy Square mansion headquarters. It was huge, in the centre of the room was a very large dining table around 18ft. long. Captain Bob, the old swindler was at one end of the table and I was at the other. It was ridiculous I could hardly hear him speak; I thought that I spoke fast till I heard him in action. Recalling all this it struck me what a snob he was, considering that he had come from such humble origins in the Ukraine.

'Want to ask you about this Department of Trade thing, I have to appear in front of them about some problems I have., this Pergamon matter. You had a spat with them if I recall.'

I nodded, sipping at the Perrier.

What's your advice on it?'

'Get a good legal team in place, hire David Freeman to run it and bring in Maurice Finer as your QC. Nobody knows more about how it works than him. They employed him to grill me.'

He grunted then started talking about share prices or something but I could see his mind ticking over, digesting all the information, he eyed me with hooded, hawkish eyes, the lunch was lovely though. Sure enough Captain Bob hired the pair. At the end of the meal he thanked me for coming and said *'If there is ever anything I can do for you'*.

Sometime after I phoned him at the *Daily Mirror* to see if he could advise me on a new business deal I was putting through in America. He blanked me; the switchboard would not even put my call through to him. After that I did not bother anymore.

Later it was found that Maxwell had contrived to improve the price of Pergamon's shares through deals with his private companies, The DTI (as they were known then) reported that Maxwell in their opinion was *'not a person who could be relied on to exercise proper stewardship of a publicly quoted company'*.

Maurice Finer representing Maxwell had fought them tooth and nail in the High Court demanding all the things that I had been denied. Such as the right to cross-examine witnesses, there were 53 witnesses called at mine. What a difference in the attitude of Mr Finer.

In 1971 around the time Arsenal won their first double, Justice Forbes was critical of the Maxwell enquiry stating:

'They had moved from an inquisitorial role to accusatory one and virtually committed the business murder of Mr Maxwell'. He added that the *'inspectors had acted contrary to the rules of national justice'*.

Thanks a lot, what about Mr Bloom? You could use the exact phrase about my time in Gutter Lane 'moved from inquisitorial to accusatory'. If anyone was 'business murdered 'it was me.

The enquiry caused Maxwell to lose Pergamon in the UK but he eventually regained control of it before he was forced to sell it when his debts ran out of control.

Maxwell, the most notorious financial bogeyman of the late 20th Century drowned on Guy Fawkes Day 1991.

Like me he loved a cruise and it was presumed he fell overboard from his luxury yacht, the *Lady Ghislaine* just off the Canary Islands, to this day nobody really knows what happened.

Rolls had gone down with debts of over £4m, they blamed it on being 'under-capitalised', but that figure was vastly inflated by 'breach of contract claims'. Most of the figures were fabricated; I think a truer figure in respect of the deficit would have been in the region of £1m. If my credit lines had not been cut and my reputation not been shredded it may have been possible to raise it and stay afloat.

No mention was ever made of the fact that people had made money on the shares in the early days when they had soared from 10p to over £2.

No mention was ever made of the fact that as the largest shareholder of Rolls Razor I was by far the biggest loser.

I was finding out very quickly and painfully that when you were down they did not kick you just once.

My De Havilland Dove

The Bentley Convertible

A glimpse of Anne driving the unique Bentley 'honeymoon express'

Chapter 17 - Love story

This chapter is written by My wife Anne and is told from her perspective. In the spring of 2013 we celebrated our 52nd anniversary.

'Love means never having to say you are sorry'

Love Story starring Ryan O'Neal /Ali McGraw

My favourite movie, but a close second is Arthur Laurent's *The Way We Were* with Barbra Streisand and Robert Redford.

The first time I saw John Bloom was in a coffee bar in Baker Street, Very early sixties, on a Sunday night. It was wintertime because I remember how cold it was. It was across a crowded room. I do not know if it was love at first sight. I am not sure if I believe in it. Perhaps you are in love from the first moment ,you just do not realise it till later.

I did not have a clue at the time who he was or what he did. He was with a group of people, he always had people around him but he stood out from the crowd, he was just different. He was cocky with his peers but with me I detected a slight nervousness, it was a curious mixture of vulnerability and arrogance - irresistible.

I was eight years younger than him but women of any age have always been more mature. The age difference never was a problem, He told me about starting a charity committee helping out with disabled kids in a Norwood Orphanage and it grew from there. John has been helping those not as fortunate as himself all his life. Even today he is so involved with helping the poor Army boys that were so badly hurt in the wars, not just giving them a day out but trying to get them jobs and lead a normal life. He has a heart as big as the Shard, that is his trouble really, too kind, too soft hearted. When Rolls Razor crashed he paid off the people that worked for him out of his own pocket. The papers never wrote about that or the many kindnesses he has done. The night he verbally assassinated Bernard Levin on the David Frost thing people saw this tough business opportunist but he only ever went after people that started on him.

We started dating soon after we met. I was living at home with my parents in Ealing I had a job as a secretary in a small features agency in Fleet Street. All the papers were based there in those days; little did I guess that in a short time I would be featured in them. The crunch came when I went on holiday to Majorca with my girl friend Caroline Wine. She later married Leslie Goldbart, one of the false friends that betrayed John when Rolls crashed. The holiday had been arranged before John came on the scene.

A couple of weeks in the sun, the holiday thing was just really starting then, I loved Majorca always did, from the first time I went there. It was to feature heavily later in the mosaics of our lives as we lived there for a while and John had the piano bar. Anyway, Caroline had booked for three weeks, one more than me. I liked the sun so much and being away from the stress of London I decided to stay on. I had told John I had gone for the fortnight and when I did not return on time he became very worried.

John being John started ringing around all the hotels on the island and eventually located mine. It was a lot harder in those times with no mobiles, Internet or texts. Having located my room he started to bombard it with calls. Problem was I was out dancing the night away under that gorgeous moonlight and did not return till two in the morning. Eventually we spoke, he told me how much he missed me, how he longed to see me and could I fly back in the morning? I did and suppose that was the moment we both knew that it was serious. Though I kept cool and played it that way for a while telling John I was not certain about things, expressing doubts as how it would work out between us.

My parents thought he was a bit wild for me. The money was coming in now and he was buying these ostentatious cars and starting to really live a high life.

In those days young people had money, probably more in real terms than many of the youngsters today. The reason being that employment was high in the 60's and if you left a job on the Friday you could start one on the Monday. The young successful people though did not have the big money that say a Premier League footballer or a Pop Star makes today. When we married the whole Arsenal team was present, imagine that today? John has told you earlier that when we first met the Beatles (the biggest group of all time) they were all on wages. John Bloom was the first young businessman to make the big bucks. I think that is why he engendered such jealousy and how people who barely knew him wanted him to fail so badly, jealousy being the root of most of the trouble in the world.

We got engaged in September of that year, waking my parents up in the middle of the night to ask for their blessings. Funny we started that evening off arguing and we ended up engaged. We were married in February 1961 two days before Valentine's Day. It was a Sunday and the reception was held in the Savoy's massive ballroom. The wedding took place in the Central Synagogue in Great Portland Street, I exercised the age old Bride's right and turned up 15 minutes late, I never saw him look so worried even when he was facing the Board of Trade's inspectors. The wedding was the social event of the year with over 500 guests.

If 'Hello' magazine had been in existence then they would have run a special edition. John's PR people had been working on it for months; it was better planned than the D-Day landings, like a Baz Luhrmann movie.

I wanted to invite just a few close friends but it had to be done like this because John had so many business acquaintances and friends. Plus he was beginning to attract the attention of the older hierarchy that were grooming him for even bigger and better things - or so we thought. The high spot of the wedding was the cakes – that is right, plural. John never did anything by halves and had two and what was the theme? You got it - kitchen appliances. One was of the classic Rolls electromatic washing machine and the other a dishwasher. There is picture of me cutting into it somewhere.

The papers called it a 'ton of love', it took four men to lift them. There is one of the John's machines in the Science Museum but they should have found a way to preserve a piece of the cake. It was a masterpiece based on the actual blueprints of the machine, taking over 150 hours to bake and make. The only other wedding cake that attracted as much attention was the one in the Richard Harris song 'McArthur Park'.

We spent our wedding night in the Savoy but no breakfast as early in the morning John was at his desk in Cricklewood.

Not for long though because we caught the afternoon train for Switzerland. At first he simply hated flying but eventually conquered his fear. The honeymoon was only three days though such was the pressure of business. However who ever said 'Money is not made lying in the shade' sure had John in mind.

There were always hassles, the press, other women, as John's fame grew so did the problems. They were not just financial either. When we first met there was another woman that was telling everyone that she and John were going to get engaged. She even tried to crash the wedding. There was all that unpleasantness in the Holford case (the next volume deals with in detail) but John told me all about that woman so it was no shock. It just came with the territory. You pay a price for everything in life, a law of nature. That is why so few show biz or high profile relationships survive. Even worse today because the women involved in these scandals know that they can earn huge amounts of money from selling their stories. In those days things were more circumspect.

When the crash came John took it very hard at first, he felt that a lot of his friends suffered as a consequence. Many people made money on him though in the early days, when the value of the shares soared. I suppose that was the toughest time of our marriage. For a while in Bulgaria I took command of the situation, fielding the avalanche of calls and trying to get John back on his feet.

A few years ago a wave of depression swept over him and almost brought him down. I think it was the strain of years of living on the edge, of fighting impossible odds and maybe caring too much about people and things that could not or were not worth fixing. He bounced back yet again, at an age when most people would settle for a quiet life. I have never met anybody with his energy or drive.

My life has had many wonderful moments. At the time you do not realise it and because our generation was at the forefront of things we had nothing to compare it to. It is only when you look back or conversely see a couple like the Beckhams emerge that it brings it home.

Here are just some random pieces from the Anne Bloom cultural scrapbook:

The best place we ever stayed was the villa called La Fiorentina on the Riviera. Elizabeth Taylor, a woman who knew a thing or two about marriage honeymooned there with Mike Todd. John had this idea about letting his top sales people stay there if they hit target. They even had the use of this fabulous American car, a white thunderbird. Another beautiful car that was stationed there was a very rare two seater Bentley Convertible, the only one ever made John informs me.

John wanted people to share in his success and motivate themselves by sampling the high life in the villa that served as a playground for successful salesman. His logic was they would endeavour to maintain it, a brilliant strategy from a business viewpoint but also from a human one. It had a pool but the joke was it was only ever 3ft deep because John could not swim.

He wrote about the music people he knew ranging from John Lennon to Jimi Hendrix, which made me think about our 'song'. The best we could come up with was 'The Girl from Ipanema', a beautiful Bossa Nova song by Astrud Gilberto that reminded us of long hot afternoons in the sun. The second most recorded song in history I understand the Beatles 'Yesterday' being the first.

John used to sing a killer version of 'Volare', the old Italian song; I think Dean Martin did a version and David Bowie. Mr Branson uses it also in one of his Virgin ads. Today John does Elvis impressions with his chum Lou Jordan. I have seen it and can confirm that it's pretty wild, especially the 'American Trilogy'. Having seen the real thing in action though...

We were lucky enough also to see Frank Sinatra in concert perhaps the greatest singer of them all.

One of our passions was watching films together, we were trying to work out our favourite movie, and you know mine, John is not too sure about his, he has a varied taste. Movies lead us to movie stars and we met a fair few over the years. Our favourite was Michael Landon, who John has rhapsodised about earlier; we were great friends with Michael and his wife at the time Lynn. We had some beautiful nights out in California, the four of us. Just hanging out together, eating out usual stuff, we were inseparable. Sadly even their marriage, which seemed incredibly strong and happy, ended in divorce, such were the pressures and temptations of fame. Hollywood murders marriages. We still stayed in touch with them even though they were apart and Lynn came to stay with us in Majorca for a while as she dealt with the breakup of her marriage.

George Best was another great friend of ours. I never followed football but he was just as big as star in his way as any movie actor. One of my favourite memories of him was when he was playing in Los Angeles and he was a regular guest at my lunch parties, casually dressed, with black sunglasses and deck shoes. I used to give them on Saturdays for the ex-pats in Los Angeles. Amongst the guests were the writers Dick Clement and Ian La Frenais whose credits included 'The Likely Lads', 'Porridge' and 'Auf Widersehen Pet'. George's life read like one of their scripts. I think had they made a film on his life the obvious choice was Warren Beatty. Not that they looked alike but both had the same predatory instincts towards woman.

I met Beatty's sister Shirley Mclaine once, John has told you about it when Peter Ustinov the raconteur held court in the Russian Tea Rooms in New York. He forgot to mention it went on for nine hours and Salvador Dali was present, the artist. Now that was surreal.

John would take me a lot to see George playing for the Aztecs the crowd loved him. Everybody did. My favourite memory of him though was in Marbella when we used to play backgammon on the beach till it got dark, the evening always ended up with us all in a bar. I always used to tell him to take care of himself but of course he didn't.

A favourite of ours was also a guy you see more on the smaller screen - Ian MacShane, famous for being in everything from 'Villain' with Richard Burton to playing drug barons in 'Miami Vice'. We were good friends with him and his wife Ruth. Whenever I am back in the country I enjoy watching his 'Lovejoy' programmes, which they show back to back on a digi channel. Our friends Dick Clement and Ian La Frenais wrote that one also.

Another great friend of mine from those days was Samantha Juste who was better known perhaps under her married name of Dolenz. Samantha was the quintessence of the swinging London dolly bird and found fame on 'Top of the Pops' where she worked alongside John's ex-Radio Caroline DJ's Tony Blackburn and Simon Dee. In the summer of love 1967 she met Monkees drummer Mickey Dolenz and they married a year later.

They lived in Laurel Canyon where we went to their star studded parties. We spent many evenings together with many people including Davy Jones, Harry Neilsson, and George Harrison with his wife Pattie Boyd.

Sometime after she had divorced Mickey. I actually introduced her to her second husband a guy called Tony Shipp, who was known as the 'Beverley Hills Vet'. It sounds like a film with Michael j Fox in the lead role but Tony was the most famous vet in town and looked after Doris Day's pooches and Olivia Newton Johns horses amongst others.

The last time we saw them they stayed with us for the Monaco Grand Prix at our villa in Antibes.

Sometimes I have sad memories of those times because a lot of those people have gone. When I was young we met many of the old guard of Hollywood royalty who were big names in the 40's and 50's; so when we met them in the 60's they were veterans then. John did not put them in because their names would not mean so much today like Cornell Wilde or Esther Williams.

Zsa Zsa Garbor was another outrageous character, the Hungarian actress and socialite was larger than life. One night the President of my charity committee Marilyn Hinton introduced my husband to the formidable Zsa Zsa, announcing him obsequiously as the 'famous John Bloom'. I watched her wince and enquire of John.

'What are you famous for?'

Clearly she did not want to share the limelight with anybody else. Zsa Zsa was married nine times.

At one of Jack Hylton 's parties one night we were introduced to Sir Donald Campbell who was a huge name then. He was a real dare devil always trying to be the fastest guy on earth. When we met him he was trying to break the water sea record in his power boat 'The Bluebird'. John was like a schoolboy around him. I had never seen him like that, except when he met the Arsenal players. Sir Donald was a true hero, a throwback from the Spitfire pilots from World War two. He was killed in January 1967 when the craft flipped over on Lake Coniston. John was upset for weeks; he lost some friends in the motor racing sport also over the years. They never found Campbell's body for years but when it was eventually buried the event was overlooked because it happened on the day of the 9/11 attack.

I risked my own life once when he sent me out scouting for a new boat for him in the South of France. It was early on in the marriage and we had not progressed to the luxury yacht stage. This was a small one about 30ft and located in this dry dock. To reach it I had to go down this rope ladder like something out of a Rider Haggard story. The problem was I was wearing a pair of high heels and a pencil skirt. Next time it was the deck shoes and chinos!

I f you ask me the secret of a long marriage I am not sure I could answer you, chemistry I suppose and friendship, I believe very profoundly in marriage, the concept of two people facing life together. Everything is a love story if you think about. I started with Ryan O'Neal and Barbara Streisand so they would be a good point to end on. In 1972 they made a comedy together called 'What's up Doc'. In a homage/satire of 'Love Story' the last dialogue in the film was Barbara saying the memorable line *'Love means never having to say you are sorry'*

Ryan tells her

'That's the dumbest thing I ever heard'

I think I can identify with that.

Anne

At the Races

La Fiorentina

The Villa Gardens

The Harbour

Anne and I in St Tropez

The fabulous Anne Bloom

Chapter 18 - We Can Be Heroes

'All the new thinking is about loss

In this it resembles all the old thinking'

Robert Hass 'Meditation at Lagunitas'

'What passing bells for those who die as cattle

Only the monstrous anger of the guns'

Wilfred Owen 'Anthem for Doomed Youth'(1893-1918)

This chapter is the last of the first volume; I saved this piece to the end because it is of particular importance to me.

All the chapters are important, you paid out for this book but this story is of huge significance to all of us really.

I was so moved by reading the following poem penned by Stephen Carr, a British Army Veteran of the Royal Military Police Close Protection Squad, that I have decided to give up a portion of my remaining life to helping the guys like Stephen. Anyhow here it is:

I did my duty, I did my best.
I hid behind my bulletproof vest

I walked the streets with gun in hand
I held the peace in a foreign land

People didn't want me there
They would often stand and stare

But my duty was to keep the peace
I tried to save a life, at least

I saw men die, I saw men suffer
Life couldn't get too much tougher

Bombs and bullets played their tune
And forced me deep in to the gloom

My duty there was never done
I worked until the passing sun

Then one day the years have passed
My memories would last and last

No corner of my mind is safe

I am haunted by that foreign place

I try to run, I try to hide
My demons always by my side

Did I serve my country true
Would I really die for you

Did I do my very best
Did I need my bombproof vest

Did I see my colleagues die
Or is it just a wicked lie

All I know is this you see
I can never be set free

The Troubles they have left their mark
They keep me trembling in the dark

So enjoy your freedom that I won
For this soldiers work is done

Copyright © Stephen Carr 2012

Stephen Carr served in the protection squad, an elite unit that was responsible for safeguarding important figures and VIP's in dangerous areas. He served in Northern Ireland twice, totalling almost six years, most of which was in plain clothes or 'under cover'. He spent a long time serving in other trouble spots but the very nature of his work and the secrecy that cloaks it forbids me from including it here.

To give you some idea of the calibre of the men that were in the unit, one of Stephen's closest buddies is now employed by the oligarch Alisher Usmanov, the richest man in Britain. In the summer of 2013 the self-made billionaire owned just less than 30% of Arsenal Football Club, but like me in the 60s he was still refused a place on the board. Alisher seems the sort of guy I could get along with very well. Apart from his passion for Arsenal Football Club he knows a thing or two about boats – owning a 110m mega yacht.

Stephen worked in Iraq as a civilian consultant for the US Military (Department of Defence) on Operation Iraqi Freedom (OIF), he was directly employed by an American, 3-star Lieutenant General in 2008/9 based in Baghdad.

Stephen is suffering from Post Traumatic Stress Disorder or PTSD.

He wishes to point out that he was not medically discharged from the Army on those grounds but however, they have since accepted that he does have PTSD, and that it was caused by his army service. This is a severe condition developed after being exposed to the threat of imminent, violent death. The symptoms of such a disorder include disturbing recurring flashbacks, the avoidance or numbing of memory and chronic levels of anxiety. Stephen told me the following.

'It is true that during my treatment for PTSD at the Combat Stress treatment centres they have identified at least eight individual military-related events that were considered life-threatening and each of them would be serious enough to cause PTSD.'

So what would that do to you? Eight times you cheated death or maybe death cheated you by making your life a living hell. Close friends die but you survive? How could your life ever be the same? I regard Stephen's poetry as a combat classic, an amazing example of modernist literature. I am encouraging him to write more, he is just so brave letting his fine words address the horrors of modern warfare. His work reminds me of the extraordinary group of poets that came out of the slaughterhouse that was the First World War names like Wilfred Owen, Robert Graves and Siegfried Sassoon.

Stephen is one of the many ex-servicemen that is helped by the charity I am involved with which is called Mission Motorsport. It is a registered Service Charity and is the official provider of disabled and adaptive motor sport.

Mission Motorsport is run by British military veterans, serving officers and motor racing professionals, it was formed in 2011 by Major James Cameron of the Royal Tank regiment who returned from commanding the British Armoured Group in Helmand Province, Afghanistan. Major Cameron is a man who instinctively leads from the front he was awarded a mention in dispatches for gallantry that year. This was an unusual honour for a commanding officer who do not often find themselves under fire. The Major was profoundly affected by the horrors that he and his men endured so instead of simply fund raising on his return, he set about finding more direct methods of support for our wounded Hero's through his chosen sport. It was immediately successful and he was formally charged by the Army to determine how much Motorsport could be used as a recovery activity. As a result the charity was launched.

I was just impressed with what they were trying to do - help rehabilitate serving personnel as well as veterans by getting them involved in the wonderful world of motorsport.

One of their key ideals was to merge the activities of the disabled with the able bodied. Here are some bullet points about Mission Motorsport's main objectives:

Inspire and rebuild confidence. In my view confidence being the key to success in life,

Help to develop new and existing skills to aid them in the future.

Develop resilience, our old friend discussed earlier in the book. If a testing environment like motorsport could help improve their ability to cope with a disability this would instil a greater degree of independence in day-to-day life.

To demonstrate to a wide audience the fine qualities of ex-service personnel that would make them more employable

To provide specialist training and direct vocational support and assistance.

The source of our clientele was from the Defence Medical Rehabilitation Unit at Headley Court and from Personnel Recovery Centres such as Tedworth House. Prior to modern warfare soldiers were always expected to be very emotionally tough and to show no sign of fear in the midst of fear.

In World War 2 it was noted that after 35 days of un-interrupted combat 98% of American soldiers manifested psychiatric problems in varying degrees.

I read with interest a broadside in the press against the BBC for falsely accusing the 'Help the Heroes 'of misspending funds. It is a very controversial issue and I really do not want to get involved in it. My gut feeling is as above; these chaps must be given jobs with the necessary training so that they can earn a decent living for the rest of their working lives. The ability to always earn and provide for their families is crucial. Far more important than any building no matter how wheel chair friendly or what a marvellous games room it had. I agree that only the best is good enough for our heroes but as always some sort of balance must be stuck between ostentation and practicality.

My wife told you in her chapter about the young John Bloom's predilection for flashy cars. Lewis Hamilton, who I saw in the pits at Silverstone, gave an interview in which he talked about his passion for collecting cars. The British ace spoke lovingly of his latest purchase a 1965 Cobra. The F1 driver it would appear calls the cars 'his girlfriends'. I owned a Cobra for a while similar to Lewis's, Peter Ustinov and myself were keen to make a business around them but the problem of servicing was against it. The Cobra remains one of the finest motorcars ever manufactured and I can understand Lewis's desire to own one.

The book started with David Bowie let's wrap it up with him. One of his best songs was 'Heroes' recorded when he lived in Berlin. The lyric ended with

'We can be heroes-just for one day'.

I do not want Stephen Carr and his mates to be heroes 'just for one day'. I want them to be a hero every day to their family, by earning a living for them.

Silverstone 30th June 2013.

The British Grand Prix, to the fan in this country the high spot of the F1 season. They used to sing about football coming home but on that day it was Formula 1 coming home. That Sunday was a cloudy, breezy day the heat wave was to follow about a week later. I left London about eight in the morning, a good friend of mine Soren arranging the transport in his Jaguar. We were taking four veterans with us to show them a good time, the next call was to collect my mate Oliver Holt, the chief sports writer for the Daily Mirror, and give him a lift to the track. It was a busy time for Oliver just then with the usual cricket and golf events plus a new Premier League season only a few weeks away and the transfer market about to explode.

Oliver Holt has a very famous mother also, the actress Eileen Derbyshire who plays Emily Nugent, the longest serving female actress in Coronation Street. Norris's best friend my wife informs me. I met her before Oliver was born back in 1963 when Lesley Conn took me to visit the cast of 'Coronation Street' on the set. Lesley knew everybody in the business and took me there for an outing. I recall meeting William Roche who took the part of Ken Barlow, our appearance on the set caused a stir because we arrived in a Rolls Royce Phantom 5. My life has had elements of a soap opera so it was good to visit the biggest of them all. I never watch it to be honest.

At Silverstone I met so many old friends I could not really list them all. One of my special chums was there though Leo Sayer. Another huge star from the 70's, his first seven singles all hit the top ten. Leo loved motor racing and had travelled all the way from his home in Australia. Leo had been managed by good friend Adam Faith, whose first seven singles also went top ten when he first burst upon the scene that was our connection. We had met up a few nights before when we had gone to the accreditation office to obtain our passes for the big day. Keith Sutton who owns one of the biggest motor sport photo-archive businesses was there also along with the living personification of Elvis Aaron Presley my friend Lou Jordan.

I sometimes think that with the help of my skin care products we have actually created the embodiment of the true King of Pop. We all ended up back at Keith's where we had an impromptu cabaret with Leo and Lou bashing out the greatest hits of Presley and Sayer. The show always goes on when Leo is in town. I joined in on a couple of Elvis numbers.

Leo signed a lovely picture for me, of him in the company of James Hunt and another old mate George Harrison that Keith conjured up out of the archives. I told you that I used to see the former Beatle at the motor racing. It must have been taken circa 1976 the year James won the World Championship after his epic battle with the Austrian Niki Lauda.

This book is just a series of amazing coincidences or reference points. Two Sundays after the British Grand Prix BBC 2 ran a programme called Hunt v Lauda (F1's Greatest Racing Rivals). A new film was also coming out about the epic battle between the English Ace and the Austrian champion. The actor playing him was even better looking than the playboy Hunt in real life. James was nearly in the George Best class for lady killing, (nearly, nobody topped George, to paraphrase the Belfast Boy 'if he had been born ugly you would never have heard of Niki Lauda'). James Hunt was the last of the Maverick drivers; he died really young at 45, like George burnt out.

I'm still mates with Niki Lauda, there's a photograph of us taken that day in book. His piercing blue eyes as bright as ever, two guys that had taken everything the world could chuck at them and more. Niki was an incredibly brave guy; his iron will carried him through that dreadful crash where he came within seconds of being burnt to death. That was the season Hunt won the world title in the last race in Japan. Niki lost an ear in the accident, the heat from the explosion was nearly 400 degrees, and it took them ten seconds to pull him out of the fireball. When I used to see him afterwards he used to joke that he was still looking for his missing ear. James Hunt used to remark that he was better looking 'after the accident'. That's the sort of guys they were, never conceded anything they never showed any weakness. If they had been born a few years earlier they would have been fighting it out in the skies rather than on the racetrack, James in a Spitfire, Niki in a Messerschmitt 109. I have many chapters on the sport, all for another day.

Christian Horner the Red Bull boss, you met him in the first chapter, gave our party a marvellous reception. He could not do enough for us, extending every courtesy and allowing our hero's total access to all areas. The Red Bull motor home was massive, spread over two floors it was more of a control centre than anything.

My special chums in the Force India team were also brilliant also, they even laid a barbecue on for us all, and there were some marvellous Indian delights to be sampled. Bernie was there of course, but he was so busy though with the demands of making sure that everything ran smoothly on the biggest day in the UK's motor racing calendar. My friend promised to schedule a slot to meet the Mission Motorsport honchos in the near future to see what assistance he could render.

Bernie let me rest up in his motor home for some of the long afternoon. It was the inner sanctum very few people have seen the inside of it. I spent a long time chatting to his delightful wife about things. Later we went for a walk about, Carole Vorderman came up to say hello. Carole like me was an avid twitter user and a big fan of F1.

The race was not brilliant; Lewis Hamilton started in pole position and in front of his home crowd was expected to win but suffered a high-speed blow out. He lost the lead on lap eight when his left rear Pirelli tyre blew out, three other drivers Felipe Masa, Jean-Eric Vergne and Sergio Perez all suffered the same fate.

It was an incredibly embarrassing day for the sport. Lewis Hamilton later said;

'What happened is just unacceptable. Safety is the biggest issue, Someone could've crashed. Behind the safety car I was thinking it was only when someone gets hurt that something will be done about it.'

Hamilton's Mercedes teammate Nico Rosberg won the race.

Sunday 7th July

The next week, there was another event at Brands Hatch in connection with Aston Martin. This time we were meeting up with a party of American veterans who had been traumatised and injured in recent conflicts. An exchange system is being set up between the American version of Mission Motorsport and us. These guys had suffered terribly in the wars. There were six of them in the party, over for a week and trying to cram as much of England in as they could. The US party was led by Grier Martin from the House of Representatives. One of the chaps had no face, not that you would have known it. Such were the marvels of technology today a completely new face was built. The following week I met a Brigadier who was gaining feedback on the day out. The Brigadier told me that he had actually seen the guy with the new face peel back his skin to brush his teeth.

Being around these guys inspired me further to help them, help myself, help the world. At the end of 'Schindler's List 'it reminded us that if you save one person you save the world. That can never be truer today.

Stephen Carr has recently obtained a job as a salesman selling Aston Martins.

Team tactics with Christian Horner

Niki Lauda - F1 Legend

Leo Sayer at Sutton Images - Silverstone 2013

James Hunt, George Harrison and Leo Sayer - Long Beach USA 1977

Leo Sayer and the Mission Motorsport Crew

US Hero's at Silverstone with Mission Motorsport

North Carolina General Assembly

House of Representatives

1023 Legislative Building

Raleigh, North Carolina 27601-1096

REPRESENTATIVE GRIER MARTIN
34TH DISTRICT - WAKE COUNTY

PHONE: (919) 733-5773
EMAIL: grier.martin@ncleg.net

September 3, 2013

Mr. John Bloom
Flat 46
Hill Street
Mayfair
London
W1J 5LZ

Dear John:

It was good to hear from you and I enjoyed our conversation. I wanted to personally thank you for all you did for us while visiting with our wounded warriors. It was indeed an honor and privilege to meet you. I would especially like to thank you for the tickets for the Aston Martin Centenary which was an amazing experience and one our veterans will never forget.

Most of all, your generosity of time that you spent with us will not be forgotten and is much appreciated.

Kindest regards,

Grier Martin

DGM/sh

Epilogue - The Last Tycoon

'Give me the ability to rage correctly'- Joe Orton

'All the 100 per cent Maverick geniuses have been so driven, so out of control with their vision, it has nearly killed them or destroyed their career'

PR Guru Mark Borkowski, who performed 'Adventure Capitalism' at the Lost Theatre in July 2013

The Last Tycoon was F. Scott Fitzgerald's last book. He died before he could finish it. It was about a movie man called Monroe Stahr. He shocked his bosses at the studio by telling them that he would make a quality film despite the fact that it would lose money.

He tells them that *'We have a duty to the public'*

I have a duty to the public, still. That is why I recently set up the skincare company called Kismet. People ask me why an old codger wants to start yet another potential business empire. To tell the truth my motivations were purely personal, I could not bear to think of my wife putting Botox into her body. To me, I had to come up with an alternative, having found some incredible anti-aging products I simply couldn't keep it to myself, so I went the tried and trusted route by taking it direct to the public at home; there is where my first fortune emanated from. So that's my project now.

Kismet is committed to offering the great skincare products, at great prices direct to the Great British Public.

I am still convinced that direct selling is the best sales channel; It offers great value for the consumer by eliminating the major overheads of the stores. With Kismet we aim to bring the Beauty store brought to your door, offering consumers the opportunity to try before they buy in a relaxed atmosphere, get great tips and advice with no time constraints or pressure to buy. We offer great deals for customers willing to host parties and will provide any customer wishing to become a consultant the best support, commissions and training in the business coupled with a rewards and incentive program that money just cannot buy.

We will also be introducing the premium Kismet Diamond range that will compete with many of the leading high-end brands at a fraction of the cost, the range will include the very latest in skincare technology with no comprises on quality guaranteed. I may be in my eighty's but I'm not done yet.

Fitzgerald saw Stahr as the last tycoon in Hollywood. Perhaps people may see me as the Last Tycoon, at one stage the youngest millionaire this country had ever seen. Now the symbol of the golden era of the 60's, a decade so flushed with success, it could not see the morbidity that lay ahead. I changed business in the same way that the Beatles changed music. My legacy is everywhere you look. I made it possible for the second generation of Jewish Businessman like Alan Sugar to change the look and culture of London Town forever. I kicked down the door; they stormed in behind me.

My legacy is a guy called Phillip Morell, an ex-Barnardo's home boy who now lives in a £15m mansion; I know for a fact this because I have visited it. Phillip lent the Royal family the barge for the Jubilee celebrations and is currently writing a book about his own extraordinary life. From which I quote from the following chapter of Phillips own forthcoming amazing rags to riches autobiography.

In The Wake Of John Bloom

'I have always been fascinated by John Bloom's methods.

He started out working as door-to-door sales man and then had gone into business in his own right selling twin tub Electromatic machines for 39 guineas which were about half the price of an equivalent model in the shops.

His success was due in no small part to the way he sold his machines through taking out full page advertisements in the news papers; a device now known as 'off the page' marketing; whereby the whole deal is explained and there is no further need of promotional support.'

My legacy is Mark Borkowski who lectures about 'the tiny piece of maverick we have in us'. The theme of his talks are that since the economic depression companies have become risk adverse and individuals should find the courage to step out of their comfort zone. The economy needs a major player in the shark tank of modern business as the same way football needs another Best, motor racing another James Hunt or music needs another Beatles to festoon it.

I ended this volume with Rolls Razor crashing and me being investigated, but the story doesn't end there, how could it? If you've enjoyed this volume then look out for volume 2 which will cover my time in America and my globetrotting adventures. My further successes, near misses and few spectacular failures, and for good measure some additional chapters on the circus that is Formula 1.

Who will grace the pages? What will they have done to leave such a lasting impression upon me, that I feel so obliged that I must share?

Well you'll just have to wait and see. Which leads us to…

I read the news today.

21st July 2013

London baked in the hottest weather for seven years; The Aussies were being thrashed in the Ashes series. I tried to catch up on what was happening on planet earth. Paul Gascoigne in more trouble charged with common assault. I always think of the images from the old black/white movies of a newspaper with a huge headline swirling around the screen.

For the press it was open season on the Ecclestone clan. Bernie had been indicted by the German prosecutors following his payment of $44m to Gerhard Gribkowsky of Bayern Landesbank. When the story broke I phoned so many of our mutual friends who were unified in their support for him and offered their total and unstinting support. What we also agreed upon was how Formula One would suffer without him at the helm. I made a point of reminding them.

'All the heads of the racing car companies were driving Ford Zephyrs before Bernie showed up on the scene.'

Poor old Tamara was in the wars to. A survey on her ludicrously expensive beauty product entitled 'Will Tamara's £375 hair potions make you look like a million dollars?' ended with her products losing out 4-2 to High Street items.

I was very disturbed to read that Tamara's husband Jay Rutland was mugged and robbed of his superb £50k gold Rolex and £20K gold bracelet as he stopped his customised Range Rover at a garage in Wanstead at 12.30am to answer a call of nature.

It is terrible that something like that can happen to law-abiding citizens,

My first thoughts were, who could the culprits be?

Was it a disgruntled investor, or someone who had not been invited to his sumptuous and champagne soaked wedding?

Fortunately the culprit was caught and awaits trial.

I was enraged that something like this could happen to a young man

Jay needs additional security, which would be an ideal job for Steven Carr to recruit some of his former army pals from the elite protection squad.

We would take them away from fighting the insurgents to take out the bad guys roaming out streets at night.

It is coming to something when a chap cannot drive his luxury car around the end of the central line at night.

After the ordeal he must have needed a holiday. He and Tamara went on a well-deserved holiday to recuperate. From the pictures I have seen in the media he is now fully recovered.

So here we are up to date at the time of writing,

As I muse, it is late at night. Summer in the City, I listened at my open window for a long time. A few nights before the Stones had played across the road at Hyde Park. I took my glass out to the kitchen, filled it with some of that expensive designer water and stood sipping it, watching my reflection. Somewhere a radio was playing, a man's voice. Not just any voice.

'Regrets? I've had a few.

But then again too few to mention'